Praise for

T0277767

DISCOVERING YOUR TEMPLE INSIGHTS

"The beauty of this book is that it helped me contemplate the powerful nature of the temple and why the Lord wants me to go there. The temple is a building of light and goodness that I love learning more about. Let the words of Aaron and Julie Bujnowski inspire you to go to the temple and feel closer to the Savior as you learn His ways and ponder the covenant path in your life. I know that you will feel lifted as you read these words about the temple. Your love for your family will deepen because of your desire to learn more about the Lord's sacred house."

—Chad Lewis, former NFL tight end for the Philadelphia Eagles
and St. Louis Rams; author of *Surround Yourself with Greatness*

"The temple is a most sacred place—a place of priesthood power. It is a place prophesied to be established before the Second Coming of the Savior. When we go there, we must learn to tap into that power more abundantly, so it will flow through us and prepare us for what will come. Aaron and Julie Bujnowski's book, *Discovering Your Temple Insights*, helps readers discover and apply deep spiritual insights from their temple worship. It provides a warm and practical approach to learning from the temple that all who read will enjoy."

—David Ridges
Author of *Temples: Sacred Symbolism, Eternal Blessings*,
Unlocking the Power of Your Priesthood, and
100 Signs of the Times: Leading Up to the Second Coming of Christ

DISCOVERING YOUR
TEMPLE
INSIGHTS

AARON & JULIE BUJNOWSKI

CFI

An imprint of Cedar Fort, Inc.
Springville, Utah

This is not an official publication of The Church of Jesus Christ of Latter-day Saints. The opinions and views expressed herein belong solely to the author and do not necessarily represent the opinions or views of Cedar Fort, Inc. Permission for the use of sources, graphics, and photos is also solely the responsibility of the author.

ISBN 13: 978-1-4621-4475-4

Published by CFI, an imprint of Cedar Fort, Inc.
2373 W. 700 S., Suite 100, Springville, UT 84663
Distributed by Cedar Fort, Inc., www.cedarfort.com

Library of Congress Control Number: 2022949780

Cover design by Courtney Proby
Cover design © 2023 Cedar Fort, Inc.

Printed in the United States of America

10 9 8 7 6 5 4 3 2 1

Printed on acid-free paper

In loving memory of Kenneth J. Bujnowski (1948–2021),
who cherished the temple and its doctrine.

Contents

Preface

Learn for Yourself

"Jesus went up into the temple, and taught . . . If any man will do [my Father's] will, he shall know of the doctrine, whether it be of God, or whether I speak of myself."

—John 7:14, 17

For members of The Church of Jesus Christ of Latter-day Saints, the temple is a most sacred building, one that we hold in the highest regard. According to the Bible Dictionary, "A temple is literally a house of the Lord, a holy sanctuary in which sacred ceremonies and ordinances of the gospel are performed by and for the living and also in behalf of the dead. A place where the Lord may come, it is the most holy of any place of worship on the earth. Only the home can compare with the temple in sacredness."[1] We are blessed not only as we enter the temple and receive temple ordinances but also as we strive to understand its doctrine and more actively apply that understanding in our everyday lives.

The temple has always been the centerpiece of the Lord's efforts to gather His people. It is the means for delivering precious covenant blessings to them. It was also meant to be a physical symbol of the Savior's actual presence and a reminder of the great work that His covenant people were called to perform. The Prophet Joseph Smith taught,

---

1. "Temple," Bible Dictionary, 734.

What was the object of gathering the Jews, or the people of God in any age of the world? . . .

> The main object was to build unto the Lord a house whereby He could reveal unto His people the ordinances of His house and the glories of His kingdom, and teach the people the way of salvation: for there are certain ordinances and principles that, when they are taught and practiced, must be done in a place or house built for that purpose.[2]

The Lord designed this sacred building to be a beacon for His people—a place that would draw them to Him. With that great purpose in mind, it stands to reason that an enhanced understanding of the holy temple and its doctrine will lead us to a more profound comprehension of our Heavenly Father, His Son, Jesus Christ, ourselves as sons and daughters of God, our role in His divine plan, our sacred origins, and our eternal destiny. Ultimately, this understanding will enable us to become more like our Heavenly Parents as we consistently act upon it.

LEARNING FROM THE TEMPLE

Prophets have always invited God's covenant children to the temple to partake of its blessings and power. In our day, President Russell M. Nelson made the same passionate plea to us:

> The temple lies at the center of strengthening our faith and spiritual fortitude because the Savior and His doctrine are the very heart of the temple. Everything taught in the temple, through instruction and through the Spirit, increases our understanding of Jesus Christ. . . . .
>
> *He* is the One who wants you to understand with great clarity exactly what you are making covenants to do. *He* is the One who wants you to experience fully His sacred ordinances. *He* wants you to comprehend your privileges, promises, and responsibilities. *He* wants you to have spiritual insights and

---

2. Joseph Smith, *History of the Church* (Salt Lake City: Deseret Book, 1978), 5:423. See also Doctrine and Covenants 124:40–41.

awakenings you've never had before. This He desires for *all* temple patrons, no matter where they live.

To each of you who has made temple covenants, I plead with you to seek—prayerfully and consistently—to understand temple covenants and ordinances. Spiritual doors will open. You will learn how to part the veil between heaven and earth, how to ask for God's angels to attend you, and how better to receive direction from heaven. Your diligent efforts to do so will reinforce and strengthen your spiritual foundation.[3]

To grasp the sublime spiritual truths offered to us in the temple more thoroughly, have the revelatory awakenings, and build the spiritual foundation of which President Nelson spoke, we present in this book an approach for gaining personal temple insights, which are learned individually via study and inspiration. Many books help you learn *about* the temple. We designed this book to help you learn *from* the temple. Our proposed approach to learning *from* the temple can be summarized in this way:

> We can gain personal spiritual insights from the temple by studying and pondering temple doctrine found in the restored gospel of Jesus Christ, by tying that learning together with information and inspiration delivered during sacred temple ordinances, and then by applying what we learned in our everyday lives.

We learn from the temple via personal inspiration from the Holy Ghost received through the perspective of temple doctrine, and we apply that revelation in the context of our own lives and experiences.

Through learning and application—study and faith—the profound meaning and personal application of temple ordinances will become increasingly apparent. However, this process is not fast; it will require a lifetime of effort. Why?

One reason is that learning is always a step-by-step process. Spiritual learning is no different. Another important reason is that we change, and our circumstances change as we mature and progress.

---

3. Russell M. Nelson, "The Temple and Your Spiritual Foundation," *Conference Report*, October 2021, emphasis in original.

Speaking from our personal experience, we witnessed this progression in our lives. We were each a young man and young woman when we first attended the Atlanta Georgia Temple to perform baptisms for the dead with members of our ward in Nashville, Tennessee. We were young single adults when we entered for our endowments, and we were only twenty-one years old when we were married and sealed in that same temple.

As we faced the various life experiences that followed—including receiving an education, getting and maintaining jobs, bearing children, losing loved ones, dealing with serious illnesses, and holding various callings—new needs emerged, requiring fresh insights from our temple experience.

During the early years of our marriage, we worshiped in the temple frequently while we attended college. We certainly learned a great deal during that time. As we matured and experienced other life events, those same temple ordinances we had so often performed during our college years had new meaning for us.

We found answers to problems we never imagined we would have. Because we had built a solid foundation of faith in the temple and its ordinances early in our marriage, and because we had sought to learn the temple's doctrine, the Lord's house continued to provide insights and direction to us as our challenges changed and increased.

The approach we present in this book is what enabled us to continue learning throughout our lifetime. We share it with you to help you on that same journey—a journey we are still on ourselves. It will help you continue to *learn how to learn from the Spirit in the temple*, which will benefit you throughout the changing circumstances of your life.

TEACHING WITH REVERENCE

In an account in the New Testament book of Acts, the apostle Phillip came across an Ethiopian man reading the book of Isaiah. Phillip asked him, "Understandest thou what thou readest?" He responded, "How can I, except some man should guide me?"[4]

4. Acts 8:30–31.

Many members may share this same sentiment regarding their temple experience—they are seeking guidance to understand more. To assist us in providing a heightened understanding of the temple to others with respect and reverence for this sacred house, Elder David A. Bednar of the Quorum of the Twelve has taught,

Many Church members are unsure about what appropriately can and cannot be said regarding the temple experience outside of the temple. . . . Two basic guidelines can help us achieve the proper understanding [of what we can discuss]:

Guideline #1. Because we love the Lord, we always should speak about His holy house with reverence. We should *not* disclose or describe the special symbols associated with the covenants we receive in sacred temple ceremonies. Neither should we discuss the holy information that we specifically promise in the temple not to reveal.

Guideline #2. The temple is the house of the Lord. Everything in the temple points us to our Savior, Jesus Christ. We *may* discuss the basic purposes of and the doctrine and principles associated with temple ordinances and covenants.[5]

This book attempts to accomplish what Elder Bednar has suggested: that we enhance our understanding by appropriately discussing the basic purposes of and the doctrine and principles associated with the temple, its ordinances, and its covenants.

With this approach in mind, we recognize and respect that the temple is holy and should be spoken of and written about with reverence. The scriptures warn us to "trifle not with sacred things"[6] and teach us "that which cometh from above is sacred."[7] However, they also encourage us to "let the solemnities of eternity rest upon [our] minds"[8] and admonish us that sacred information "must be spoken

5. David A. Bednar, "Prepared to Obtain Every Needful Thing," Conference Report, April 2019; emphasis added.
6. Doctrine and Covenants 6:12.
7. Doctrine and Covenants 63:64.
8. Doctrine and Covenants 43:34.

with care, and by constraint of the Spirit; and *in this there is no condemnation.*"[9]

With these warnings and encouragements in mind, we carefully and prayerfully prepared this book. Naturally, we do not disclose sacred details about temple ordinances, but we provide an approach for you to gain inspired insights from the Spirit for yourselves. We hope it will help you on your journey to a higher spiritual understanding in the Lord's house as the Holy Spirit teaches us "the deep things of God"[10] found there.

LET THE HOLY SPIRIT GUIDE

The Holy Ghost is our ultimate spiritual teacher. We must learn for ourselves from Him while in the temple. We designed this book to be a helpful tool in that sacred process. Although this book is a useful resource, it can never replace the personal work and effort required for you to receive your own personal insights from the Spirit.

As you exercise your individual effort to study, seek, and listen, the Lord will bless you with light and enlightenment. We know because He has blessed us in this way as we have put in our own effort to learn, listen, and act.

May that personal guidance from the Spirit during your sacred temple experience always be the light that you follow. Your life and the lives of those you love and serve will be blessed as you allow the temple to help you become the son or daughter of God He intends you to be.

THE STRUCTURE OF THIS BOOK

Because we intend to help you learn *from* the temple, we structured this book as a guide and workbook. It has two major parts: (1) The Patterns and Purposes of Temples and (2) Understanding and Applying Temple Doctrine and Principles.

In part 1, "The Patterns and Purposes of Temples," we wrote two chapters to help you understand *how* the temple teaches and *why* the

---

9. Doctrine and Covenants 63:64; emphasis added.
10. 1 Corinthians 2:10.

temple exists. It is easier to learn from the temple if you understand its teaching approach and its reason for being.

In part 2, "Understanding and Applying Temple Doctrine and Principles," fifteen chapters cover fundamental doctrine and principles found in the temple and its ordinances. These concepts are generally known gospel doctrine and principles, and their explanations can be found in many publications produced by the Church and written by other authors.

You may ask, "Why discuss these well-known points of gospel doctrine and principles in a book on temple insights?"

First, many may not recognize that the temple teaches these basic truths in abundance. They may miss precious learning and application experiences because they are "looking beyond the mark"[11] for esoteric concepts and mystic messages instead of searching the "plain and precious"[12] truth of God found in the temple. Temple doctrine is applied gospel doctrine.

Second, we wanted to help kick-start your process to search, learn, and apply temple doctrine by gathering its most salient concepts into one place. We hope this book becomes a resource as you begin and continue your journey of spiritual learning from the Holy Ghost in the temple.

Finally, we wanted to tie these points of doctrine and principles to the temple in a way that refreshes them in your minds. We want to help you learn them anew—taking a fresh point of view through the lens of temple ordinances. We hope you have this renewal each time you worship there.

Each chapter presents key concepts for its primary topic printed in bold text, with supporting details following. We include scriptures and quotes related to the doctrine and principles being presented. We also offer our own insights gained through study and experience, sharing a few examples from our lives of how we learned or applied temple doctrine and principles to specific challenges or opportunities we faced.[13] Sharing our insights and applications should enhance and

11. Jacob 4:14.
12. 2 Nephi 19:3.
13. Although we cowrote this book, many of these experiences are written in the first person because we felt it was important to get the personal perspective of that individual. Each chapter begins with one of these first-person experiences. When they are shared in the book, they are marked with a section break called "Personal Application," and we give the name of the person who is speaking for clarity.

not replace or interfere with your own personal journey of inspiration, communion with the Spirit, and personal application.

As mentioned previously, we do not discuss specifics of temple ordinances. You must go there yourself and tie the information presented in this book to their proper place in the temple. In this process, the Holy Ghost will enlighten your mind and spirit, and you will discover precious insights and applications for yourself.

To further help your personal understanding and application, we offer a list of questions to consider at the end of each chapter, along with space for inspired answers that come to your mind. We hope this will deepen your understanding and encourage personal application.

ALL ARE ALIKE UNTO GOD

We wrote this book based on our own study and experiences, which constitute many years of making Jesus Christ and His temple the center of our discipleship. Although we have served in various local leadership positions, we don't have any special credentials regarding the temple or temple work. We are not scholars or General Authorities. We are just "normal" members.

In our view, this normalcy is the beauty of the temple. It is open and available to all members. "All are alike unto God."[14] Anyone with the desire to learn from it can come and partake of its rich blessings if they choose to put in the effort and "apply unto it."[15] Rank-and-file members, local leaders, scholars, and General Authorities can *all* receive inspiration and power in the Lord's house.

We share some of our experiences and insights here, and we invite you to have and record your own. In these efforts your love of the temple will blossom, and your spiritual foundation will strengthen.

We know the Lord will bless and guide you as you humbly seek Him in the temple. It is His house, and He desires to meet you there. So, begin your search now, and continue it in the holy temple. It is truly a journey of a lifetime!

---

14. 2 Nephi 26:33.
15. Doctrine and Covenants 8:4.

PART 1

The Patterns and Purposes of Temples

The patterns and purposes of the temple have created a beautiful mosaic in our spiritual lives. Each time we attend, we are enriched and edified by them. When we had the privilege of seeing our daughter, Breanna, marry her high school sweetheart, Tanner, in the Dallas Texas Temple, we witnessed those same patterns and purposes begin to bless their young lives. They can bless us all as we seek to understand them.

Therefore, to set the stage for discovering insights from the temple, we must understand its underlying *patterns*. The temple has a unique and distinctive approach to its teaching and covenant-making. When we know this pattern, we will have an improved context for our spiritual experience there. This understanding enables us to move past the "mechanics" or the outward performances and move on to the "symbolism" or inward spiritual meaning as that understanding grows. What we take *from* the temple will likewise grow.

We must also comprehend the fundamental *purposes* of temples, which open our spiritual aperture to our rationale for being there. They provide the texture and richness that deepen our experience because we understand *why* we are there. A more profound understanding of the purpose for the temple and its ordinances creates the lasting impressions which ensure the temple goes through us, rather than us merely going through it. It moves us past memorization and on to application. It takes us past process and gives us power.

Let's learn more about both the patterns and purposes of temples as we begin our efforts to learn *from* the House of the Lord.

Chapter 1

Temple Patterns

"The word for temple in Latin, templum, means the same thing as template. . . . The temple is also an observatory. That is what templum is—a place where you take your bearings on things."

—Hugh W. Nibley [1]

This chapter covers patterns used in the ordinances, administration, and design of the temple, including the use of symbolism. Understanding *how* the temple teaches is crucial because it will enhance our ability to learn *from* it. We started this journey as youth when we first attended the temple, and it's a journey we are still on and will continue together here with you.

Personal Application: Julie

When Aaron and I were both teenagers attending the same high school, I was not a member of The Church of Jesus Christ of Latter-day Saints. Aaron introduced me to the missionaries, and I took the discussions. Unfortunately, my parents did not allow

---

1. Hugh W. Nibley, *Temple and Cosmos* (Salt Lake City: Deseret Book, 1992), Chapter 1: The Meaning of the Temple, 19.

me to join at that time. However, I would regularly go to Church meetings and youth activities with him.

When our ward would travel three hours from Nashville, Tennessee, to the Atlanta Georgia Temple for baptisms, I would go with them. Unable to enter, I would walk around the temple grounds while the others were inside performing ordinances. I would look at the beautiful spire, the stained glass windows, and the pretty flowers. I felt a peace I never experienced elsewhere.

The temple became a symbol of all the eternal blessings I wanted in my life. When I eventually joined the Church in October 1989 at the age of eighteen and was finally able to enter the temple myself in May 1990, those early faith-filled sacrifices amplified the meaning of the temple for me. As my understanding of temple patterns has grown, it has enabled me to continue learning from the temple, which has sustained me to this day.

The temple is a sacred space, the literal House of the Lord. The temple is a special building set apart as a holy space, separate from the "profane" or "common" things of this world.[2] Within it, we perform sacred saving ordinances for the living and the dead. The temple is made holy by priesthood dedication, priesthood ordinances, and the presence of the Lord. It is literally the "house of God." [3]

The temple and everything associated with it point to Jesus Christ—the Son of the living God and the Savior and Redeemer of the world—and to His infinite and eternal Atonement. He must be the focus of our temple worship because only through Him can we become like our Heavenly Parents. He is the Holy One, and His house is a holy house.

The temple is a pattern—a template—for us individually and collectively to show us what we can and must become as sons and daughters of Heavenly Parents. As we pattern our lives after its teachings, we will become more like Jesus Christ. The temple is also a compass

---

2. See Donald W. Parry, *Temples of the Ancient World* (Salt Lake City: Deseret Book, 1994), xiii–xiv.

3. Doctrine and Covenants 88:119.

of sorts, pointing us to the Father and the Son and helping us get our bearings in a world of confusion and temptation.[4]

Everything we do in the Church before we enter the temple prepares us for the ordinances received there. Everything we receive in the temple prepares us for what happens in our lives after we leave.

As President Nelson taught, "The temple is the object of every activity, every lesson, every progressive step in the Church. All of our efforts in proclaiming the gospel, perfecting the Saints, and redeeming the dead lead to the holy temple."[5] Therefore, we must often return to remember and renew its sacred knowledge and power. Doing so will embed its pattern in us and will manifest its power through us.

On the temple is inscribed the words, "The House of the Lord." It is the house of Jesus Christ, a place of His actual presence. Also written on the temple is the phrase "Holiness to the Lord." The word "to" suggests we should bring holiness there, a divine injunction to enter worthily.[6] He is holy, and His house is sacred. Therefore, we must also strive to be worthy of being there. Only then will we take a piece of its holiness with us.

Being worthy is not the same as being perfect. "Worthy" means to be sufficiently qualified. Elder Marvin J. Ashton, formerly of the Quorum of the Twelve, taught, "Worthiness is a process, and perfection is an eternal trek. We can be worthy to enjoy certain privileges without being perfect."[7]

The questions asked in two temple recommend interviews ensure our worthiness, which is a preamble to the holiness given as the Holy Spirit sanctifies us. When we answer those questions sincerely, the presiding officers will certify our worthiness.

The temple orients, sanctifies, teaches, and enables us to become like the Savior. It is His house. When we enter, we bring Him *our* worthiness, and when we leave, we can take a piece of *His* holiness with us.

---

4. See Donald W. Parry, *Temples of the Ancient World*, Introduction, xi–xxiv. See also Hugh W. Nibley, *Temple and Cosmos*, 19.
5. Russell M. Nelson, "Prepare for the Blessings of the Temple," *Liahona*, October 2010.
6. "For God hath not called us unto uncleanness, but unto holiness" (1 Thessalonians 4:7).
7. Marvin J. Ashton, "On Being Worthy," Conference Report, April 1989.

The teaching in the temple is both literal and figurative, real and symbolic. The temple contains a mix of literal and symbolic teachings, which are embedded in the words and actions of its ordinances. When we ponder and differentiate between those realities, a rich, profound learning experience will occur.

By using symbolic and literal teaching, our temple experience is simultaneously spiritual and practical. It encompasses the most profound and expansive concepts of God and heaven, along with the most useful "real-world" application of sublime gospel doctrine. This duality is part of the temple's meaning as a "house of order."[8]

It takes time and effort to learn via symbols, and we must have patience as we mature in our ability. On one occasion, President David O. McKay shared his journey of understanding temple symbolism:

> There are two things in every Temple: [1] Mechanics, to set forth certain ideals, and [2] symbolism, what those mechanics symbolize. I saw only the mechanics when I first went through the Temple. I did not see the spiritual. I did not see the symbolism of spirituality. . . . [The temple] is simple in the mechanical part of it, but sublime and eternal in its significance [in the symbolic part of it].[9]

The "mechanics" that President McKay describes are all the processes and actions we participate in during temple ordinances. Like him, we can mature in our spiritual understanding of the temple as we seek the deeper meaning and symbolism of temple ordinances and move beyond the "mechanics" that we experience.

For those things that are symbolic, we must realize symbols have multiple levels and layers of meaning.[10] When we see or hear something while in the temple, we should ask ourselves, "What does it

---

8. Doctrine and Covenants 88:119.

9. Gregory Prince and William Robert Wright, *David O. McKay and the Rise of Modern Mormonism* (Salt Lake City: University of Utah Press, 2005), 277.

10. For example, a stop sign is typically red and is shaped in an octagon. This symbol means an automobile must "stop" at an intersection where it is posted. Thinking more expansively, we can see that a stop sign also represents the broader concepts of traffic laws, orderly conduct, braking systems, driving skills, and a whole host of other non-driving "stop" or "pause" related concepts and actions, depending on the way a person uses a "stop" symbol.

mean or represent?" as often as we ask, "What does it encourage me to do?" Most importantly, we should always ask, "What does it enable me to become?" When we look at the temple through these introspective lenses, we will expand our vision and deepen our understanding.

Through symbolism, the temple gives "milk" to the person who is early on his or her spiritual journey, and it provides "meat" to the more spiritually advanced person.[11] It obscures truth for the spiritually immature while exposing truth to those who have spiritually prepared themselves.

Understanding the temple's symbolism gives us the truth we need and the divine pattern to understand and apply it to our unique personal situation.

The physical design of the temple is a collection of spiritual symbols. The physical design of the temple—although somewhat variable and customized between temples—contains common elements that symbolize and enhance its purpose. We describe a few here.

Outside the temple, spires point heavenward to remind us of the proper direction of our focus, intent, and source of strength, which is Jesus Christ. An angel Moroni with his trumpet symbolically calls for the House of Israel's gathering to the Lord's house, an invitation for us to hasten our efforts in that great work. Granite used for the exterior symbolizes a solid, unwavering foundation of truth built on Jesus Christ; it should not change with time.

The temple cornerstone also represents Jesus Christ, who is the cornerstone of our faith. Water features remind us of the fountain of all righteousness, Jesus Christ, and the living waters He offers us. Plants and flowers represent life and the Life-giver. Many newer temples also have a *Christus* statue on their grounds, an ever-present reminder that the temple is the house of the living Christ.[12]

---

11. See 1 Corinthians 3:2.
12. The original *Christus* is a nineteenth-century marble statue of the resurrected Jesus by Bertel Thorvaldsen. It is located in the Evangelical Lutheran Church in Denmark's Church of Our Lady in Copenhagen. In April 2020, The Church of Jesus Christ of Latter-day Saints adopted an official symbol with the *Christus* statue at its center.

Inside the temple, stained glass windows allow light into the "House of Light" while keeping the sacred precincts separate from the world, representing the revelation we should receive and the common or profane ideas we should shun. Doors keep out the profane and keep in the sacred. Garden scenes and potted plants represent life and growth. Representations of intertwined squares and circles represent the place where the earth and its four corners join with heaven and its eternal expansiveness. This sacred place of heavenly intersection is the temple.[13] The white clothing we wear symbolizes purity, reminds us of our worthiness, and represents His victory over sin and death, which will eventually perfect us.

In the baptistry, the font rests on the backs of twelve oxen, representing the twelve tribes of Israel. A symbolic animal represented each tribe. The ox represented the tribe of Joseph, which is an appropriate symbol in the temple because Joseph, through Ephraim and Manasseh, is the tribe that bears the bulk of the load as we gather Israel in the latter days.

We should soak in and ponder all visual cues given to us from the moment we step on the sacred temple grounds to enhance and deepen our experience while there.[14] When we go to a temple, we will often walk around the temple grounds observing its many unique features. Those reverent moments have confirmed for us on numerous occasions that the temple is the literal house of God.

You can find more details and associated symbolism in a temple's physical design than we can enumerate here. We would suggest reading any of the many resources available on this topic to deepen your understanding.[15]

---

13. See Hugh W. Nibley, *Temple and Cosmos*, "Chapter 4: The Circle and the Square," 139–173.
14. For a more detailed and expansive description of many physical elements on early Church temples, which will help to explain symbolism on modern temples more completely, see Matthew B. Brown and Paul Thomas Smith, *Symbols in Stone* (Salt Lake City: Covenant Communications, Inc., 2003) and Matthew B. Brown, *The Gate of Heaven* (Salt Lake City: Covenant Communications, Inc., 1999).
15. For an in-depth treatment of temple symbolism, see Alonzo L. Gaskill, *Sacred Symbols* (Salt Lake City: Cedar Fort, 2019), Amy Hardison, *Understanding the Symbols, Covenants, and Ordinances of the Temple* (Salt Lake City: Covenant Communications, Inc., 2016), Donald W. Perry, *175 Temple Symbols* (Salt Lake City: Deseret Book, 2020), and Jack M. Lyon, *Understanding Temple Symbols Through Scripture, History, and Art* (Salt Lake City: Deseret Book, 2016).

We use ceremony in the performance of temple ordinances.
One reference defines "ceremony" as "an act or series of acts performed according to a traditional or prescribed form."[16] The ceremony associated with temple ordinances is unique in the lives of members of the Church. Little in our previous spiritual life is a close enough parallel to prepare us for this experience adequately. For some, this peculiarity and unfamiliarity cause anxiety and stress. A few may even experience aversion. These feelings may persist even after the first encounter.

Understandably, the temple is a most distinctive experience, requiring patience, diligence, and love of the Savior to understand and embrace. If we feel unsettled by our temple experience, perhaps we should remember the feeling of comfort and acceptance we felt in some of our previous spiritual experiences, such as attending a special conference or meeting.

As we might recall, these experiences only required our passive participation. In contrast, the temple experience involves our active engagement, which requires us to learn specific mechanics. These actions can be off-putting for some and even agonizing for others.[17]

Fortunately, familiarity can help us feel comfortable and—in time—even uplifted as we move past the mechanics of the ordinances and on to the precious symbolism they contain. Prayers for peace throughout this unique experience can bring us accelerated comfort. Genuine curiosity and interest can open our minds and improve our attitudes.

In time, these distinctive experiences can provide the same comfort and acceptance we have felt elsewhere in our covenant journey if we will but open our hearts and minds to their more expansive meaning and application.

Personal Application: Aaron and Julie

A comparative mental model to help us accept and understand the need for the temple's ceremonies may be the coronation

---

16. "Ceremony," *Oxford Dictionary of English* (Oxford: Oxford University Press, 2010), 284.
17. Likewise, preparing and delivering a talk, which requires much effort and action on our part, is off-putting and agonizing for many.

of a new king or queen. We learned about coronations when we took a trip to London, England, in 2005.

Previous requirements as a prince or princess are far less intense than when the individual assumes the throne. To impress upon the person's mind the importance of this new responsibility, he or she participates in a coronation event, requiring the prince or princess to go through a series of confirmation activities. Each of these requires the individual to perform certain ceremonies and make individual commitments.

Some previously in this position may have felt uneasy about the great responsibility they are assuming and may have felt anxiety, antipathy, or even aversion during the bestowal process. However, it would not be unexpected to place these requirements upon one who will undertake such a significant endeavor.

During the endowment and sealing ceremonies, the promises given to us are similar. They give us eternally significant responsibilities as future kings and queens, so they require us to do more than to participate passively as we receive them. Great blessings are always tied to great commitments!

We use special symbols and gestures in temple ordinances. Special symbols and gestures are an integral part of the pattern and ceremony of temple worship. They are not disclosed or described outside of the temple. However, a few basic principles can help us comprehend how they might fit into the context of our spiritual lives.

Each sacred symbol or gesture delivered and received during temple ordinances represents the covenants and commitments we make and is a tangible reminder of all the information and teachings associated with them. They are simple methods of enabling us to recall the broader and deeper details, nuances, and implications of what we agreed to and learned. They remind us to keep our covenants, encourage others to keep theirs, and symbolically identify when faithful acceptance and compliance with covenants occurs.

Testing our knowledge of these symbols and gestures provides a figurative accounting of whether we have fully lived up to their associated obligations. Recalling them represents a measure of progress and development in becoming like our Heavenly Parents by living our covenants. These tests are not just a measure of performance in remembering the symbols and gestures themselves.

We keep specific details about temple ordinances private. Certain aspects of temple worship are not disclosed outside of the temple. The sacred nature of this information symbolizes the holiness of the obligations associated with temple ordinances.

We should take covenants seriously. The stern warnings and admonitions about not discussing the temple's ceremonies and their associated symbols outside of the temple encourage our sacred sobriety and seriousness. They impress upon our minds the need for reverence and respect for their respective covenants and their associated obligations and blessings.

Detailed information related to temple ordinances is holy. Sacred information can only be passed to those worthy and prepared to receive it and those who have willingly reciprocated the spiritual trust He offers us. This willingness proves to Him and us the actual direction of our hearts and desires, ideally to be holy like Him. Keeping this holy information private is another reminder of the higher worthiness we should aspire to achieve.

Our agreement not to disclose certain information outside the temple also represents our relationship with Heavenly Father and Jesus Christ, to whom alone we will give a final accounting at some point in the future and through whom alone we receive blessings. We must understand the closeness the Father feels to us and the close spiritual relationship He wishes to have with each of His children. We should treasure this special relationship, as portrayed, symbolized, and encouraged by the guarding of these sacred pieces of information. Guarding them is a symbol and expression of the love He has for each of us and of the love we have for Him.

The Church is striving to help members and friends understand more about the temple and its processes by publicly sharing allowable information. For example, videos of the temple garment and temple ceremonial clothing are posted on the Church's website.[18] The covenants

---

18. See "Sacred Temple Clothing," https://www.churchofjesuschrist.org/temples/
sacred-temple-clothing?lang=eng.

we make in the temple are outlined in the Church's *General Handbook of Instructions*.[19] As Elder Bednar of the Quorum of the Twelve also taught, "We *may* discuss the basic purposes of and the doctrine and principles associated with temple ordinances and covenants."[20]

We *can* talk about a number of topics outside of the temple. For the specific information we are asked to keep private, we can use that as a token of trust by our Heavenly Father to demonstrate reverence for His house, which will grow our deep respect and love for Him.

What is absent in the temple is instructive. We gain spiritual learning from what we do *not* find in the temple's ordinances or administration. We see no distinctions in attire; all individuals dress similarly, wearing simple white clothing. All are treated equally. We have no titles for patrons; we only call each other "brother" and "sister."

We do not find disorder and randomness in the administration of ordinances. Ordinance workers perform all ordinances with as much exactness and order as possible because they have prepared and practiced beforehand. We do not witness frantic, chaotic, or hurried behaviors; we only witness simple, peaceful, diligent actions by workers and patrons alike. We experience no complexity; we only experience sacred simplicity.

All these "absences" represent what will be missing in the eternities and what should be absent in our family, ecclesiastical, and professional lives outside the temple. We should carry this pattern with us into the eternities.

Ultimately, the temple is a "house of learning."[21] The temple utilizes an inspired teaching model to instruct all those who enter it.

---

19. See General Handbook, Chapter 27.2 for a summary of the endowment and for a discussion of the covenants made during that ordinance, accessed February 6, 2021, https://www.churchofjesuschrist.org/study/manual/general-handbook/27–temple-ordinances-for-the-living?lang=eng#title_number12.
20. David A. Bednar, "Prepared to Obtain Every Needful Thing," Conference Report, April 2019; emphasis added.
21. See Doctrine and Covenants 88:119.

Elder John A. Widtsoe, formerly of the Quorum of the Twelve, shared four distinct parts to this teaching method:[22]

> *The preparatory ordinances.* The preparatory ordinances enable the participant to be ready for what he or she will receive later. They cleanse us, set us apart, and shield or protect us as we start the next phase of our journey to become heirs of eternal life. They are symbolic of the Father's patience and long-suffering with us while He slowly and carefully prepares us to progress towards our ultimate divine destiny.

> *The learning environment.* The temple teaches using the spoken word, conversations, and actions by ordinance workers, pictorial and cinematic representations, symbols and symbolism, and patrons' participation. These teaching elements are typical of standard academic methods performed in a classroom or lecture hall. They require the same level of attentiveness and concentration a diligent student would give in such settings.

> *Covenants.* A covenant is a promise to give life to knowledge. Knowledge is only serviceable if we use it. Covenants simultaneously guard moral agency and enable the assured delivery of blessings by encouraging us to act.

> *Tests of knowledge.* We symbolically experience an accounting of our performance against our covenants and a measure of our overall developmental progress through tests of knowledge in the temple ceremonies. These tests are (a) an accounting of what we learned, (b) a measure of our performance in keeping the covenants made, and (c) a measure of our progress in becoming like the Savior. The tests do not just validate what we know, but they are a symbol of what we have done and, ultimately, what we have become. They are also symbolic of the tests and trials of mortality, which serve to develop in us the godly character the Father wants us to have.

These teaching methods are designed to deepen and personalize our learning, enabling us to gain the most from our temple experience.

---

22. See John A. Widtsoe, "Temple Worship," *The Utah Genealogical and Historical Magazine*, Vol. XII, April 1921, 58–59 for a full discussion of these four elements, https://babel.hathitrust.org/cgi/pt?id=njp.32101042555944&view=1up&seq=76.

By understanding *how* we are taught, we will be more prepared to comprehend *what* we are taught.

QUESTIONS TO CONSIDER

1. What patterns did you observe in the temple during your last visit? What meaning do they have for you? How can the temple be a pattern for your life?
2. What symbols most impressed you during your last visit to the temple? What meaning or application might they have in your life?
3. What does the phrase, "Holiness to the Lord" mean to you? Why is holiness important to your temple experience? How can you increase your personal holiness?

NOTES AND INSIGHTS

_____

_____

_____

_____

_____

_____

_____

_____

_____

_____

Chapter 2

Temple Purposes

"Temples are the great repositories of eternal
life . . . waiting for the children of God to come up
and bring their offerings of broken hearts and contrite
spirits, and draw upon [that] treasure."

—Franklin D. Richards[1]

This chapter covers the various purposes of the temple: the binding and sealing of families for eternity, the receipt of spiritual power and revelation, and the development of a Christlike character. Ultimately, the temple's purpose is to bring us to Jesus Christ. As we understand *why* the temple exists, we will be more prepared to take advantage of *what* we can receive *from* it.

Personal Application: Julie

The temple is a place of spiritual purpose and power. I have witnessed its power in our lives many times. I share one meaningful experience here. Aaron's father, Ken, was raised by his single mother and her parents because his father left their home when he was a little boy. Ken never really knew his father, only

---

1. Franklin D. Richards cited in Truman G. Madsen, *The Temple: Where Heaven Meets Earth* (Salt Lake City: Deseret Book, 2008), 44.

making contact as an adult shortly before his father passed away. He related to Aaron that he harbored harsh feelings toward his father because of that absence.

In 1998, we helped Aaron's parents find all the information necessary to perform the temple work for Ken's father and mother. We flew to Seattle, Washington, where Aaron's parents were living, to perform the ordinances with them. At that time, his parents were serving as temple workers in the Seattle Washington Temple, and they received permission to perform the ordinances for Ken's parents. Aaron acted as proxy for his grandfather, Joseph Thomas Bujnowski, and I acted as proxy for his grandmother, Margaret Ruth Kanya.

Ken told us afterward that while he was performing the ordinances for his father, all the ill will and bad feelings he had felt for many years melted away. He miraculously felt reconciled and healed spiritually. He understood that although his father's actions had caused him years of heartache, the Savior's Atonement allowed father and son to be reconciled in Christ.

Each of us can feel this type of healing and reconciling power when we faithfully attend the temple. The temple will bring us the miracle of the Atonement in tangible ways. Healing is one of the most precious gifts we take from our temple experience—one of its key purposes.

The temple offers required, saving ordinances for all humankind. All men and women who have reached the age of accountability must accept the gospel of Jesus Christ and receive all its saving ordinances to qualify for exaltation. In His great mercy, the Savior provided a way for those who died without access to obtain them.

Those who have died are now in the world of spirits. There, ministers of righteousness teach them the principles of salvation contained in the gospel of Jesus Christ. They can freely accept or reject the saving doctrine and principles.[2] Those who accept must still receive ordinances to progress.

Because we must perform ordinances while in mortality, the Savior provided a way for those of us still living to receive those ordinances on behalf of the dead—vicariously. This activity by proxy occurs in

2. See Isaiah 24:22; John 5:25; 1 Peter 3:18–20; 4:6; Doctrine and Covenants 138.

dedicated temples, where we stand in the place of the dead to receive ordinances for them.[3] They must still accept those ordinances while in the spirit world, which guards their agency. In this way, they become perfected even as we become perfected while serving them.[4]

Unfortunately, those who die cannot have a fulness of joy in the spirit world until (1) they learn the principles of the gospel of Jesus Christ, (2) the vicarious ordinances of salvation are performed on their behalf, and (3) they willingly accept them. Until that occurs, they cannot progress, which is a condition we cannot fully comprehend. Elder D. Todd Christofferson has said,

> I have pondered this at some length wanting to better understand the condition of spirits beyond the veil. I was given to understand that the situation of those who die without the gospel and its saving ordinances, even those who did their best and were decent people by our standards, *is less than desirable.*
>
> It cannot be paradise for any until they have accepted the gospel of Jesus Christ, repented of their sins insofar as they can, and entered into the covenant and received a remission of their sins through the baptisms of water and Spirit. Therefore, it is not a small thing where we have the means to provide them a baptism that we neglect or delay the opportunity.[5]

Therefore, we must enable our kindred dead to receive the ordinances that will allow them to progress and move into spirit paradise!

In the temple, we receive saving ordinances for ourselves, and we perform these same ordinances vicariously for those who passed away before receiving them. The temple is a "house of faith"[6] where we put our beliefs into practice and act on future promised blessings for ourselves and our kindred dead.

The ordinances performed in the temple include baptisms and confirmations, the endowment with its initiatory ordinances, and the sealing

---

3. See 1 Corinthians 15:29; Doctrine and Covenants 128.
4. See Doctrine and Covenants 128:15.
5. D. Todd Christofferson, "How Beautiful Thy Temples, Lord," BYU Family History Fireside—Joseph Smith Building, March 8, 2002; emphasis added.
6. Doctrine and Covenants 88:119.

ordinances to bind spouses and families together for eternity. In the temple, we only perform baptisms and confirmations for the dead, whereas we complete the other ordinances for both the living and the dead.

Most unique is the endowment ceremony. In his description of the endowment, Brigham Young said,

> Your endowment is, to receive all those ordinances in the House of the Lord, which are necessary for you, after you have departed this life, to enable you to walk back to the presence of the Father, passing the angels who stand as sentinels, being enabled to give them the key words, the signs and tokens, pertaining to the Holy Priesthood, and gain your eternal exaltation in spite of earth and hell.[7]

Endowment means "gift." This ordinance gives us the precious gifts of knowledge, understanding, and covenant blessings. Ultimately, it gives us the gift of priesthood and spiritual power.

We will find great joy in performing vicarious ordinances for our ancestors. It is among the most precious work we can do.

Personal Application: Julie

Aaron and I have been actively involved in family history research for many years. Through that process, we have collected the names of thousands of our ancestors. We have experienced miraculous events when names are quite literally given to us, an indication that our ancestors want their work completed.

Many years before she passed away, my grandmother was contacted by a family historian to gather information on her maternal line. The authors put that information into a large hardback book. Only a few copies of that precious resource were published, and she gave us one.

Years later, a relative told us of another book about my grandmother's paternal line with the names of that side's ancestors in it. We went to a small rural library in Tennessee, where Aaron and I photocopied more than three hundred pages of my ancestors' names.

---

7. Brigham Young cited in *Journal of Discourses*, 2:31.

On another occasion, an aged relative in a distant city called us out of the blue and said that she was sending us information on Aaron's paternal relatives in Poland. She sent a link to a video with someone walking around a cemetery recording many headstones, along with the Polish translation of dates and names.

Each time we go through the process of documenting the names in the Family Search database and then performing the ordinances in the temple, we feel incredible peace. While in the temple performing ordinances for certain names, we feel great anxiety for the work to be completed.

Through these sacred experiences, we have received the assurance that many of our ancestors are very desirous of receiving their saving ordinances. We also feel similar anxiety about providing them. All of us receive blessings through this most important process.

Sacred saving covenants are voluntarily made during temple ordinances. The temple is a "house of covenants." Covenants are two-way agreements, and we make them when we receive ordinances. Temple covenants are between the patron and the Lord, either in person for themselves or vicariously for those who have died. They activate or give life to the knowledge we receive there. They encourage us to act on what we learn. These temple covenants are foundational stepping stones on the path to exaltation. They continue the journey begun at baptism along what is called "the covenant path."

In the temple, we covenant to keep the law of obedience, the law of sacrifice, the law of the gospel (the higher law), and the law of chastity, and we covenant to accept the law of consecration. We also make commitments to avoid specific acts of irreverence, rebellion, and impurity. Finally, when we are married, we covenant to fulfill our divine roles as husband and wife.[8]

Why would we need to covenant to keep these specific laws in the temple when we have already made the baptismal covenant to take

---

8. See General Handbook, chapter 27.2 for a summary of the endowment and for a discussion of the covenants made during that ordinance, accessed February 6, 2021, https://www.churchofjesuschrist.org/study/manual/general-hand-book/27–temple-ordinances-for-the-living?lang=eng#title_number12.

upon us the name of Christ, keep His commandments (which include these laws), and always remember Him?

Temple covenants move us beyond what a disciple of Christ would do and toward what an heir of a heavenly throne would do. They are the higher requirements of sons and daughters, beyond those of followers. The covenants of baptism qualify us as disciples of Jesus Christ; the covenants of the temple qualify us as literal sons and daughters of God, heirs of His kingdom, kings and queens, priests and priestesses.

The temple enables us to become like our Heavenly Parents. In their most complete expression, the temple and its ordinances, covenants, and processes teach and develop in us the character, traits, qualities, personalities, and attributes of godliness. The temple shows us why and how our Heavenly Parents and their Beloved Son behave and make decisions so we might act like and, ultimately, become like them.

Because we feel the Spirit in the temple more powerfully and because the Spirit is the enabler and enhancer of all godly characteristics, the temple is the most powerful place we have on the earth for the character of Christ to be developed and enhanced in us. Therefore, the temple is a house of glory[9]—His current glory and our eventual glory.

We learn of His character (1) in the presentation and the administration of the ordinances, (2) in the content and context of the covenants and promises themselves, and (3) in the way we approach honoring and keeping our commitments and using our learning, which we validate by tests of our knowledge in the temple and by our choices outside the temple.

This ascent to the character of godliness or "the measure of the stature of the fulness of Christ"[10] is the ultimate purpose for all ordinances we receive. We witness them most poignantly demonstrated in temple ordinances performed in the House of the Lord, where heaven and earth meet. The temple is where we commit to the highest laws of eternal progress and where we see them portrayed dramatically and symbolically.

Our hearts are changed and humbled, and we are reborn and refined when we take full advantage of our time in the temple. This rebirth happens

---

9. See Doctrine and Covenants 88:119.
10. Ephesians 4:13.

each time we go. Thus, we, like our Savior, grow "grace for grace"[11] and "line upon line and precept upon precept,"[12] slowly becoming more like Him. Elder David A. Bednar of the Quorum of the Twelve has taught,

> Our hearts—the sum total of our desires, affections, intentions, motives, and attitudes—define who we are and determine what we will become. *And the essence of the Lord's work is changing, turning, and purifying hearts through gospel covenants and priesthood ordinances.*
>
> We do not build or enter holy temples solely to have a memorable individual or family experience. Rather, the covenants received and the ordinances performed in temples are essential to the sanctifying of our hearts and for the ultimate exaltation of God's sons and daughters.[13]

Thus, through temple ordinances, we are enabled to become more like our Heavenly Parents, which is the final goal of mortality.

Temples are places of selfless service. Due to their perfect meekness and humility, the Father and the Son are utterly selfless and giving in their character and actions. They invite us to be equally as generous in our ministry. "Because he laid down his life for us . . . we ought to lay down our lives for the brethren [and sisters]." [14]

Selfless service is inherent in the very design of the work for the dead. We model and adopt this service-centric orientation when we do vicarious ordinances in the temple. For this reason, we cannot be made perfect without our dead, and they cannot be made perfect without us.[15]

The performance of vicarious temple ordinances is of utmost importance, and it helps us become more like the dead as we become

---

11. Doctrine and Covenants 93:12–13, 19–20.
12. Doctrine and Covenants 98:12; 128:21.
13. David A. Bednar, "Let This House Be Built to My Name," Conference Report, April 2020; emphasis added.
14. 1 John 3:16.
15. See Doctrine and Covenants 128:15.

"saviors on mount Zion."[16] President Gordon B. Hinckley said, "I think that vicarious work for the dead more nearly approaches the vicarious sacrifice of the Savior Himself than any other work of which I know."[17]

This connected relationship or kinship with our ancestors is symbolic of the saving relationship we have with the Father and the Son. Performing vicarious temple work is indicative of our desire to truly become like Them in thought, word, and deed.

Personal Application: Aaron and Julie

We are personal witnesses of selfless temple service. On one occasion, we went to the temple to perform the sealings of a large number of our relatives. We were excited and anxious to complete their work. When we arrived at the sealing room, few patrons were there, but there was just enough to accomplish the work of sealing sons and daughters to their parents.

One sister had been there for quite some time. Although she was tired and ready to leave, she realized that if she departed, we would not be able to complete the many ordinances we were so anxious to perform. Sacrificing herself, she stayed until we finished all our names. We were so grateful for her sacrifice that day.

Members often make these kinds of personal sacrifices to perform temple work, which is a similitude of their Savior and His supreme sacrifice. Sacrifice is another way the temple enables us to be more like Him.

We receive priesthood power in the temple. The promise of spiritual power is the ultimate gift we receive within the walls of the House of the Lord.[18] We partake of the "power of godliness"[19]

---

16. Obadiah 1:21.
17. Gordon B. Hinckley, "Excerpts from Recent Addresses of President Gordon B. Hinckley," *Ensign*, January 1998, 73.
18. See Doctrine and Covenants 109:22–23.
19. Doctrine and Covenants 84:20–21.

that comes through the ordinances and covenants of the priesthood, which form the covenant path. The covenant path is the priesthood path for both men and women. It is the path to priesthood and spiritual power for all.

This power enables our posterity and us (1) to become like our Heavenly Father, in terms of our purpose and characteristics, (2) to bind ourselves to our spouse, children, and God for eternity, (3) to carry out our assignments and stewardships within the family and within the kingdom, and (4) to overcome all our enemies, including sin and death, to endure all our trials and tribulations, and to find healing and reconciliation.

The temple personalizes and amplifies spiritual power via its covenants and symbols. Through that power, the temple can edify us if we are in a time of peace, comfort us if we are in a time of turmoil, and guide us if we are in a time of doubt or confusion.

The temple has the power to heal families, broken hearts, and myriad "sorrow that the eye can't see."[20] It can bring reconciliation where there was once separation. All this healing comes through Jesus Christ and His infinite Atonement.

This power is priesthood power, which is delivered by the power of the Holy Ghost. God promises it to all His faithful covenant sons and daughters. It grows with each saving ordinance until we receive an eventual fulness.

Elder John A. Widtsoe, formerly of the Quorum of the Twelve, taught, "A temple is a place in which those whom he has chosen are endowed with power from on high. And what is power? Knowledge made alive and useful that is intelligence; and intelligence in action that is power. Our temples give us power—a power based on enlarged knowledge and intelligence—a power from on high, of a quality with God's own power."[21] Ultimately, temple power is the power to become like Him.

---

20. "Lord, I Would Follow Thee," *Hymns*, no. 220.
21. John A. Widtsoe, "Temple Worship," *The Utah Genealogical and Historical Magazine*, Vol. XII, April 1921, 55, accessed February 6, 2021, https://babel.hathitrust.org/cgi/pt?id=njp.32101042555944&view=1up&seq=73&skin=2021.

Temples are places of revelation. A temple is a place of revelation and light because heaven and earth intersect within its walls. It is a "house of prayer,"[22] where we can actively petition for blessings and favors and where deity can respond to our requests. While there, we can reverently commune with the Spirit. We can receive guidance to aid us on our mortal journey and strength that empowers us to become more like our Savior.

When facing unique, unexpected, or seemingly incomprehensible issues in mortality, we most likely need a greater understanding of how to apply previously revealed doctrine and principles to the situation and not new doctrine or principles. Revelation in the temple can provide us a fresh understanding to solve these types of problems, giving us a more abundant, nuanced insight into how to apply truth we have already received.

The Spirit we feel in the temple can also help us understand our divine purpose—who we are and who we can become. Sister Sheri L. Dew, a former counselor in the Relief Society General Presidency, taught, "There is nothing more vital to our success and our happiness here than learning to hear the voice of the Spirit. It is the Spirit who reveals to us our identity—which isn't just who we are but who we have always been. And that when we know, our lives take on a sense of purpose so stunning that we can never be the same again."[23]

Jesus Christ is the "Prince of Peace,"[24] so His house is a "House of Peace." Peace is a primary mode of communication by the Spirit, and it is an important way the revelation will come to us in the temple.

The Holy Spirit is subtle and gentle, so the mode of revelation, communication, and teaching in the temple is the most sublime and pure we can experience. To commune with Him, we must be more worthy, more attentive, and more alert than anywhere else because He may communicate to us information we *need* in addition to information we *want*.

---

22. Doctrine and Covenants 88:119.
23. Sheri L. Dew, "Knowing Who You Are—And Who You Have Always Been," Brigham Young University Women's Conference. Provo, Utah: Brigham Young University, May 4, 2001, accessed January 31, 2021, https://womensconference.ce.byu.edu/sites/womensconference.ce.byu.edu/files/dew_sheri_2.pdf.
24. Isaiah 9:6.

We may come to the temple with a question we want to be answered and leave with an answer to a question He wants us to discover. Pondering reverently while there will assist us in receiving those divine, personal messages.

We can "hear" more clearly in the temple, not necessarily because the voice of the Lord is louder there, but most often because the distractions of the world and the influence of the adversary are absent there. Therefore, the sacred subtlety of the Spirit can give way to light and enlightenment.

The only thing we bring into the temple is us, so the only things that can distract us in the temple are our own imperfections, biases, and other natural man or woman tendencies and personal idiosyncrasies. We are invited to "cease from all [our] light speeches, from all laughter, from all [our] lustful desires, from all [our] pride and light-mindedness, and from all [our] wicked doings."[25] The extent to which we leave these distractions behind governs what we can and will receive while in the temple.

President Joseph F. Smith taught us the importance of this soberness of mind, which directly applies to our time in the temple:

> The Lord has called upon us to be a sober-minded people, not given to much laughter, frivolity and light-mindedness, but to consider thoughtfully and thoroughly the things of his kingdom that we may be prepared in all things to understand the glorious truths of the gospel, and be prepared for blessings to come. . . .
>
> I do not believe the Lord intends and desires that we should pull a long face and look sanctimonious and hypocritical. I think he expects us to be happy and of a cheerful countenance, but he does not expect of us the indulgence in boisterous and unseemly conduct and the seeking after the vain and foolish things which amuse and entertain the world.[26]

---

25. Doctrine and Covenants 88:121.
26. Joseph F. Smith, Conference Report, October 1916, 70.

With this reverent and solemn attitude, the temple can open to us the windows of heaven, such that divine information more freely flows to us and through us.

Personal Application: Julie

Several years ago, we were contemplating a move from Houston, Texas, to Dallas, Texas, because of a new job opportunity Aaron received after graduating from business school. The job could be done from either Dallas or Houston. We had lived in the Houston area for seven years and had grown quite comfortable there. Therefore, we had decided not to move so our two children would not have to change schools and so we could maintain the many friendships we had made in our ward and community.

We went to the Houston temple to receive a confirmation that Houston was the right place for us. During a sealing session, Aaron received a distinct impression when thinking about staying in Houston. It came in the form of a single word to his mind: Danger!

We discussed this inspiration after the sealing session while still in the temple. Later, when we changed our prayer and asked about moving to Dallas, a feeling of peace came. This feeling confirmed that the Lord's will was for us to move, which we did. We moved forward in faith, not having the complete picture but trusting that the Lord knew what was best for our family. Only years later did we discover the danger we avoided due to this move. We were so thankful for the Lord's goodness in giving us an answer we were not seeking—one that would immensely bless our family.

We can all have similar experiences in the Lord's house. It can be a sacred source of inspiration for each of us if we will but let it.

Only in temples are families sealed together for eternity. Families are essential to developing the character of godliness. In the marriage relationship, love, kindness, tenderness, gentleness, and service can be developed and demonstrated daily. We can more quickly identify and correct developmental gaps in this sacred relationship.

We develop and test these godly characteristics regularly in the family relationship. The love of an earthly family is an extension of our heavenly family's love, and this love is critical to enabling and encouraging our progress.

Families are sealed in the temple by a person holding the priesthood sealing authority. They are joined by this "welding link" into "a whole and a complete and a perfect union,"[27] which endures eternally. Welding is the process by which two different metals are heated and then combined to form a single strong alloy. This forged union is symbolic of how distinct members of a family are bound together as one through temple sealings.

A "whole and a complete and a perfect union" is a relationship bound not just by emotions, love, and acts of service but also by covenant and priesthood power. The combination of all these elements forges the link and makes the knowledge and relationship active and eternal. The outcome of an eternal union will be the ability to have spirit children and to assist in their eternal progression.

A person can love and emotionally connect to his or her family in mortality. This truth is given eternal life and validity via the covenant they make with those family members in holy temples, which binds them together eternally. If their relationship is only given life via the mortal marriage contract, then their *commitment* ends at death even if their *love* continues, for this world's civic authority ends when mortal life is complete.[28]

Only in the family's eternal continuance will we fully realize our ultimate purpose of becoming like our Heavenly Parents. And this eternal promise is only made in holy temples.

The temple gives us a "perfect brightness of hope."[29] Hope is one of the most precious blessings we receive from regular temple worship.

---

27. Doctrine and Covenants 128:18.
28. See Doctrine and Covenants 132:7.
29. 2 Nephi 31:20.

It is a positive expectation for the future. Hope is the glimmer of light at the end of a long, dark tunnel of trouble and distress.

Elder Neal A. Maxwell, formerly of the Quorum of the Twelve, taught, "Christ-centered hope is a very specific and particularized hope. It is focused on the great realities of the resurrection, eternal life, a better world, and Christ's triumphant second coming 'things as they really will be.'"[30]

Moroni likewise taught, "And what is it that ye shall hope for? Behold I say unto you that ye shall have hope through the Atonement of Christ and the power of his resurrection, to be raised unto life eternal, and this because of your faith in him according to the promise."[31]

A Christ-centered hope, therefore, is one in which we expect to receive the eternal promises given to us in the scriptures and through our covenants. Those who have had the faith to enter into the waters of baptism, receive the Holy Ghost, and then strive to endure to the end along the covenant path have the hope of "eternal life."[32] "Wherefore, [they have the hope that] all things are theirs, whether life or death, or things present, or things to come, all are theirs and they are Christ's, and Christ is God's."[33] They hope to become "heirs of God, and joint-heirs with Christ."[34]

The temple provides us with this type of hope. Through its ordinances, we understand the literal reality of God, His plan, our Savior, and our purpose. We receive concrete covenants that offer sure promises of blessings, both here and in eternity.

The temple's brilliance is that it brings heaven down to earth and makes it palpable and understandable. In this setting, our hope is no longer ethereal or vague. It becomes real and tangible. Because of the temple, we "might with surety hope for a better world," which becomes "an anchor to the souls of men [and women]."[35]

---

30. Neal A. Maxwell, *Notwithstanding My Weakness* (Salt Lake City: Deseret Book, 1981), 40–41.
31. Moroni 7:41.
32. 2 Nephi 31:20.
33. Doctrine and Covenants 76:59.
34. Romans 8:17.
35. Ether 12:4.

With this anchor in place, our "perfect brightness of hope"[36] stabilizes and sustains us in the ups and downs of mortal life. Hope provides *perspective*. It provides *purpose*. Ultimately, hope provides *peace*.

Personal Application: Julie

We have found the precious hope offered by the temple in our own lives. Aaron's father suddenly passed away from a heart attack on April 3, 2021, the day before Easter. It shocked the entire family. Although it was a difficult time for all, Aaron took it particularly hard. He and his father were golfing buddies, and they had been able to spend a great deal of time golfing together during the pandemic.

Aaron spoke at his father's funeral. At the close of his talk, he spoke of the hope that the Atonement brought him and likewise brings to all who have similarly experienced personal tragedies:

> *To every person in the congregation today who—like us—has lost a loved one, to every individual who has felt physical pain or mental anguish, to every person who has struggled under a load of any type, I invite you to come unto Christ, for "[His] yoke is easy, and [His] burden is light" (Matt. 11:30). I testify of His living reality. He lives! So, come unto Christ and renew your hope in Him.*
>
> *It is my prayer that at this time of loss and grief, we can remember the Atonement of our Lord and Savior Jesus Christ, and reconfirm our hope in Him, "which hope we have as an anchor of the soul" (Heb. 6:19). May we feel the desire to rejoice in His glorious sacrifice, for all the hope that it brings us.[37]*

---

36. 2 Nephi 31:20.

37. Aaron M. Bujnowski, "Seek This Jesus," address delivered at the funeral of Kenneth J. Bujnowski, April 9, 2021. https://www.dropbox.com/s/lw1kod-5j6n7e675/Seek%20This%20Jesus.pdf?dl=0.

The temple is the embodiment and the conduit of Jesus Christ's peace and healing. He can deliver and amplify hope, which is a stabilizing anchor during the storms of life. That Christ-centered hope is among the most precious purposes of the holy temple.

QUESTIONS TO CONSIDER

1. What do the ordinances of the temple mean in your life? How have they blessed you and your family?
2. How do temple covenants increase your spiritual power? How has that occurred in your life?
3. How can the temple and its ordinances provide you with hope in a situation you are currently facing?

NOTES AND INSIGHTS

_____

_____

_____

_____

_____

_____

_____

_____

_____

PART 2

Understanding and Applying Temple Doctrine and Principles

The remainder of this book discusses temple doctrine and principles and encourages you to deepen your understanding of them. These preparatory actions will be foundational in your efforts to learn *from* the temple, for the Lord can only enhance what you bring to His house. Without these basic ingredients, your spiritual "meal" in the temple will be lacking. With them, it will be a glorious "feast of fat things."[38]

Personal Application: Aaron

In 2018, I went with the youth of the Frisco Texas Stake to the Nauvoo Temple. To prepare for our special trip, we spent time in the months prior teaching the youth about the locations they would visit and about the Church history events that occurred there.

On our way from Dallas–Fort Worth to Nauvoo, we stopped in Independence and Adam-ondi-Ahman, Missouri, and we visited the Liberty Jail. In each of these locations, we learned of the Saints' zeal to receive the blessings of the temple, which was tragically delayed due to the persecution they experienced. At Liberty, we learned of the "prison-temple experience"[39] that resulted in Doctrine and Covenants 121–123. In Nauvoo, we learned that despite those earlier difficulties, the Saints built a magnificent temple where they received all the precious priesthood blessings they sought.

---

38. Doctrine and Covenants 58:8.
39. Jeffrey R. Holland, "Lessons from Liberty Jail." CES Fireside. Provo, Utah: Brigham Young University, September 7, 2008, accessed February 6, 2021, https://speeches.byu.edu/talks/jeffrey-r-holland/lessons-liberty-jail/.

Our time in Nauvoo and at its rebuilt temple was filled with many learning experiences for all involved. It was a privilege to be in the temple with the youth from our ward, for whom I was their bishop. These youth yearned to learn more about the temple and its ordinances, and they were thrilled when we were able to teach them while we were together in Nauvoo. On this occasion, the temple was, indeed, a "house of learning."[40]

Their learning on that trip was enhanced by our efforts to prepare them beforehand, just as our time in the temple is enhanced by our preparatory efforts outside of it.

KEYS TO UNDERSTANDING

In the temple, we receive "keys" to spiritual knowledge, even the "key of the knowledge of God."[41] In this context, keys unlock understanding.[42] These temple keys are patterns or blueprints that enable us to understand how we can become more like our Heavenly Parents as we apply the temple's doctrine and principles to our everyday lives.

Our path to becoming like our Heavenly Parents can be difficult to see and navigate because of the darkness and troubles we experience in mortality. This uncertainty, confusion, or blindness for how to become like them is one meaning of the phrase the "mystery of godliness,"[43] or rephrasing it, the "mystery of how to become godly." Becoming more like our Heavenly Parents is understood by those who clearly see and apply truth, but it is a "mystery" and remains unknown to those who do not.

Personal experience and individual communion with the Spirit while in the temple will enable us to receive the keys to the mystery of becoming godly. We can then use them to unlock or decode sacred insights for our understanding and future application. As we discussed

---

40. Doctrine and Covenants 88:119.
41. Doctrine and Covenants 84:19–21.
42. These keys can include priesthood keys. However, we wish to emphasize the word "key" in terms of its application to the *understanding* and *insight* the temple provides, which are available to all people, not just priesthood key holders.
43. 1 Timothy 3:16; Doctrine and Covenants 19:10.

earlier in this book, the temple is a divine compass that points us to our intended destination as heirs of eternal life. Therefore, there must be no barriers to our sublime, personal communion with the Spirit in the temple where we can get direction for our lives, including ignorance of or unfamiliarity with temple doctrine.

KNOW THE TEMPLE'S DOCTRINE

We can more effectively receive and use the temple's keys of understanding when we have a more refined knowledge of its doctrine and principles. Learning the doctrine and principles of the restored gospel of Jesus Christ found in the temple will enable us to access their more profound meaning and improve their application. The temple links, unifies, and systematizes these truths and presents them in a way that gives them life.

Joseph Smith taught, "A man [or a woman] is saved no faster than he [or she] gets knowledge."[44] The Lord added, "It is *impossible* for a man [or a woman] to be saved in ignorance."[45]

The knowledge referred to in these statements is not only an *intellectual understanding* of truth, but it also includes the *experiential comprehension* that comes from *acting on and applying truth*. Accordingly, it is impossible to receive answers to our significant questions in the temple unless we get knowledge "by study and also by faith"[46]—in other words, by learning and then acting on what we have learned. The proper application of knowledge is what the scriptures call *intelligence*,[47] and intelligence creates character.

---

44. Joseph Smith, *History of the Church*, 5:392.
45. Doctrine and Covenants 131:6; emphasis added.
46. Doctrine and Covenants 88:118.
47. See Doctrine and Covenants 93:30, 36. The word "intelligence" in the scriptures has several meanings: (1) Intelligence is the eternal identify of each child of God, which was not created or made. This intelligence was clothed with a spirit body by our Heavenly Parents; (2) Intelligence is the application of knowledge. Knowledge is the mental retainment and recall of facts and information, or it is the information itself. Intelligence is the wise use of knowledge, or it is applied knowledge; and (3) Intelligence is mental, emotional, and spiritual acuity or aptitude. It is our ability to learn, feel, and embrace the truths of the world, of people and their emotions, and of God.

In the remainder of the book, we summarize essential points of temple doctrine and their related principles. They are a foundation for what we might learn and experience *within* the temple and what we might apply *outside* the temple.

We share scriptures, insights from Church leaders and gospel scholars, and insights from our own study and various life experiences. We share a few experiences that the temple's doctrine helped us resolve, and we share other experiences that helped us understand the temple's doctrine. We hope to add to your ability to discover temple insights that we may all be "edified and rejoice together"[48] as you seek for yours.

We organized various points of doctrine into chapters with associated subtopics. The bolded and italicized subtopics within each chapter align to specific concepts we can learn from the temple. Each chapter is self-contained yet often linked to topics in other chapters due to the interrelated nature of gospel doctrine and principles. We attempted to avoid overt duplication, but some may remain to enhance and complete the discussion of a particular topic.

This doctrinal summary is not comprehensive, but it covers the most salient and relevant themes for our temple experience. It is also not authoritative nor meant to represent the official position of the Church. We simply wrote it to be a helpful and insightful summary for those seeking to gain more from their temple experience. We gathered these essential points of temple doctrine together and presented them here in one place to help kick-start and supplement your learning process.

These points of temple doctrine and principles include the subjects listed below, organized by chapter and divided into three major sections:

Section 1: The Father, the Son, and the Plan

- The Nature of God and His Purpose
- Our Savior Jesus Christ
  - His Living Reality and His Character
  - His Roles and His Name
  - His Infinite Atonement and His Doctrine
- The Plan of Salvation

---

48. Doctrine and Covenants 50:22.

Section 2: The Children of God and Their Exaltation

- Our Divine Nature and Potential
- Agency, Choice, and Accountability
- Commandments and Covenants
- The Fall and Its Effects
- Justice and Mercy
- Sacrifice and Consecration
- The Creation and Destiny of the Earth
- The Eternal Family

Section 3: Divine Helps and Warnings

- Priesthood Power
- Our Discipleship and Social Relationships
- Divine Truth and the Ministers of God
- Evil and the Adversary

WHY TEMPLE DOCTRINE?

Why is a focus on temple doctrine so crucial to our eternal progression generally and to our temple experience specifically? Elder Boyd K. Packer, formerly of the Quorum of the Twelve, insightfully taught, "True doctrine, understood, changes attitudes and behavior. The study of the doctrines of the gospel will improve behavior quicker than a study of behavior will improve behavior."[49]

Doctrine grounds us in eternal truth. When applied, it builds and fortifies a godly character, and character is what changes behaviors. Eventually, a perfect character makes us like God.

In our efforts to become more like our Heavenly Parents by developing their same godly character, we often proactively seek ways to understand and apply these and other gospel doctrine and principles in our lives. Other times, issues, challenges, or questions present us with unsolicited but developmentally essential opportunities for

---

49. Boyd K. Packer, "Little Children," Conference Report, October 1986.

increased understanding and application of doctrine. In either case, knowing and applying temple doctrine is paramount.

THE PROCESS FOR DISCOVERY

How can you use the temple as a divine help and guide to understand and apply its doctrine and principles? How do you receive and use the keys of spiritual wisdom at the temple that unlock the mysteries of godliness for you? We would suggest following a revelatory process patterned after one taught by Elder Richard G. Scott, formerly of the Quorum of the Twelve.[50] We outline it for you below.

First, you can ask your Heavenly Father in humble prayer, "What doctrine or principles taught in the temple are most relevant to the current understanding I'm seeking or to the current issue I'm facing?" We provide the subjects summarized in this book as one potential source of ideas. As you prayerfully consider this question, you can write down the doctrine and principles you feel impressed with as being most applicable.

Second, you can diligently study these selected points of doctrine. As President Russell M. Nelson taught, "Good inspiration is based upon good information."[51] You can turn to the scriptures and use the Topical Guide, Bible Dictionary, and Guide to the Scriptures to look up and read every relevant passage pertaining to them. The scriptures and quotes provided in this book may also be a resource for your study. You can write down what you learn and the impressions you receive in the "Notes and Insights" sections of this book or in your personal journal. You may even want to keep a special temple journal, where you record your temple insights.

Third, you should go to the temple and, during the ordinances, seek greater insight into the doctrine and principles you identified by asking the following:

---

50. See Richard G. Scott, "To Acquire Spiritual Guidance," Conference Report, October 2009.
51. Russell M. Nelson, "Revelation for the Church, Revelation for our Lives," Conference Report, April 2018.

- What did I learn about those points of doctrine today?
- How did the symbols I experienced relate to them, and what do they mean for me?
- How can I apply what I have learned to the situation I am facing?

During temple ordinances, you may see patterns or receive impressions that unlock your understanding. They are the "keys" that will help you unlock the mystery you seek. After the ordinances, you can reverently sit in the temple and ponder, looking for new impressions or further guidance. When new insights come, they will be additional keys. Later—perhaps in a private, reverent place in your home—you could write down your thoughts and feelings while they are fresh on your mind. You could ask your Heavenly Father, "What more do you want me to know?" Then, you can record any additional inspiration or keys to understanding that may come.

Fourth, you can begin to apply what you have learned. Often, greater insight comes as you begin to act in faith on what you have already been given. As President Gordon B. Hinckley encouraged, "Get on your knees and ask for the blessings of the Lord; then stand on your feet and do what you are asked to do."[52] You must *use* the keys of spiritual knowledge the Spirit provides you to receive the blessings you seek.[53]

Finally, you can repeat this process of doctrinal learning—asking, studying, pondering, attending the temple, writing down impressions, and applying what you learn—until you feel the peace of knowing that you are on an inspired path forward. Final confirmation that the Lord approves your direction will surely come to you as you diligently seek for it.

---

52. Gordon B. Hinckley, "To the Women of the Church," Conference Report, October 2003.
53. See Mosiah 4:10: "If you believe all these things, see that ye *do* them" (emphasis added).

GO FORWARD WITH FAITH

As you read and ponder the points of doctrine summarized in the remainder of this book, you should seek personal insights about them from the Spirit and your personal experience. You may begin to identify information that could help you with a current issue or question you are facing. You may feel impressed that a particular doctrine is one you need to understand and apply to spiritually grow. Or you may find a doctrinal concept interesting and want to learn more.

Whatever your reason, you can use the process described above to enhance your learning outside the temple. As you carry those thoughts into the temple, your efforts will prepare you to receive even greater light and knowledge in the House of the Lord. The insights you learn *from* the temple will sustain you as you strive to apply them on your lifelong journey of Christian discipleship along the covenant path.

Now, let's dive into temple doctrine and principles together!

Section 1

The Father, the Son, and the Plan

No book on learning from the temple would be complete without a thorough discussion of our Heavenly Father, His Beloved Son, Jesus Christ, and His plan of salvation. Although they may seem like rudimentary topics, understanding them is critical to comprehending the temple and its ordinances.

Several years ago, President Russell M. Nelson challenged the young adults of the Church to undertake a deep study of the Savior, Jesus Christ. He invited them to look up all scriptures related to Him and prayerfully consider their meaning. He had done so himself. What he said about his experience was astonishing: "I read and underlined every verse cited about Jesus Christ, as listed under the main heading and the 57 subtitles in the Topical Guide. When I finished that exciting exercise, my wife asked me what impact it had on me. I told her, 'I am a different man!'"[1]

At that point, President Nelson had been an Apostle for more than thirty years. He had traveled around the world as one of the Savior's special witnesses. However, when he studied the Savior more thoroughly and thoughtfully, the experience helped him grow in his testimony of the Lord. It helped him become a better disciple and witness of Christ. So, we thought, "If this exercise could accomplish such spiritual growth for him, it can certainly help us as well!"

We had always tried to make our Savior the center of our marriage and family. We consistently taught our children about Christ throughout their lives. Even on vacation, we tried to find opportunities to teach them about their Savior. Despite those previous efforts, we took President Nelson's invitation to heart and made a renewed effort to learn about our Savior. This section came out of our desire to learn even more about Him.

---

1. Russell M. Nelson, "Drawing the Power of Jesus Christ into Our Lives," Conference Report, April 2017.

As you read this section of the book, we invite you to do the same thing. Thoughtfully and prayerfully study about your Heavenly Father, His Son, and His plan of salvation. New understanding will come as the Spirit whispers to you. Then, with that deepened testimony, your experience in the temple—the Lord's house—will provide you with additional precious personal insights about these most important points of doctrine and how they apply to you.

Chapter 3

The Nature of God and His Purpose

"When we understand who God is, who we are, how He loves us, and what His plan is for us, fear evaporates . . . [and] our concern over worldly things vanishes."

—John H. Groberg[1]

This chapter covers our Heavenly Father—who He is, what He does, and why He does it. We have come to realize that He is both omnipotent and present, powerful and personal. Learning these points of doctrine will help us prepare for what we might learn about Him from the temple and how that understanding can apply to us.

Personal Application: Aaron

Between my freshman and sophomore years in high school, our small ward youth group took a trip from Nashville, Tennessee, to Palmyra, New York, to attend the Hill Cumorah Pageant. We drove there, staying at members' homes along the way.

---

1. John H. Groberg, "The Power of God's Love," Conference Report, October 2004.

*I remember the fun games we played in the van, the break-
fasts the young men made for the young women, and the sights
we saw along the way. However, one personal experience stands
out for me.*

*On the evening of the pageant, I recall laying in the grass
looking up at the beautiful stars in the sky. I could hear the sounds
from the show, but for some reason, I was focused on that beautiful night sky. I began to wonder to myself if my Heavenly Father
knew I was there. Did He know me?*

*As I pondered this question, I felt a peace I didn't recall feel-
ing before. It seemed to be an assurance that, among the hundreds
of people at the pageant and the billions more around the world,
I was known of Him. He knew me!*

*I've thought about that experience in the years since. I've
wondered if I can know Him as well as He knows me. As I have
tried to learn more about my Heavenly Father, my love for Him
and my desire to be like Him has grown. Knowing Him has led
me to become more like Him. With that desire firmly in place, the
temple has become a reservoir of understanding for who God is,
what He wants for me, and how I might accomplish it.*

**We must understand the character, characteristics, and
attributes of Heavenly Father to become like Him.** The temple
teaches us the literal reality of God, showing us who He is and how
He works.[2] Joseph Smith taught, "Three things are necessary in
order that any rational and intelligent being may exercise faith in
God unto life and salvation. First, the idea that He actually exists.
Secondly, a correct idea of His character, perfections, and attributes.
Thirdly, an actual knowledge that the course of life which he is pur-
suing is according to His will."[3]

---

2. Many Christian sects believe in a God "without body, parts, and passions."
   Members of The Church of Jesus Christ of Latter-day Saints, however, believe
   in a Heavenly Father with a physical yet glorified body.
3. Joseph Smith, *Lectures on Faith*, comp. N.B. Lundwall (Salt Lake City: Deseret
   Book, 1835), 3:2–5, 33.

What are the "character, perfections, and attributes" of God? The temple answers this question for us, as do our holy scriptures.

The Father is called "Man of Holiness."[4] Through His Son, He has said, "Behold, I am God; Man of Holiness is my name; Man of Counsel is my name; and Endless and Eternal is my name, also."[5] This holy Man abounds with pure and holy attributes. The scriptures are replete with descriptions of His godly attributes and with encouragement for us to develop them.

Herein lies the secret to the universe—the most powerful eternal beings are meek, humble, loving, kind, gentle, temperate, long-suffering, and patient.

They are obedient, diligent, active, giving, sacrificing, and resolute.

They are perfectly just and perfectly merciful.

They are without hypocrisy and guile.

They chasten and correct, but they do so with love and kindness.

They are full of charity, love unfeigned, and pure knowledge, along with every other conceivable positive attribute.

These are the character traits and their associated behaviors that are required to eternally do the selfless work of perfecting imperfect and sometimes irrational human beings like all of us.[6]

In the ordinances of salvation, we covenant to develop these godly attributes and "put off the natural man [and woman]."[7] In the temple, we see these attributes portrayed in the presentation and delivery of the ordinances. Outside the temple, we see them demonstrated in the everyday lives of faithful disciples of Christ and good, honorable people everywhere.

---

4. Moses 6:57.
5. Moses 7:35. The Son speaks with "divine investiture of authority," which means His words are spoken as if the Father Himself said them.
6. For a description of many of these godly attributes, see the following scriptures: Psalm 45:7; 51:1; Proverbs 3:12; Isaiah 63:7; Jeremiah 9:24; Romans 12; 2 Corinthians 6:2–10; Galatians 5:22–23; Ephesians 4:1–2, 31–32; Philippians 2:3; 4:8; Colossians 1:23; 1 Timothy 3:2–4; 4:12; Titus 2:1–12; James 3:17–18; 2 Peter 1:4–8; 1 John 3:8–12, 18–21; Alma 7:23, 9:26; Moroni 7:45–48; Doctrine and Covenants 4; 121; Abraham 3:17.
7. Mosiah 3:19.

***We must develop godly characteristics to become like our
Heavenly Parents and to do their work.*** We must strive to develop
the attributes of deity to become like our Heavenly Parents. The Savior,
who was our perfect model, commands us to be "even as I am"[8] and
"be ye holy; for I am holy."[9] As Joseph Smith taught, "If you wish
to go where God is, you must be like God, or possess the principles
which God possesses."[10]

The entirety of the gospel of Jesus Christ, including all its teachings, ordinances, and covenants, is focused on enabling us to become
like our Heavenly Parents—on developing their godly traits, attributes, and characteristics. The sole purpose of our life on the earth is
to have experiences that enable us to develop and demonstrate those
divine characteristics, using the restored gospel of Jesus Christ as our
guide.

Why do we need these traits? If we are to become like our Heavenly
Parents, then we will be engaged in the work of salvation for eternity.
This work requires eternal beings to work with imperfect and some-
times irrational humans for eternity.

All parents know from experience that to be effective, they need
love, patience, and longsuffering, among myriad other positive traits.
Heavenly Father needs these characteristics to work with us effectively,
and we will, likewise, need them to work under His direction for eternity. Eternal selflessness is His work—a work to which we aspire as
His sons and daughters.

Unfortunately, our mortal nature contends against our spiritual
nature.[11] Therefore, we must change our very nature to become more
like our Heavenly Parents. To assist us in becoming like them, facilitate the development of their traits, and overcome our carnal desires,
we should seek the gifts of the Spirit because the Holy Spirit is the
enabler of these attributes in us. He works on us from the inside out.
President Ezra Taft Benson taught,

---

8. 3 Nephi 27:27.
9. 1 Peter 1:16.
10. Joseph Smith, *Teachings of the Prophet Joseph Smith*, comp. Joseph Fielding
Smith (Salt Lake City: Deseret Book, 1976), 216.
11. See Mosiah 15:5, 16:3, 27:25; Alma 12:31, 13:28; Helaman 3:16.

The Lord works from the inside out. The world works from the outside in. The world would take people out of the slums. Christ takes the slums out of people, and then they take themselves out of the slums. The world would mold men [and women] by changing their environment. Christ changes men [and women], who then change their environment. The world would shape human behavior, but *Christ can change human nature.*[12]

The Spirit will enable us to demonstrate godly attributes more consistently, embedding them in our very character and souls. By doing so over a lifetime and beyond, we will eventually become like our Heavenly Parents, and when our Brother, the Savior, appears, "we shall be like him; for we shall see him as he is"[13] and as we are. Of the Spirit's role in enabling the character of Christ in us, Elder Parley P. Pratt, formerly of the Quorum of the Twelve, taught,

> The gift of the Holy Spirit . . . quickens all the intellectual faculties, increases, enlarges, expands, and purifies all the natural passions and affections, and adapts them, by the gift of wisdom, to their lawful use. . . .
>
> It inspires virtue, kindness, goodness, tenderness, gentleness, and charity. It develops beauty of person, form, and features. It tends to health, vigor, animation, and social feeling. It invigorates all the faculties of the physical and intellectual man [or woman].[14]

President George Q. Cannon, formerly of the First Presidency, further taught, "No man [or woman] ought to say, 'Oh, I cannot help this [mortal weakness]; it is my nature.' He [or she] is not justified in it, for the reason that God has promised to . . . give [spiritual] gifts

---

12. Ezra Taft Benson, "Born of God," Conference Report, October 1985; emphasis added.
13. See 1 John 3:2; Moroni 7:48.
14. Parley P. Pratt, *Key to the Science of Theology* (Salt Lake City: Deseret Book, 1979), 61.

that will eradicate [our weaknesses]."[15] Therefore, It Is our great opportunity to pray for the gifts of the Spirit that will make us perfect or complete.

Truthfully, godly characteristics are gifts of God through the Spirit. Our sustained efforts are necessary but are insufficient for their full development. So, we must always humbly seek the Spirit's influence and companionship while in mortality to receive the gift of godly traits.

God the Eternal Father has a sacred and sole purpose focused on His children. The primary purpose of God the Eternal Father is to "bring to pass the immortality and eternal life of man [and woman]."[16] This chief purpose is a focus on us and not on Himself. His only intent is to help us become like Him—to acquire His divine traits and attributes.

He is utterly selfless and never changing in His purpose. The scriptures and the temple portray Him and His Son executing on it repeatedly and personally. Their actions are a model for us to follow when we minister to others as sons and daughters of Heavenly Parents.

Even though God's primary *purpose* does not change, He may adjust His *methods* over time and across cultures to accomplish His great work of perfecting us. We should not become concerned or confused when we observe these differences. We should always ask, "How will this particular approach help me or others become more like Him?" Thoughtful consideration will eventually give way to improved understanding and insight.

His methods may include allowing us to learn and develop through the difficulties and trials of life. Although seemingly contradictory, He knows that these experiences can refine us and help us to spiritually grow, even if they cause us pain and heartache in the moment. He loves us and acutely feels our pain, and He helps us through the experience because He knows it will benefit us.

---

15. George Q. Cannon, "Seeking Spiritual Gifts," *Ensign*, April 2016, 80.
16. Moses 1:39.

Personal Application: Aaron

Let me share a personal story that helped me to experience in a very real way how the Father gives us experiences to accomplish His purpose. It also helped me understand the great love our Father in Heaven has for us as His children during that process. When our daughter was about three years old, she developed a medical condition that became a chronic health problem. Multiple occurrences of this issue raised a concern that there may have been a physical reason for her symptoms.

To determine if there was an underlying physical abnormality, doctors ordered a test for which she would have to remain awake to make an accurate medical assessment. Julie and I were there to help Breanna remain calm because they knew there would be some pain and discomfort involved.

They had Breanna lie on the table while they began to prepare her for the test. An innocent child, she had no concept of what was about to occur because she had never experienced anything like it before in her young life. However, she trusted in us, and we reassured her that everything would be okay.

According to the plan laid out to us by the doctors, I stood at the head of the examination table to hold Breanna's shoulders, and Julie stood at her feet. Nurses also positioned themselves around her to hold her steady during the procedure. We all knew there would be pain and discomfort for our sweet little girl, but this test was the only way for us to be sure there was not a more severe problem with her health.

As the test began, Breanna's passive, quiet demeanor turned to one of pain and distress. She began to cry and squirm, trying to remove herself from our grasp as we all held her still.

With an anguished voice, she looked at me and cried, "Daddy, why are you doing this to me?"

I softly replied, "We're doing this because we love you and want you to get better."

No more painful or heart-wrenching words could have been spoken to me, her father, who loved her with all my heart. Her words echoed those of the Savior who, while suffering the extreme pains on the cross, cried out to His Father: "My God, my God, why hast thou forsaken me?"[17]

At that moment—the instant of the most intense physical pain for my daughter and the time of the most emotional pain for me—I understood in a very real way what our Father in Heaven must have felt to see His Son, His only Son, suffering without relief. He feels the same pain for any of His children who suffer in the near term, even when He knows that suffering will bring blessings in the long term.

This experience gave me the assurance that the Father's desire and purpose is to see us grow spiritually—even amid distress— and that He will be there with us as we progress.

The Father personally ministers to us, His children. The temple shows us, and the scriptures teach us, that the Father is intimately aware of our lives' details. He is personally involved either directly, by His or His Son's interventions, or indirectly, by directing ministers of righteousness who act on their behalf. "God is mindful of every people."[18]

With comforting watchfulness, the Lord affirmed, "Mine eyes are upon you."[19] The Father loves His children unfailingly. He finds joy in our successes and feels pain and sorrow at our failures. He reaches out to us, so He is with us as we experience both. He wants to remain close as He helps us develop His divine attributes.

The methods He uses may be customized to the time and the culture in which He must do His work and the specific needs and personalities of the individuals to whom He ministers, but His intent is always the same. With the personalized care of a loving parent, the Father accommodates our strengths and addresses our weaknesses, one by one.

When we pray, read scriptures, and attend the temple, we are close to Him, and He wants to be close to us. "Draw near unto me and I

---

17. Matthew 27:46; emphasis added.
18. Alma 26:37.
19. Doctrine and Covenants 38:7.

will draw near unto you."[20] He wants to bridge the gap that exists because of our mortality and His immortality. He wants to be close to us because He loves us.

Drawing ourselves close to Him is called *worship*. In the case of the temple, we call it "temple worship." When He brings Himself close to us, He is *ministering*. Because He is our Father, it could also be called godly *parenting*. Our worshiping and His ministering come from our love for Him and His love for us. As such, the temple is assuredly a house of love.

All God's children have experienced His love and personal ministry in some fashion, even if we do not immediately recognize His influence. Our temple experience reminds us of this sacred fact, one that we should always remember and cherish. As we do, our love for our Heavenly Father will be real and ever-present, a tender evidence of our relationship with Him.

QUESTIONS TO CONSIDER

1. What are the ways the temple can help you understand that your Heavenly Father knows you personally? What evidences of His presence have you recently experienced in your life?
2. What characteristics of God do you most desire to develop? What small changes can you make today that will help you develop them? How can the temple help you?
3. How do you feel when you have the Holy Spirit with you? What impressions did He give you about how you might become more like Heavenly Father during your last visit to the temple? What have you done with them?
4. How can the temple help you understand your eternal purpose? In what ways are your temple covenants helping you to achieve it?

---

20. Doctrine and Covenants 88:63.

NOTES AND INSIGHTS

_____

_____

_____

_____

_____

_____

_____

_____

_____

Chapter 4

Our Savior Jesus Christ

"Jesus is my friend. . . . None other can take His place.
None other ever will. . . . He is the Lamb of God,
to whom I bow and through whom
I approach my Father in Heaven."

—Gordon B. Hinckley[1]

This chapter covers our Savior, Jesus Christ. He is everything to His disciples. This topic is so expansive that we present the core doctrine and principles related to Him in three specific areas: (1) His living reality and His character, (2) His roles and His name, and (3) His infinite Atonement and His doctrine. Because He is the central figure of the temple and the Father's plan for us, this is a most sacred topic. We recommend you visit and revisit it, each time deepening your understanding of and relationship with your Savior.

Personal Application: Julie

Although Aaron was born into the Church, I was not. I was raised in another Christian faith. My grandmother, Lila Lee Haskins, was a very faithful member of her Christian church.

---

1. Gordon B. Hinckley, "My Testimony," Conference Report, April 2000.

She was a God-fearing person who read the Bible and attended Sunday services. She sang in her church choir and contributed to her church cookbook.

Granny taught me about Jesus. She told me stories from His life and made sure I knew who He was. She showed me how the petals of blossoms on the dogwood tree are in the form of a cross, a reminder of the sacrifice of Jesus Christ. She made sure that Christmas and Easter focused on Christ. Because of her example and teachings, I came to know that Jesus was my Savior.

Before I joined the Church, I had a belief in my Savior. But after I made the covenant to follow Him through baptism into His Church, I felt connected to Him. Since that time, my faith has grown as I have tried to live my baptismal covenant and have made other promises on the covenant path.

Now, my knowledge of Him is sure, and my faith in Him is bright and strong. He has sustained me through the ups and downs of my life. I love Him and want to be one of His faithful disciples. As I faithfully attend the temple, I continue to deepen my understanding of and love for my Savior.

HIS LIVING REALITY AND HIS CHARACTER

The temple testifies of the living reality and divinity of our Lord and Savior, Jesus Christ. Jesus Christ is the premortal Jehovah, the First Born and Only Begotten of the Father. He stands at the Father's right hand and has been delegated all power by Him. The temple testifies of Him.

Every prophet—both ancient and modern—has also testified of Him as His special witness. Their testimonies are a chorus of voices that enable *us* to know Him because *they* know Him. In the year 2000, all fifteen prophets and apostles of our dispensation testified,

We offer our testimony of the reality of [Jesus Christ's] matchless life and the infinite virtue of His great atoning sacrifice. None other has had so profound an influence upon all who have lived and will yet live upon the earth. . . .

He gave His life to atone for the sins of all mankind. His was a great vicarious gift in behalf of all who would ever live upon the earth. He rose from the grave to "become the firstfruits of them that slept" (1 Corinthians 15:20). . . .

We bear testimony, as His duly ordained Apostles—that Jesus is the Living Christ, the immortal Son of God. He is the great King Immanuel, who stands today on the right hand of His Father. He is the light, the life, and the hope of the world. His way is the path that leads to happiness in this life and eternal life in the world to come. God be thanked for the matchless gift of His divine Son.[2]

What great peace it should give us to know that we have living prophets who know Him and who, as Elder Boyd K. Packer testified, "have *that* witness."[3]

The character of Jesus Christ is the earthly embodiment and our perfect example of the Father's traits. During His mortal ministry, Jesus Christ developed and demonstrated a perfect character. It is what Elder Neal A. Maxwell, formerly of the Quorum of the Twelve, called "the character of Christ."[4]

The Savior came to model for us the character and attributes of His Father. They are separate beings, but they have the same traits. He always pointed us to His Father, and He did it most notably in demonstrating these characteristics of godliness. Jesus taught, "He that hath seen me hath seen the Father."[5]

Jesus Christ was the only perfect human, although He was unique because He was fully human and became wholly divine as He grew

---

2. "The Living Christ: The Testimony of the Apostles" (Salt Lake City: The Church of Jesus Christ of Latter-day Saints, January 1, 2000).
3. Boyd K. Packer, "The Spirit Beareth Record," Conference Report, April 1971.
4. Neal A. Maxwell, cited in David A. Bednar, "The Character of Christ," BYU–Idaho Religion Symposium, January 25, 2003, https://www2.byui.edu/presentations/transcripts/religionsymposium/2003_01_25_bednar.htm.
5. John 14:9.

"grace for grace."[6] Like us, He was "tempted in all points,"[7] but unlike us, He resisted them all.[8] Therefore, He was our perfect exemplar of overcoming the adversary and the natural man or woman.[9]

We see Him in others when we observe and recognize areas of perfection in them. These include a superior intellect, an adept sense of humor, pure compassion, an engaging personality, a splendidly kind and selfless attitude, and so on. They are examples of Him in these areas of strength and refinement. "Because as he is, so are we in this world."[10]

The temple models many of these godly traits and shows how we might develop them all via covenants and our own choices in living those covenants. It encourages and enables us to become like our Master by developing His traits. Of the importance of these attributes, Elder Neal A. Maxwell, formerly of the Quorum of the Twelve, taught, "For the serious disciple, the cardinal attributes exemplified by Jesus are not optional. These developmental milestones take the form of traits, traits that mark the trail to be traveled. After all, should not Latter-day Saints have a special interest in what is required to become a Saint, virtue by virtue and quality by quality?"[11]

All of us should desire to develop and use these precious traits in our lives.

Personal Application: Aaron

There have been countless people in my life who have demonstrated the character of Christ. The following story illustrates such character.[12] When I was in high school, my Young Men president was named Doug. He was a kind and loving man who actively involved himself in our lives. He always made sure the things that

---

6. Doctrine and Covenants 93:12.
7. Hebrews 4:15.
8. See Doctrine and Covenants 20:22.
9. See 1 Peter 2:21.
10. 1 John 4:17.
11. Neal A. Maxwell, "In Him All Things Hold Together," *BYU Speeches* (Provo: Brigham Young University, March 31, 1991), accessed March 31, 2021, https://speeches.byu.edu/talks/neal-a-maxwell/in-him-all-things-hold-together/.
12. Story used with permission.

were important to us as youth were also important to him. I will always remember him attending the state marching band contest, where Julie and I performed in the finals. He saw our potential, and he treated us accordingly.

When I applied to college, my first choice was Brigham Young University (BYU) in Provo, Utah. Doug encouraged me to apply because he had deep connections to the school. He had attended the university as a young adult, his father worked there as an administrator, and his brother-in-law, Brad, worked there as a professor.

Because money was tight in our family, I had never been to the campus or even to the state of Utah before flying out to attend school after being accepted. So, I purchased a plane ticket, packed my bags, and headed out to BYU in the fall of 1989. I had no idea what the campus looked like, other than the pictures I had seen in brochures.

The day I arrived, and I was waiting at Doug's childhood home when his brother-in-law, Brad, stopped by. We chatted a bit, and I told him I was excited to start school. Then, he asked if I had ever been to the campus. When I told him I had not, he was astonished. He invited me to go with him to an event he was about to attend on campus. He said if I participated in the event with him, he would give me a driving tour of campus on the way to the meeting. I excitedly accepted.

Brad drove me around BYU's campus, describing the various buildings and recounting the school's history. He was a friendly and knowledgeable tour guide. We parked the car and went into a large concert hall on campus. As we walked down the corridor to the front of the auditorium, I looked up and saw that it was packed with youth waiting for Brad to speak.[13] We walked to the

---

13. I don't know how many people were in attendance that day, but the concert hall I described had a capacity of more than one thousand seats. I recall that the room was very full that day. Coming from a place where there were only five or six Church members in my high school of almost two thousand students, this was the greatest number of Church youth I had ever seen.

front of the hall, and Brad told the people waiting for him, "Sorry I'm late! I've got your opening prayer," and he pointed to me.

It turns out that Doug's brother-in-law was Brad Wilcox, one of the most popular youth speakers in the Church, who is currently serving as a member of the General Young Men Presidency. Because I had no family or close connections to Utah other than people at church, I was completely unaware of Brad's notoriety. I just knew him to be Doug's brother-in-law, a great guy who would visit us in Nashville, Tennessee, now and then. Doug never "talked up" Brad, and Brad never acted as someone important.

These humble men helped an inexperienced young man from a distant state begin his time at a large university in a wonderful and kindly way. Doug went out of his way to help me get to BYU's campus. On that memorable day when I arrived, Brad was willing to be late to a significant event to spend time with me. Their character was and still is one of humility and Christlike service. How grateful I am for them and others like them who are a Christlike light to the world.

The Savior has two foundational traits—meekness and humility—from which spring all others. Of all Jesus Christ's perfect qualities, two merit special consideration by us: meekness and humility.[14] Mormon taught us the sublime truth that *"none* is acceptable before God, *save* the meek and lowly in heart."[15] Why would Mormon put such importance on these two foundational attributes? He does it because they are the gateway to every other godly trait we desire to have, including charity or perfect love—the ultimate, defining characteristic of deity.[16]

Meekness and humility are the two traits that fueled the Savior's perfect submissiveness to His Father and His perfect love for us.

---

14. For two excellent discourses on meekness, see Neal A. Maxwell, "Meek and Lowly," *BYU Speeches* (Provo: Brigham Young University, October 21, 1986), and Neal A. Maxwell, "Meekly Drenched in Destiny," *BYU Speeches* (Provo: Brigham Young University, September 5, 1982).

15. Moroni 7:44; emphasis added. Humility and "lowliness of heart" are synonymous.

16. See 1 John 4.

Jesus declared, "I seek not mine own will, but the will of the Father which hath sent me."[17] He willingly "yieldeth himself" to the will of the Father.[18] At the height of His agony in Gethsemane, Jesus expressed His lifelong unfailing submissiveness to His Father in this heartfelt statement: "Nevertheless, not *my* will, but *thine* be done."[19]

Jesus expressed His eternal unfailing love for us in this statement: "Greater love hath no man than this, that a man lay down his life for his friends."[20] Submissiveness and love allowed Jesus Christ to complete the exacting demands of the Atonement, which brought the possibility of redemption to us all. His meekness and humility enabled His sacrifice and our salvation.[21]

Given meekness and humility were the foundation of His submissiveness and love, Jesus made a most compelling invitation and promise to us that amplifies our need to develop these two traits. It is the only statement on record in which He personally describes His own character traits. He beckoned, "Take my yoke upon you, and learn of me; *for I am meek and lowly in heart*: and ye shall find rest unto your souls."[22]

If we are to develop these two foundational traits to find our rest, we should more thoroughly understand them.

What is humility? Humility—or being lowly in heart—is the subtraction of self, a "freedom from pride or arrogance."[23] The humble do not think they are better or more important than others or God.[24] They recognize their dependence on God and others, and they are open to receiving input, direction, teaching, and help from them. Being humble requires meekness.

---

17. John 5:30. See also John 4:34; 6:38; 8:29; Doctrine and Covenants 19:24.
18. 1 Nephi 19:10. See also Doctrine and Covenants 19:2.
19. Luke 22:42; emphasis added.
20. John 15:13.
21. See Doctrine and Covenants 19:15 and 1 Nephi 19:9.
22. Matthew 11:29; emphasis added. See also Doctrine and Covenants 19:23: "Learn of me, and listen to my words, walk in the meekness of my Spirit, and you shall have peace in me."
23. "Humility," www.merriam-webster.com.
24. Humility is "the quality of having a modest or low view of one's importance" ("Humility," *Oxford Dictionary of English* [Oxford: Oxford University Press, 2010], 854.)

What is meekness? Certainly, it encompasses an attitude of kindness and gentleness. However, meekness is much more. It is also the appropriate control of power and passions. Research by one scholar revealed that the original Greek word, πραυτησ, which was translated into English as "meek," was originally thought of as "discipline that controls power." Ancient military leaders used this word to describe powerful war horses, where confidence and constraint were necessary to harness and use the horse's physical might at the right time and circumstances. This author summarized his research by saying, "Meekness provides a self-effacement, empathy and kindness needed to nurture relationships responsively, yet combined with it is the perceptiveness to discern . . . how and when to put aside acquiescence in order to intervene with greater assertiveness and discipline. . . . In short, meekness is about personal power consciously controlled and generously shared, not foregone."[25]

Therefore, meekness is not weakness. It is the strength of character that enables a person to treat others with kindness and have enough self-control to be bold and assertive only when necessary. Speaking of the strength of meekness, Elder David A. Bednar of the Quorum of the Twelve has taught,

> Meekness is a defining attribute of the Redeemer and is distinguished by righteous responsiveness, willing submissiveness, and strong self-restraint. . . .
>
> The Christlike quality of meekness often is misunderstood in our contemporary world. Meekness is strong, not weak; active, not passive; courageous, not timid; restrained, not excessive; modest, not self-aggrandizing; and gracious, not brash. A meek person is not easily provoked, pretentious, or overbearing and readily acknowledges the accomplishments of others.[26]

Therefore, the meek are gentle, kind, and submissive, and they are simultaneously strong, powerful, and resilient. They have a perfect

---

25. David Molyneaux, "'Blessed Are the Meek, for They Shall Inherit the Earth'— An Aspiration Applicable to Business?" *Journal of Business Ethics* (Netherlands: Kluwer Academic Publishers, 2003), 48:359–360.

26. David A. Bednar, "Meek and Lowly of Heart," Conference Report, April 2018.

balance of gentleness and strength, of kindness and confidence, and of patience and power. They are temperate but teeming with energy.

They manage and objectively control personal or organizational authority with concerted discernment and perfect confidence of when, where, and how this power should be used and why. They exhibit self-control of carnal passions, righteous indignation, and instinctive retorts, even amid temptations, trials, and persecutions.

The meek consistently demonstrate tenderness and mildness— even when under duress and particularly when personally attacked. They are mild and forgiving but not eternally tolerant or passive, directly but kindly delivering appropriate consequences when discerned as necessary. They are not powerless or pacifistic but rather calmly objective, followed by passionate, decisive, and even risky intervention when needed.

These behaviors set the foundation for every other godly trait, including God's ultimate defining characteristic, charity.

The perfect love of Jesus Christ—or charity—is His ultimate, defining characteristic. Charity is the culmination of all Jesus Christ's defining characteristics. John the Beloved taught, "God is love."[27] It defines who He is. His pure love is the driver for all He does for us, including the extreme sacrifice performed during His infinite Atonement. Because the temple is the "House of God," it is also a "House of love."

Charity is the ultimate gift and the most significant godly trait that we can receive, now or in eternity. As Mormon taught, "Charity is the pure love of Christ, and it endureth forever; and whoso is found possessed of it at the last day, it shall be well with him."[28] "Charity never faileth" and is described as the "greatest of all" gifts.[29]

Charity "is not an act but a condition or state of being [one becomes]."[30] However, we can best understand the divine attribute of

---

27. 1 John 4:8.
28. Moroni 7:45.
29. See Moroni 7:46; 1 Corinthians 13:8.
30. Dallin H. Oaks, "The Challenge to Become," Conference Report, October 2000.

charity by its associated behaviors and actions, which are evidence it is in operation and proof of what a person has become.[31]

Below, we expand on the meaning of charity's associated behaviors as described in our scriptures. We hope to provide an elevated understanding, so we can more consistently seek this most precious godly trait.[32]

Suffereth long—Endures, does not tire in, incessantly complain or bemoan during, or quickly give up due to adversity or opposition. Sustains or endures difficulties, challenges, or resistance for extended periods while still maintaining a positive outlook or kindly approach. Continues forward faithfully and positively despite any obstacle or hardship he or she might face and irrespective of its source, whether through circumstance or due to the actions and agency of others.

Kind—Has a sensitivity toward the needs of others. Is soft, gentle, kind-hearted, caring, affectionate, loving, warm, considerate, helpful, thoughtful, unselfish, understanding, benevolent, friendly, hospitable, charitable, and generous.

Vaunteth not itself—Is not a braggart and not someone who overtly enhances his or her public image for personal gain. Does not push him or herself above others, but seeks to serve and edify them selflessly, quietly.

Envieth not—Does not covet or have a resentful longing for things that belong to another, whether they are possessions, professions, honors, talents, skills, traits, callings, assignments, opportunities, family arrangements, luck, good fortune, or anything else that is given to or received by another person, especially when it seems to be more than he or she receives, or more than the other person seems to deserve.

---

31. See 1 Corinthians 13; Moroni 7:44–48; Doctrine and Covenants 121:41–46 for a full description of charity.
32. The outward evidences of charity are listed in Moroni 7:45 and 1 Corinthians 13:4–7. The actions listed in Doctrine and Covenants 121:41–43 are also evidences of charity.

Doth not behave itself unseemingly—Does not behave indecently, unbecomingly, or in an unholy or impure manner.

Not puffed up—Is not prideful, boastful, or conceited. Is not self-centered or vain. Is not condescending of others who seemingly have less and is not critical of those who apparently have more.

Seeketh not her own—Seeks to turn his, her, or others' attention toward God or the needs of others, not toward him or herself. Puts the needs of others and God's kingdom ahead of his or her own needs and desires.

Is not easily provoked—Is not quick to anger, easily irritated, or quickly exasperated. Controls power and passions, especially any negative emotion (anger, fear, jealousy, and so on). Does not react but chooses a response based on the desired outcome. Does not keep a ledger of imputed wrongs.

Thinketh no evil—Has no secret agenda, no private desire for personal gain, no hidden or unrepentant iniquity. Is not hypocritical and is without guile (deceit, duplicity, or betrayal). Assumes positive intent in the unknown rationale for the actions of others. Thinks the best of others. Ponders positive, upright, righteous, kind, and loving ideas and ideals. Wishes the best for others, including enemies, despite their actions or opinions, both stated and unstated.

Rejoiceth not in iniquity—Delights in noble and holy accomplishments, no matter the source. Embraces anything good or praiseworthy. Rejects anything gross, degrading, basal, sinful, lustful, lewd, or wicked. Despises the natural man or woman. Abhors unrighteousness, filthiness, lasciviousness, grossness, and baseness.

Rejoiceth in the truth—Delights in the everlasting truths of the gospel. Always seeks higher truths. Supplements learned truth with revealed truth.

Uses persuasion—Uses a gentle, subtle influence. Influences not by coercion or force but by invitation, enticement, and encouragement.

Has love unfeigned—Demonstrates authentic, heartfelt love and service for the individual that is not fake or deceitful and without ulterior motives.

Beareth all things—Takes on heavy loads, responsibilities, stewardships, and burdens and does it willingly and without complaint or resentment.

Believeth all things—Has faith in all things given by the Father through His Spirit or His servants. Acts on that belief without perfect knowledge.

Hopeth all things—Has a positive expectation of blessings to come, based on faith, despite his or her present condition or state.

Endureth all things—Perseveres through all trials, tribulations, difficulties, opposition, chastisement, or any other problem—however heart-wrenching—that the Lord sees fit to inflict upon the person. Realizes all opposition provides experience and endows the person with humility, meekness, and every other godly attribute of Heavenly Father. Moves through difficulty and trial in a positive, faith-filled manner while still recognizing and not ignoring the pain, heartache, and exhaustion of such experiences.

All things—In all the aforementioned evidence of charity, *all means all*. With charity, we will believe, bear, hope, and endure every spiritual, ecclesiastical, physical, mental, emotional, interpersonal, social, societal, familial, political, environmental, or organizational issue, opportunity, opinion, fact, or claim we face.

Mormon invited us all to develop this most important of all traits, charity so that we can become like our Savior. He implored,

Wherefore, my beloved brethren [and sisters], pray unto the Father with all the energy of heart, *that ye may be filled with this love*, which he hath bestowed upon all who are true followers of his Son, Jesus Christ;

That ye may become the sons [and daughters] of God; that when he shall appear *we shall be like him*, for we shall see him as he is; that we may have this hope; that we may be purified even as he is pure.[33]

May we all heed his urgent invitation!

HIS ROLES AND HIS NAME

Jesus Christ plays the central role in the Father's plan of salvation. Jesus Christ is involved in, empowers, and leads every aspect of the Father's plan for His children. He has said, "I am over all, and in all, and through all, and search all things."[34] He is the center of the temple.

Jesus Christ is the only Begotten Son of the Father.[35] He is the enabler of the Father's plan of salvation and the facilitator of it. He is the Word through which the Father has always done His work.[36]

As the premortal Jehovah, Jesus was the Creator of the universe.[37] As the mortal Messiah, He was the Lamb of God, sent to be an offering for sin. Following His resurrection, He became the eternal Savior and Redeemer, directing the work of salvation through His servants, the prophets.

In the final day, Jesus Christ will be our Judge and our Advocate,[38] evaluating and assisting us with perfect justice and mercy. Between now and then, He is our Comforter and Enabler, facilitating and enabling our rigorous walk through mortality.

---

33. Moroni 7:48; emphasis added.
34. Doctrine and Covenants 63:59.
35. See John 1:14; 2 Nephi 25:12; Alma 12:33–34; Doctrine and Covenants 76:23.
36. John 1:1.
37. See Colossians 1:16; Hebrews 1:2; Mosiah 3:8; Helaman 14:12.
38. See Moroni 10:34; Doctrine and Covenants 29:5.

Everything in the temple and everything in the gospel points us to Jesus Christ.[39] Why do all things point to Him? Because "no other name [is] given nor any other way or means whereby salvation can come unto the children of men, only in and through the name of Christ, the Lord Omnipotent."[40]

We must depend solely on Him because He is our Savior and Redeemer. Without Him, all are lost; with Him, all is possible. Nephi affirmed what His disciples do to put Him at their center: "We talk of Christ, we rejoice in Christ, we preach of Christ, we prophesy of Christ, and we write according to our prophecies, that our children may know to what source they may look for a remission of their sins."[41] These are the behaviors of faithful disciples of Christ throughout the ages.

Jesus Christ is our Savior and Redeemer. Jesus Christ is the Messiah, meaning the Anointed One, He whom the Father chose to satisfy the demands of exacting justice fully so that He could offer abundant mercy to an imperfect but willing set of covenant sons and daughters. The temple affirms this most critical role.

The Savior came to offer Himself as a vicarious sacrifice for sin. Only He could make this infinite and eternal sacrifice because only He was perfect and outside of the reach of divine justice. Only He was in the unique position to redeem us from our sins because only He knew no sin.

By performing His great atoning sacrifice, He saves us from death because He will resurrect all people one day. Because He fully met the demands of justice for all children of God, He can save us from sin as we humbly come to Him, accept and live His doctrine, and endure to the end. His atoning sacrifice allows Him to claim the "rights of mercy," or the right to extend mercy to any who sincerely come unto Him.[42] The scriptures describe, and the temple demonstrates, ways He heals, saves, and redeems us.

---

39. See 2 Nephi 11:4; Jacob 4:5; Alma 33:19; Moses 6:63.
40. Mosiah 3:17. See also Alma 38:9; Doctrine and Covenants 18:23.
41. 2 Nephi 25:26.
42. See Moroni 7:27–28.

To "redeem" is to "buy back." We are "bought with a price"[43]—the high price of the blood He shed for us. He redeems us by trading His perfect life for our imperfect life.[44] To "reconcile" is to restore. He reconciles us to God by enabling us to qualify to come back into the presence of the Father, sanctified from sin and acquitted of the consequences of sin.

Jesus Christ is our Judge and Advocate. Jesus Christ fully paid for every sin and transgression of every child of God with His infinite and eternal Atonement. Because of His Atonement, Jesus Christ stands as both the Judge[45] and the Advocate[46] of all people.

As our Judge, He evaluates us against His merciful law, the gospel law. As our Advocate, He pleads with the Father on our behalf, seeking mercy wherever possible. He stands alone in these roles. As Jacob taught, "The keeper of the gate is the Holy One of Israel; and he employeth no servant there." [47]

The infinite and eternal nature of His Atonement can allow the Savior to acquit us[48] and sanctify us[49] "according to the power of his deliverance."[50] He paid for every sin and transgression, so He can make anything we've done irrelevant and wipe anything clean if He, in His perfect judgment, chooses to do it.

The Savior will not violate the laws of justice and mercy. He will allow every negative consequence to remain, especially to those who were disobedient and unrepentant after having full knowledge of the gospel, having full accountability and capacity to act, and having

---

43. 1 Corinthians 6:20.
44. If we qualify for salvation by living the doctrine of Christ, Jesus Christ literally offers His perfect life to the Father in lieu of our imperfect life. For all intents and purposes in the eyes of the Father's perfect justice, we will be accepted as if we had lived the Savior's perfect life. See Philippians 3:9; 2 Corinthians 5:21; Romans 5:19; 2 Nephi 2:3; Jeremiah 23:6.
45. Moroni 10:34.
46. See Doctrine and Covenants 29:5; 32:3; 45:3; 62:1; 110:4.
47. 2 Nephi 9:41.
48. To acquit is to free us from the consequences of sin.
49. To sanctify is to cleanse us from the sullying effects of sin.
50. Alma 7:13.

been clearly and consistently commanded to repent. "For of him unto whom much is given much is required; and he who sins against the greater light shall receive the greater condemnation."[51]

He will also give out the fullest extent of mercy due to every individual who has reached the age of accountability, for He is "merciful unto those who confess their sins with humble hearts."[52] The Savior will base His decision on His perfect judgment of how we complied with gospel law—His law—considering what our situation may have been during mortality. Joseph Smith taught,

> [The Lord] will award judgment or mercy to all nations according to their several deserts, their means of obtaining intelligence, the laws by which they are governed, the facilities afforded them of obtaining correct information, and His inscrutable designs. . . .
>
> God judges men [and women] according to the use they make of the light which He gives them.[53]

Elder M. Russell Ballard of the Quorum of the Twelve likewise taught, "I feel that judgment for sin is not always as cut-and-dried as some of us seem to think. . . . I feel that the Lord also recognizes differences in intent and circumstances . . . When he does judge us, I feel he will take all things into consideration: our genetic and chemical makeup, our mental state, our intellectual capacity, the teachings we have received, the traditions of our fathers, our health, and so forth."[54]

When the Lord judges us, He is judging how much of His mercy we can access based on our circumstances, what we've done and, ultimately, what we've become. We are already condemned because of our sins, transgressions, and mistakes. Therefore, His role as Judge is to determine the extent of our redemption because of our repentance and faith

---

51. Doctrine and Covenants 82:3. In Alma 9:23, we also read that it is "more tolerable" for those who have impediments to receiving and living the gospel than those who had full ability to accept and live covenants but who chose not to.
52. Doctrine and Covenants 61:2.
53. Joseph Smith, *Teachings of the Prophet Joseph Smith*, 218, 303.
54. M. Russell Ballard, "Suicide: Some Things We Know, and Some We Do Not," *Ensign*, October 1987.

in Him. As our Advocate, His role is to petition for the greatest mercy and the least punishment possible. In His roles as Judge and Advocate, He will not be pushing us down to condemn us; He will be trying to lift us up to redeem us from the condemnation we created for ourselves.

We must trust that He will be perfectly equitable toward all circumstances, including the most unfair, we or those we love may face. He will deliver mercy "according as [his] will, suiting his mercies according to the conditions of the children of men."[55] Elder Dale G. Renlund of the Quorum of the Twelve recently taught us about infuriating unfairness:

> Some unfairness cannot be explained; inexplicable unfairness is infuriating. . . . In unfair situations, one of our tasks is to trust that "all that is unfair about life can be made right through the Atonement of Jesus Christ." Jesus Christ overcame the world and "absorbed" all unfairness. Because of Him, we can have peace in this world and be of good cheer. If we let Him, Jesus Christ will consecrate the unfairness for our gain. He will not just console us and restore what was lost; He will use the unfairness for our benefit.[56]

Indeed, Jesus Christ is "full of grace, equity, and truth" in His judgments, and He is "full of patience, mercy, and long-suffering" in His ministry.[57] His "grace is sufficient"[58] to absorb and absolve anything and everything wrong in our lives. We must always believe this eternal fact; we must trust *Him* to make all things right.

In all cases, we must always do our best to qualify for His mercy. He judges our best on the light and truth we have received and what we are legitimately able to do with that knowledge, according to the expression of our agency available to us. When we have done our best, which is unique for each of us, *He* delivers us through His infinite and eternal Atonement.

---

55. Doctrine and Covenants 46:15.
56. Dale G. Renlund, "Infuriating Unfairness," Conference Report, April 2021.
57. Alma 9:26.
58. Ether 12:26.

Jesus Christ is our Comforter and Enabler. The temple teaches us of the Savior's ability and willingness to comfort and strengthen us. Jesus Christ fully took upon Himself every temptation, pain, affliction, infirmity, and sickness any child of God would ever bear, so He can fully comfort and succor us when we experience any of them ourselves. He did this so He might "know according to the flesh how to succor his people."[59]

To "succor" is to "give assistance or aid." It comes from the Latin word *succurrere*, which means to "run to the help of."[60] He helps bear our load and makes it light on our shoulders. He soothes our heartache and heartbreak with perfect empathy and perfect love. He rescues us from despair, worry, and pain by sending us peace. He lifts the burden of guilt by extending us forgiveness upon our repentance.

His Atonement also allows Him to enable and strengthen us to do His work, overcome any trial or issue of mortality, and become like Him. Of the enabling and strengthening power of the Savior through His Atonement, Elder David A. Bednar of the Quorum of the Twelve taught,

> Most of us clearly understand that the Atonement is for sinners. I am not so sure, however, that we know and understand that the Atonement is also for saints—for good men and women who are obedient and worthy and conscientious and who are striving to become better and serve more faithfully. . . .
>
> The gospel of the Savior is not simply about avoiding bad in our lives; it also is essentially about doing and becoming good. And the Atonement provides help for us to overcome and avoid bad and to do and become good. There is help from the Savior for the entire journey of life—from bad to good to better and to change our very nature.[61]

---

59. Alma 7:11–12.
60. "Succour," *Oxford Dictionary of English*, 1777.
61. David A. Bednar, "In the Strength of the Lord," *BYU Speeches* (Provo: Brigham Young University, October 23, 2001), accessed February 6, 2021, https://speeches.byu.edu/talks/david-a-bednar/strength-lord/.

Jesus Christ changes us from natural men and women into spiritual men and women with divine characteristics even as we submit our will to Him. He works via the Holy Ghost, which is the conduit of His redeeming and enabling power.

The name of Jesus Christ has unquestionable divine power. In the scriptures, the ordinances of salvation, and the temple, we are shown the inherent power of the name of Jesus Christ. His name represents all that He is, including all His godly traits and His purpose to bring to pass our immortality and eternal life. His name is synonymous with authority and power[62]—the power to act, the power of covenants, the power to heal, the power to bless, the power to pray, the power to reveal, and, ultimately, the power to become like Him.

When one of His servants invokes His name for sacred purposes, the outcomes are unquestionable and assured. The same is true when a person takes upon him or herself that sacred name via covenant. He infuses them with His power.

This name is holy and should be spoken and used with utmost reverence. He promised to put His name in the temple,[63] which implies His presence will be in His holy house if we are worthy and do not drive Him out. It also means we who have taken His name upon us will experience His presence more fully in the temple as we submit ourselves unto Him there.

When we are willing to accept His name by covenant, we express our willingness to accept His sacrifice and receive all the blessings of it. As Elder Dallin H. Oaks, current President of the Quorum of the Twelve, taught, "Our willingness to take upon us the name of Jesus Christ affirms our commitment to do all that we can to be counted among those whom he will choose to stand at his right hand and be called by his name at the last day."[64] We agree to follow Him, be His disciples, and join Him in His work

---

62. See Acts 4:7.
63. See Doctrine and Covenants 110:7.
64. Dallin H. Oaks, "Taking Upon Us the Name of Jesus Christ," Conference Report, April 1985.

to save and help our brothers and sisters. We commit to be called by His name and, ultimately, become like Him.[65]

HIS INFINITE ATONEMENT AND DOCTRINE

The Atonement of Jesus Christ is the central act of the plan of salvation. Jesus Christ's great, vicarious act of supreme sacrifice is called the Atonement. He completed the Atonement when He voluntarily took upon Himself every sin, transgression, pain, and sickness of every son and daughter of Heavenly Father in the Garden of Gethsemane,[66] when He willingly offered Himself and His perfect life as a sacrifice upon the cross at Calvary,[67] and when He took up His life and emerged from the Garden Tomb as the first resurrected person on the third day, conquering sin and death.[68]

Jesus Christ and His Atonement are the central themes of the scriptures and the temple. Understanding them is the most profound key to all spiritual knowledge we can obtain in this life and through our temple experience. It unlocks our ability to apply gospel knowledge in all circumstances, and it enhances our capability to become more like Him.

Every symbol, ceremony, and action in the temple points toward Jesus Christ's great and glorious act of Atonement—vicariously performed on our behalf—and to Him who completed it. All gospel doctrine and principles center on this redemptive action and its divine Actor, Jesus the Christ.

If we face a severe issue, we benefit by pondering how we could resolve it through Jesus Christ and His Atonement. He is the Way through all the problems, trials, challenges, and opportunities of life. He is, indeed, the Hope and Light of the World.

---

65. See Mosiah 5:7–15; Doctrine and Covenants 18:24–25.
66. See Matthew 26, Mark 14, Luke 22.
67. See Matthew 27, Mark 15, Luke 23, John 19.
68. See Matthew 28, Mark 16, Luke 24, John 20.

The meaning of the word "Atonement" helps us understand its purpose and blessings. Because Jesus Christ and His infinite Atonement are the central themes of the temple, understanding the meaning of the word "Atonement" across various languages helps us to comprehend more completely what it does for us.[69]

The primary word for atonement in Hebrew is *kafar*, meaning "to cover, to wipe out, or to forgive." The Hebrew word *teshnva* is also used for atonement, and it means "a return to God." Other Hebrew words affiliated with the concept of atonement are *yeshiva*, which means "sitting down" or *yeshuv*, which means "to have a place because a person has returned home."

All these Hebrew words together reference "sitting down with" or "being reconciled to" the Father once again, having been prepared and purified to be in His holy presence.

In Arabic, the words *kafara* or *kafata* describe atonement. They represent "a close embrace," meaning the Father lovingly embraces us upon our return to Him.

In English, the word "atonement" means "at-one-ment," which means "to be at one with" or "to be reconciled to" God. It suggests that whatever is broken in our lives can be repaired by Him.

Therefore, taking all these various meanings together, the concept of atonement means to return to a former state, return home and be lovingly and longingly welcomed back, and repair what is broken or amiss. These actions are portrayed and taught repeatedly in our temple experience. What a comforting and hopeful reality to know that through Jesus Christ, we may once again see our Heavenly Parents and qualify to live in Their presence!

Jesus Christ redeems us through the power of His Atonement. As taught in the temple, the Atonement gave Jesus Christ the power to save and succor us. However, we must remember that the *person* Jesus Christ has this power, not the *act* of the Atonement. President Russell M. Nelson clarified this distinction when he taught,

---

69. See Hugh W. Nibley, "The Atonement of Jesus Christ, Part 1," *Ensign*, July 1990 for a full treatment of the origins of the word "atonement." See also Russell M. Nelson, "The Atonement," Conference Report, October 1996.

There is no amorphous entity called "the Atonement" upon which we may call for succor, healing, forgiveness, or power. Jesus Christ is the source. Sacred terms such as *Atonement* and *Resurrection* describe what the Savior did, according to the Father's plan, so that we may live with hope in this life and gain eternal life in the world to come. The Savior's atoning sacrifice—the central act of all human history—is best understood and appreciated when we expressly and clearly connect it to Him.[70]

Therefore, Jesus Christ redeems, saves, and enables. His Atonement gives Him this power, but He wields it on our behalf. We should speak of the Savior acting *through* the Atonement rather than speaking of the Atonement itself acting. As a result, we should look to Him to receive the power of His infinite and eternal Atonement. So, let us come unto Him for the hope and healing we seek!

Jesus Christ's Atonement is fully comprehensive. The temple helps us understand the expansive and fully comprehensive scope of the Savior's Atonement. The scriptures describe the scope and scale of the Savior's Atonement as being "infinite and eternal."[71] Therefore, we should learn what the words "infinite" and "eternal" mean when applied to the Atonement's breadth and depth. It gives us the merciful understanding that He can resolve every problem, dysfunction, or injustice. His power to save and heal is limitless!

Infinite

The word "infinite" describes the Atonement's scope and coverage. It represents the *outward* dimensions of the Atonement.[72] It was infinite in the following ways:

---

70. Russell M. Nelson, "Drawing the Power of Jesus Christ Into Our Lives," Conference Report, April 2017.
71. Alma 34:9–14.
72. See Russell M. Nelson, "The Atonement," Conference Report, October 1996 for a full discussion of "infinite."

1. In the divinity of the one sacrificed (Jesus was perfect in every way).
2. In power (He received all power and can deliver us and give all or a portion of it to us).
3. In duration (its effect is unlimited and without end).
4. In coverage for all humankind (men, women, and children), for all living things (plants, animals, and all types of life), for all worlds (excludes no creation of Heavenly Father), for all times (past, present, and future).
5. In intensity and suffering by Him (the pain, anguish, and sorrow He felt).
6. In depth (all manner of death, sin, suffering, disease, and pain).
7. In love for us (His perfect charity).
8. In blessings it bestows (the magnitude of the blessings that await).

Eternal

The word "eternal" describes the Person who performed the Atonement and the type of sacrifice embodied by it.[73] An eternal being performed it, so He could not be killed. The Savior had to willingly give up His life to die. By doing so, His willing sacrifice gave Him the power to redeem all humankind eternally. This descriptor represents the *inward* dimension of the Atonement.

With this understanding, we should have infinite and eternal hope amid a terribly difficult world. He has no limit to His power to save and succor us; only we limit Him. As a friend of ours often says, "My God is a big God!"[74] The Savior and His Atonement should be the light in our darkness, a beacon that beckons us home to our "promised land" of peace and reconciliation because He can resolve all issues and heal all pain through the power of His Atonement.

---

73. "Eternal" is a descriptor of the Savior. For example, if He punishes, it is an "eternal punishment" because it is His punishment (see Doctrine and Covenants 19:8–12). Therefore, "eternal atonement" is His Atonement.
74. Used with permission.

Jesus Christ's Atonement is intimately personal. The temple
helps us understand the highly personal nature of our relationship
with the Savior. Jesus Christ's infinite and eternal Atonement gave
Him the power to heal us and the perspective to understand us. It
was not only the *defining* act of all history, but it was the most *intimate* act. Elder Neal A. Maxwell, formerly of the Quorum of the
Twelve, taught,

> Jesus' daily mortal experiences and His ministry, to be sure,
> acquainted Him by observation with a sample of human
> sicknesses, grief, pains, sorrows, and infirmities which are
> 'common to man' (1 Corinthians 10:13). But the agonies of the
> Atonement were infinite and first-hand! Since not all human
> sorrow and pain is connected to sin, the full intensiveness of
> the Atonement involved bearing our pains, infirmities, and
> sicknesses, as well as our sins.
>
> Whatever our sufferings, we can safely 'cast our care
> upon him; for he careth for [us]' (1 Peter 5:7). *Jesus is a fully
> comprehending Christ.* The Atonement, then, was infinite in
> the divineness of the one sacrificed, in the comprehensiveness
> of its coverage, and in the intensiveness—incomprehensible to
> us—of the Savior's suffering.[75]

It should give us great comfort to know that irrespective of our
sin or suffering, our Savior knows by personal experience what we
are feeling. Isaiah wrote, "He hath borne *our* griefs, and carried *our*
sorrows . . . and with *his* stripes we are healed."[76] He felt our exact
pain and sorrow. We have no more intimate and personal Friend and
Comforter than Jesus Christ.

***Gospel law and the doctrine of Christ are merciful expressions
of Jesus Christ's Atonement.*** Jesus Christ fully met the requirements

---

75. Neal A. Maxwell, *Not My Will, But Thine* (Salt Lake City: Deseret Book, 2008), 54–55; emphasis added.
76. Isaiah 53:4–5; emphasis added.

of the perfect law[77]—first for Himself and then vicariously for us. Therefore, instead of meeting the exacting demands of the perfect law, we can obey the gospel law—founded on the "doctrine of Christ"[78]—which He gives us as a substitute. We covenant to obey the gospel law in the temple.

The word "gospel" is derived from the English word *godspel*, meaning "good news." What is this good news? The scriptures give us the answer: Jesus Christ and His infinite Atonement are the good news! In the Doctrine and Covenants we read, "This is the gospel, the glad tidings . . . That he came into the world, even Jesus, to be crucified for the world, and to bear the sins of the world, and to sanctify the world, and to cleanse it from all unrighteousness; That through him all might be saved whom the Father had put into his power and made by him."[79]

What is His gospel law? Gospel law is the system of rules that gives us access to the blessings of His Atonement. His law is a higher law, one which requires not only our thoughts, words, and deeds but also the alignment of our desires and intentions with His will.[80] Fortunately, gospel law is a merciful law that provides a pathway for repentance and cleansing through Him even when we imperfectly keep it.

What is His doctrine, the doctrine of Christ? His doctrine states that men and women can receive salvation through (1) faith in the Lord Jesus Christ, (2) repentance, (3) baptism by immersion for the remission of sins, (4) the laying on of hands for the gift of the Holy Ghost, and (5) enduring to the end, meaning continuing to have faith

---

77. The perfect law is the requirement that a person perfectly comply with all the Father's commandments to fully merit and earn his or her eternal reward. Only Jesus Christ met the demands of this most stringent law.
78. 2 Nephi 31:2.
79. Doctrine and Covenants 76:40–42.
80. See Matthew 4, 5, 6 for a full description of higher expectations of our intentions *and* our actions under gospel law given by the Savior in the Sermon on the Mount. This contrasts with the expectations of our actions only under the Mosaic law.

by acting on all other invitations and covenants required by the Lord and by repenting consistently throughout our lives.[81]

How does His doctrine relate to His gospel? They are the same! We are taught, "This is my gospel—repentance and baptism by water, and then cometh the baptism of fire and the Holy Ghost, even the Comforter, which showeth all things, and teacheth the peaceable things of the kingdom."[82] The "good news" is that we are saved by Jesus—and by Him alone—as we imperfectly but willingly live the doctrine of Christ.

As His covenant disciples, we must center all things in Him. We must rely "*wholly* upon the merits of him who is mighty to save."[83] When we focus all things on Him and do our best to align with gospel law and with the doctrine of Christ, we put Him in a position to advocate for us before the Father effectively. He is bound to do so when we tie ourselves to Him by covenant. "I, the Lord, am bound when ye do what I say; but when ye do not what I say, ye have no promise."[84]

May we make and always keep those covenants!

QUESTIONS TO CONSIDER

1. In what ways are you developing the "character of Christ" in your life? How can your temple covenants assist you in your efforts?
2. What did you learn about Jesus Christ and His infinite Atonement during your last visit to the temple? Why is that important to your life now?
3. In what ways can you make Jesus Christ the center of your life? How can the temple help you accomplish them?

---

81. See 2 Nephi 31:13–16; Doctrine and Covenants 19:31; 3 Nephi 27:20; Moroni 8:25.
82. Doctrine and Covenants 39:6.
83. 2 Nephi 31:19.
84. Doctrine and Covenants 82:10.

NOTES AND INSIGHTS

_____

_____

_____

_____

_____

_____

_____

_____

_____

_____

Chapter 5

The Plan of Salvation

*"We are not left alone to wander through mortality
without knowing of the master plan which the Lord
has designed for His children."*

—L. Tom Perry[1]

This chapter summarizes the Father's plan of salvation.[2] Temple work is a vital part of His plan to save all His children. We have experienced its blessings as we have performed temple and family history work for thousands of our ancestors. Temple ordinances amply teach the doctrine of His plan. A renewed understanding of this *plan of happiness* or *plan of mercy* will enable us to draw out new insights and applications when we worship in the Lord's house.

Personal Application: Julie

Some years ago, I was searching for more information on my maternal grandmother's family. Thomas Bedford Jett is my great-, great-, great-grandfather on that side. At the time, I

---

1. L. Tom Perry, "The Plan of Salvation," Conference Report, October 2006.
2. See "Lesson 2: The Plan of Salvation," *Preach My Gospel* (Salt Lake City: The Church of Jesus Christ of Latter-day Saints, 2019) for a more expansive treatment of this topic.

knew his name, but I did not have the names, dates, and places for his wives and his children. I searched for a good while when I decided to post a request on the internet in a genealogy chat board asking if anyone had information on Thomas Bedford Jett. After some time had passed, a distant cousin I did not know contacted me and said that his father would have information on my family line.

I contacted this individual, and, miraculously, he mailed me eleven pages of family history, which included all the names, dates, and places for Thomas Bedford Jett's family. Receiving this information out of the blue was, for us, a cry from the dust. My ancestors seemed to be pleading with me, saying, "We are well and are hoping you will rescue us."

We immediately began to do the temple work for these precious ancestors who had waited so long for their ordinances. After performing all their baptisms and endowments, we took the names to the temple to seal the family members together for eternity.

When we got to the children of Thomas Bedford and his third wife, Talitha, the sealer asked if we would like to perform the sealings of all six sons to the parents simultaneously. Typically, each child would be sealed to his or her parents one at a time, but on this day, he asked if we would like to perform all the sons together. We joyously agreed.

Aaron and I acted as proxies for Thomas Bedford and Talitha, and six brethren were proxies for their six sons. While kneeling at the altar with three sons to my right and three sons to my left, a wave of emotion came over me as I thought about the great reunion that must be happening on the other side of the veil.

I had looked many times at a picture of this family with its eight children. Now, in my mind's eye, I could see family members embracing one another with deep joy and heartfelt appreciation for the gift of salvation they had been offered. At that moment, I had a powerful spiritual confirmation that these ordinances were legitimate and that the members of this good family accepted them.

The work we do in the temple is vital to the salvation of those who have passed on. We stand as "Saviors on Mount Zion"[3] in bringing the reconciliation and redemption of Jesus Christ's Atonement to them. Thus, we, like the Savior, offer them blessings they could not receive on their own. In turn, we are refined and perfected by our service and sacrifice.

We lived together with our Heavenly Parents and the rest of humanity during our premortal life. The ordinances of the temple and the scriptures of the Restoration confirm the reality of our premortal lives. This doctrine is unique to the restored gospel of Jesus Christ as the rest of Christianity has lost this plain and precious truth.

Before this life, we lived together as spirit beings with Heavenly Parents, created by them from intelligences that had existed eternally. In the Doctrine and Covenants we learn, "Intelligence, or the light of truth, was not created or made, neither indeed can be."[4] All of humanity was created by Them, making us all spirit siblings—brothers and sisters in God. Not having physical bodies, as did our Heavenly Parents, we could not progress or receive a "fulness of joy."[5]

However, we were individual spirit beings with distinct personalities, unique gifts and talents, and heartfelt desires. From the beginning, the Father gave us the great gift of agency, by which we could use our talents and act upon our desires as we progressed to become like Him. Agency was our most precious gift, one He emphatically honored.

The Father's plan of salvation for His children has eternal importance. To become like Him, the Father proposed a plan for our progression. In His plan, we would come into mortality, gain a physical body, be instructed in the knowledge of good and evil, be given commandments as boundaries, and then be tested and tried as we experienced opposition to the truths and commandments He gave us.

---

3. See Obadiah 1:21.
4. Doctrine and Covenants 93:29.
5. Doctrine and Covenants 93:33.

He said, "We will prove them herewith, to see if they will do all things whatsoever the Lord their God shall command them."[6]

This life was designed to be a great test of our agency, of whether we would freely choose to follow His path. These experiences would be the means for us to develop His traits and characteristics, those we would need to work together with Him for the salvation of His children for eternity.

The plan would preserve our agency, but because of choices we would make, we would not return to live with Heavenly Father again without the help of a Savior. The plan to enable us to become like Him is called the "plan of salvation," the "plan of redemption," the "plan of happiness," or, ultimately, the "plan of mercy."[7]

His plan would require One of His children to come to earth, live a perfect life and be free of the divine demands of justice, and willingly sacrifice Himself for all His brothers and sisters. In this way, He would vicariously pay the full demands of justice and, thereby, be able to offer mercy to them. Above all, He would return all glory to the Father, requiring infinite humility and meekness.

Jehovah—the premortal Jesus of Nazareth—was the only One capable of accomplishing this most eternally critical role and of humbly and meekly returning all glory to the Father. "Here am I, send me" was His response to the Father's question of "Whom shall I send?"[8] The beloved Son said, "Father, thy will be done, and the glory be thine forever."[9] The Father accepted Jehovah's humble offering, and we all confirmed His choice with our sustaining actions.

We participated in a tremendous premortal war initiated by Lucifer, the enemy of all righteousness. Unfortunately, Lucifer, the enemy of all righteousness, opposed the Father's plan. He offered to fulfill the Father's plan, but in his approach, he would usurp the Father's power and glory for himself and, in the process, destroy our agency.[10]

6. Abraham 3:25.
7. See Alma 42:5, 8, 13, 15.
8. Abraham 3:22–28.
9. Moses 4:2.
10. See Moses 4:1–4; Isaiah 14:12–17.

In Lucifer's scheme, he would convince his brothers and sisters to choose him as the savior, but he had no interest nor ability to carry out an atonement as laid out in the Father's plan. This path was too hard for him and did not give him all power.

So, he devised an alternative path, which would be easier for him and would be more enticing to his listeners. His proposal would not require a perfect Savior or an atoning sacrifice. His plan would supposedly save everyone and not lose one soul, but to do so, he needed them to give up their agency. His demand was a consummate act of manipulation by the supreme narcissist. He was not interested in our benefit, only in his. His offer was a power play for him, not a sacrifice for us.

The adversary could try to save all at least three ways, but in doing so he would cleverly destroy agency:

1. He could force or compel people to be righteous, ensuring their exact obedience. In this way, he would guarantee compliance with eternal law and obviate agency.[11]
2. He could not give people a choice to be wicked; he could limit options and opposition and thereby destroy their agency.[12]
3. He could convince them that he would save all humankind irrespective of their choices because he could redefine "right and wrong" as part of his gospel. In this way, there would not be consequences for their acts, destroying their agency by making choices irrelevant.[13]

He surely employed all these ideologies and methods in his opposing efforts, just as he does today. This multi-pronged method ensured that he would entice and ensnare the broadest number of people

---

11. This approach is used by many individuals and organizations where compulsion and force generate compliance.
12. This seductive philosophy is one of "no choice, no consequence," which is opposed to the Father's plan of "choice *and* consequence." It eliminates commandments to limit choice, whereas the Father provides commandments to enhance choice.
13. This ideology is the worldly doctrine of many who believe that individuals "define" right and wrong, called moral relativism.

possible. Some who would oppose direct force would surely give in to indirect coercion.

This opposition grew to be a "war in heaven" where the followers of Christ fought against the followers of the adversary, prevailing "by the word of their testimony."[14] Of this war in heaven, Joseph Smith taught, "The contention in heaven was—Jesus said there would be certain souls that would not be saved; and the devil said he could save them all, and laid his plans before the grand council, who gave their vote in favor of Jesus Christ. So the devil rose up in rebellion against God, and was cast down, with all who put up their heads for him."[15]

The Father rejected Lucifer's plan, and by doing so, He guarded our agency.[16] With that rejection, the adversary chose to rebel against the Father wholeheartedly.

Devastatingly, one-third of all our Heavenly Parents' children followed Lucifer, who led the rebellion. They were all cast out into the earth due to their opposition to the Father's plan. They were never able to receive a physical body and became forever lost and miserable because this choice permanently halted their eternal progress. Elder David A. Bednar of the Quorum of the Twelve has taught,

> Satan does not have a body, and his eternal progress has been halted. Just as water flowing in a riverbed is stopped by a dam, so the adversary's eternal progress is thwarted because he does not have a physical body. Because of his rebellion, Lucifer has denied himself all of the mortal blessings and experiences made possible through a tabernacle of flesh and bones. One of the potent scriptural meanings of the word *damned* is illustrated in his inability to continue progressing and becoming like our Heavenly Father.[17]

---

14. Revelation 12:7–11.
15. Joseph Smith, *Teachings of the Prophet Joseph Smith*, 357.
16. All that the Father and Son do is designed to protect and enable our agency because they know that our agency is the most powerful enabler of our godly characteristics.
17. David A. Bednar, "Watchful Unto Prayer Continually," Conference Report, October 2019.

We must be cognizant of the adversary's hatred of the Father for casting him out and his abhorrence of us for following the Father's plan. His opposition of us continues and is amplified in mortality.

Mortality—the second estate—is eternally important to the Father's plan for His children. Two-thirds of God's children received the opportunity to come to the earth and to pass through what is called their "second estate," having been faithful in their "first estate"[18] or their premortal estate.

This mortal experience would allow His children to progress and eventually become like their Heavenly Parents. We are now living in this second estate as glorious spirit children of God clothed with imperfect mortal bodies, imbued with agency, and offered the chance for accelerated progression through the experiences of mortality.

Unfortunately, the spiritual war continues in the mortal world just as it commenced in the premortal world,[19] with the unseen hosts of Lucifer opposing the work of the Lord and with the valiant followers of Christ contending against them with their testimonies.

The trials of mortality and the temptations of the adversary and his minions provide the opposition required to use our agency and to develop the godly traits required to live with Him again. Only then, we will be prepared to perform His work of salvation for eternity.

The veil over mortality is a necessary element of the Father's plan. We cannot remember our premortal life. This absence of recall is called "the veil." This term also refers to the separation of the spirit realm from our earthly realm. It allows us to begin this life in innocence and continue our lives free of overt interaction with those in the spirit world, which protects our agency and allows us to "walk by faith"[20] while here.

The temple affirms the existence of the veil, as do the scriptures. They teach us that learning and applying gospel principles, heeding

---

18. Jude 1:6.
19. See Doctrine and Covenants 76:29.
20. 1 Corinthians 16:13.

the teachings of authorized ministers, and seeking personal experience with deity are all ways to overcome its effects.

The temple helps us pierce the veil by enabling us to fulfill the command to remember—remember the Savior and His sacrifice, remember who we are, remember whose we are, remember the source of our blessings, remember our covenants, remember our purpose and mission, recognize the reality and the threat of the adversary, and remember our ability to conquer darkness through the power of Christ!

Men and women were foreordained and prepared for their earthly work during their premortal life. The temple testifies that the Lord foreordained men and women to accomplish His work while in mortality and fulfill their specifically identified purpose. Joseph Smith taught, "Every man [or woman] who has a calling to minister to the inhabitants of the world was ordained to that very purpose in the Grand Council of heaven before this world was."[21]

We were "called and prepared from the foundation of the world according to the foreknowledge of God." [22] In the premortal realm, we "received [our] first lessons . . . and were prepared . . . to labor in his vineyard."[23]

In what way were we prepared? We learned the doctrine of Christ and the plan of salvation. We learned about our roles and duties. We learned these plans and principles when we knew there would be an eventual veil over our minds. Perhaps, in some way, that training imprinted on our spirits specific skills, characteristics, traits, and talents we believed would come out naturally during mortality.

We should not misconstrue the doctrine of foreordination with the idea that those born in the covenant in this life or those who receive specific blessings or callings were the only valiant ones in the premortal existence. Surely, valiant souls were born into the covenant, just as valiant souls were born outside of the covenant. If it were not so, our missionary efforts would be ineffective.

---

21. Joseph Smith, *History of the Church*, 6:364.
22. Alma 13:3.
23. Doctrine and Covenants 138:56.

Foreordination does not mean *predestination*. Each person must make positive choices to qualify for those long-ago promised blessings. The Lord did not guarantee any promised blessing. Only by aligning our will with the will of the Father will blessings flow.[24]

What is most important is that we make the most of our opportunities in this life, so we may be found faithful to what we have received and what we could act upon while in mortality. President Spencer W. Kimball taught,

> In the world before we came here, faithful women were given certain assignments while faithful men were foreordained to certain priesthood tasks. While we do not now remember the particulars, this does not alter the glorious reality of what we once agreed to. You are accountable for those things which long ago were expected of you just as are those we sustain as prophets and apostles![25]

We must always strive to live up to our duties while in mortality. Only then will the promised blessings flow.

Personal Application: Aaron

My father was not born into the Church. However, I believe that his conversion story is evidence that he was prepared before he was born to receive the gospel. My brother told this story in his eulogy at Dad's funeral.[26] He related,

> *Dad was raised as a devout Catholic, and he planned to enter the ministry as a Catholic priest after graduating from Holy Innocents high school [in Pittsburgh,*

---

24. Foreordination is not predestination. Foreordination is that men and women were set apart to certain roles or blessings in mortality. Only through their faithfulness would these be given. Predestination is the false idea that a person is destined to receive certain blessings or callings, irrespective of his or her faithfulness.
25. Spencer W. Kimball, "The Role of Righteous Women," Conference Report, October 1979.
26. Story used with permission.

Pennsylvania]. However, due to the Vietnam war, he enlisted in the Air Force in 1967 at the age of 17. He became a radar operator and was stationed in Iceland, California, and then the Philippines.

While in California, he met a fellow corpsman who happened to be a member of The Church of Jesus Christ of Latter-day Saints. The religious conversations he had with his LDS friend fueled his curiosity in the Church, which led him to do some further investigation. He visited the library of the community college where he was taking some classes to look for some books that would provide more information about the Church. He said that there were many anti-Mormon books in the library's religion section, but the book he happened to pull from the shelf was A Marvelous Work and a Wonder by Elder LeGrand Richards, [a former member of the Quorum of the Twelve].

After reading this wonderful book, he asked his friend to arrange discussions with the missionaries, and he was soon after baptized a member of The Church of Jesus Christ of Latter-day Saints. Years later, my dad was called to be a Seventy in his stake, which at the time required ordination by an apostle. And it so happened that the visiting apostle who ordained my dad was Elder LeGrand Richards, the man whose book was instrumental in my dad's conversion.[27]

My father always considered the divine symmetry of his rendezvous with Elder Richards evidence that he was foreordained to be introduced to the Church. He felt satisfied that his righteous choices had allowed him to realize premortally promised blessings.

This account is a precious family story that reminds us of our mission in life, one to which we were commissioned before we were born.

---

27. John K. Bujnowski, "Kenneth John Bujnowski Eulogy," April 9, 2021. https://www.dropbox.com/s/ujbav4d8c7egugm/04.07.21%20Ken%20Bujnowski%20Eulogy.pdf?dl=0.

The scattering and gathering of Israel are part of the Father's plan. The Father wanted as many of His children to return to Him as possible. He also wanted to protect and promote His sacred covenants, with their priesthood power and eternal blessings. So, He gave the house of Israel stewardship over the covenant, and He used the process of scattering them throughout the world to put His covenant people in a position to bring the rest of His children home. He is now gathering Israel on both sides of the veil through ministering, missionary, and temple work. President Russell M. Nelson has said, "That gathering is the most important thing taking place on earth today. Nothing else compares in magnitude, nothing else compares in importance, nothing else compares in majesty."[28]

The post-mortal spirit world and the work of salvation happening within it are critical to the Father's plan of mercy. One of the great truths restored in this last dispensation is the reality of the postmortal spirit world and the critical work of salvation going on there. This work is the focus of modern temples.

When we die, our spirits and our bodies separate. Our bodies return to the dust.[29] However, our spirits live on and move into the spirit world, where they await the resurrection. "The dead look at the long absence of their spirits from their bodies as a bondage"[30] because their progress is more limited than when alive in mortality. Only one spirit world exists, but it has two separated sections: spirit paradise and spirit prison.

Spirit paradise: "Those who are righteous are received into a state of happiness, which is called paradise, a state of peace, where they shall rest from all their troubles and from all care, and sorrow." [31] These are individuals "who had been faithful

---

28. Russel M. Nelson and Wendy W. Nelson, "Hope of Israel," Worldwide Youth Devotional, Salt Lake City, Utah, June 3, 2018.
29. See Genesis 3:14.
30. Doctrine and Covenants 138:50.
31. Alma 40:12.

in the testimony of Jesus while they lived in mortality."[32] "Among the righteous [in the spirit world] there [is] peace."[33]

Spirit prison: The wicked, the rebellious, and those who have not made or have not kept sacred covenants will be constrained to reside in a portion of the spirit world called "spirit prison,"[34] where they wait in "a state of awful, fearful."[35] For, "where these are, darkness reign[s]." [36]

When Jesus Christ went to the spirit world following His death, He initiated the great work of salvation for those who had not yet received the gospel. In a great revelation given on October 3, 1919, President Joseph F. Smith saw the ministry of the Savior in the world of spirits and the organization of the great work of salvation there. He saw righteous priesthood holders who were sent to preach to the spirits in prison[37]

President Smith also clarified the great role sisters have in proclaiming the gospel among the dead in the world of spirits:

Who is going to preach the gospel to the women? Who is going to carry the testimony of Jesus Christ to the hearts of the women who have passed away without a knowledge of the gospel? Well, to my mind it is a simple thing.

These good sisters who have been set apart, ordained to the work, called to it, authorized by the authority of the Holy Priesthood to minister [to other women], in the House of God

---

32. Doctrine and Covenants 138:12.
33. Doctrine and Covenants 138:22.
34. 1 Peter 3:19.
35. Alma 40:13–14.
36. Doctrine and Covenants 138:22. See also Doctrine and Covenants 88:32. In speaking of those in spirit prison, the prophet Joseph Smith taught, "The great misery of departed spirits in the world of spirits, where they go after death, is to know that they come short of the glory that others enjoy and that they might have enjoyed themselves, and they are their own accusers" (Joseph Smith, *History of the Church*, 5:425.)
37. Doctrine and Covenants 138:18–21, 30–32; emphasis added.

for the living and for the dead, will be fully authorized and empowered to preach the gospel and minister to the women.[38]

Individuals in the spirit world who accept the gospel and accept the vicarious ordinances performed on their behalf in holy temples will be allowed to go into spirit paradise, receive their rest, and begin to work for the salvation of their brothers and sisters. "The dead who repent will be redeemed, through obedience to the [vicariously received] ordinances of the house of God."[39]

The work of salvation among the dead is evidence of the great mercy of the Savior, who wants to judge all children of God equitably. "For this cause was the gospel preached also to them that are dead, that they might be judged according to men in the flesh, but live according to God in the Spirit."[40]

The vicarious ordinance work for the dead performed in temples is of inestimable importance. Having provided the means whereby the dead could receive the fulness of the gospel, the Savior also needed to provide a way for them to receive the ordinances of salvation, which we can only perform in mortality. He restored through the prophet Joseph Smith the eternal truth that we can perform ordinances by proxy for those who have already passed away.[41] This vicarious activity is the great work we perform in modern temples.

We cannot fully estimate or fathom the great worth of this work to those who have accepted the gospel and await in spirit prison. Of this fact, President Wilford Woodruff encouragingly taught,

> Our mission is more extended and extensive than we realize. . . . We are bordering upon the millennium. We are living in the great and last dispensation, in the which the God of Israel expects us, his servants, his sons and daughters, to

---

38. Joseph F. Smith, Ed. John A. Widtsoe, *Gospel Doctrine* (Salt Lake City: Deseret Book, 1986), 461.
39. Doctrine and Covenants 138:58.
40. 1 Peter 4:6.
41. See Doctrine and Covenants 128.

perform the work which has been left to our charge. It is our duty to build these temples. It is our duty to enter into them and redeem our dead. . . .

Our forefathers are looking to us to attend to this work. They are watching over us with great anxiety, and are desirous that we should finish these temples and attend to certain ordinances for them, so that in the morning of the resurrection they can come forth and enjoy the same blessings that we enjoy.[42]

This position of "Saviors upon Mount Zion"[43] is a tremendous responsibility for each covenant son or daughter of God, one where we truly learn to be more like our Father in Heaven.

Kingdoms of glory await all God's sons and daughters, except those few who are of perdition. Following the resurrection of the dead and at the Final Judgment, all children of God will be consigned to their eternal reward by our perfect Judge, Jesus Christ. Due to His infinite and eternal sacrifice, nearly all children of God will mercifully inherit a kingdom of glory. This glorious truth demonstrates the exactness of His justice and the expansiveness of His mercy.

The glory of each kingdom will manifest in the resurrected bodies of those assigned to it because they lived commensurate with its requirements and laws while on earth.[44] They will go to a place where they will "enjoy that which they were *willing* to receive."[45] The only exceptions to inheriting a kingdom of glory are those very few unfortunate individuals cast into outer darkness, where no glory exists. The scriptures of the restoration detail each of these eternal destinations.[46]

In the temple, we are symbolically shown the differences between each of the kingdoms of glory, taught how to inherit them, and given a representation of their increasingly ascending glory. This teaching

---

42. Wilford Woodruff cited in Journal of Discourses, 23:330– 331.
43. Obadiah 1:21
44. See 1 Corinthians 15:40–42; Doctrine and Covenants 88:37–40.
45. Doctrine and Covenants 88:32, 34; emphasis added.
46. See Doctrine and Covenants 76 for a full description of all the degrees of glory and of outer darkness.

is accomplished through ascending various floor levels or by lighting and design changes between rooms.

The Lord taught us, "Unto every kingdom is given a law; and unto every law there are certain bounds and conditions. All beings who abide not those conditions are not justified [in obtaining their respective kingdom]."[47] We briefly describe below what we learn in the restored gospel of Jesus Christ about the kingdoms of glory and outer darkness with their respective laws, bounds, and conditions.

Celestial kingdom

The celestial kingdom is the highest kingdom of glory, and it is where God the Father, His Son Jesus Christ, and the Holy Ghost dwell. Its splendor is compared to the sun, meaning it is exceedingly brilliant; it creates light instead of reflecting it; it purifies and refines; and it is a source of life.

We learn in the temple that the celestial kingdom is a social place where families and friends will interact and work together freely and lovingly. Celestial individuals will be resurrected in the morning of the first resurrection in what is called "the resurrection of the just."[48]

Those who inherit this kingdom are all who made and kept sacred covenants with God, who valiantly accepted and bore testimony of Jesus Christ, and who "overcame by faith" in mortality.[49] To "overcome by faith" means they sincerely repented of their sins and transgressions, and they endured difficulty and uncertainty by moving forward despite only having a partial knowledge or an incomplete understanding. They lived as influenced by the Holy Ghost, striving to submit to the will of the Father in all things.

Having done all the Lord commanded, they "shall overcome all things"[50] in the final judgment and will inherit exaltation. They are "just men [and women] made perfect through Jesus the mediator of

---

47. Doctrine and Covenants 88:38–39.
48. See Doctrine and Covenants 76:50, 64–65; 88:20–22, 28–29.
49. Doctrine and Covenants 76:53.
50. Doctrine and Covenants 76:60.

the new covenant,"[51] Through His Atonement, they will become like their Heavenly Parents. President Joseph F. Smith declared,

> The Lord has made it possible for us to become members of the Church of the Firstborn [or heirs of the celestial kingdom], by receiving the blessings of the house of the Lord and overcoming all things. Thus we become heirs, 'priests, and kings [and queens and priestesses], who have received of his fulness, and of his glory,' who shall 'dwell in the presence of God and his Christ forever and ever,' with full exaltation.[52]

Also included in this kingdom are people who never received the gospel's fulness in mortality but who wholly embraced it in the world of spirits and who accepted the vicarious ordinances performed for them.[53]

This earth will become the celestial kingdom.[54] Its inhabitants will engage in the work of salvation, together with their Heavenly Parents and the Son, for eternity. For this reason, celestial beings must have all the traits of godliness to enable them to work to save and glorify imperfect and sometimes irrational mortals.

Within the celestial kingdom are three degrees of glory. Those who have entered and kept the new and everlasting covenant of marriage inherit the highest.[55] Prophets have often emphasized that God will make allowances later for those who did not have this opportunity in mortality.[56] What comforting promises for every one of us!

---

51. Doctrine and Covenants 76:69.
52. Joseph Fielding Smith, *Doctrines of Salvation* (Salt Lake City: Deseret Book, 1954), 2:41–42.
53. See Doctrine and Covenants 76:50–70, 92–95 for a full description of the celestial kingdom of glory and the persons who inherit it.
54. See Doctrine and Covenants 130:9; 88:17–20, 25–26.
55. See Doctrine and Covenants 131:1–4.
56. Of this truth, President Lorenzo Snow taught, "If a young man or a young woman has no opportunity of getting married, and they live faithful lives up to the time of their death, they will have all the blessings, exaltation, and glory that any man or woman will have who had this opportunity and improved it. That is sure and positive" (Lorenzo Snow, *The Teachings of Lorenzo Snow*, comp. Clyde J. Williams [Salt Lake City: Bookcraft, 1984], 138.)

Terrestrial kingdom

The terrestrial kingdom is the middle kingdom of glory, where Jesus Christ will visit and where the Holy Ghost is in operation. Its glory is compared to the moon, which only reflects light from the sun and is far less brilliant.[57] Terrestrial individuals will come forth in the afternoon of the first resurrection.

Those who inherit this kingdom "are they who are honorable men [and women] of the earth, who were blinded by the craftiness of men."[58] An honorable person is a person who is generally good and law-abiding. He or she is likely to be religious and faith-oriented, to be kind and generous to others, to serve in the community, to advocate for social justice, and to be regarded as a "good person."

Terrestrial persons had a belief in Jesus Christ and lived as influenced by the light of Christ, consistently choosing right over wrong in most cases. These honorable individuals were offered, understood, and could freely act upon the fulness of gospel truth but were blinded by the world's influence and allurements. Therefore, they did not accept it or did not live it fully, but they continue to do good and to be good.

They may have wanted to keep parts of the gospel law, but they were unwilling to submit to the entire law. Unfortunately, they "died without law,"[59] meaning they refused to be bound by the full gospel law that would have blessed them with celestial glory.

Even if their choices allow them to remain "honorable and good" in mortality, they did not enable them to be "excellent and valiant" by the Lord's standards. The scriptures describe them as those "who were not valiant in their testimony of Jesus," so they

---

57. According to scientific measurements, the moon is ~400,000 times dimmer than the sun, which is instructive when comparing the difference between celestial and terrestrial glory. As measured on the magnitude scale, a logarithmic scale where lower numbers are brighter, the moon is -12.7 and the sun is -26.7. To convert that magnitude scale to a power, it is $2.512^{(-12.7-(-26.7))}$ = 2.512^{14} = ~400,000. See https://www.discovermagazine.com/the-sciences/bafact-math-the-sun-is-400–000–times-brighter-than-the-full-moon for a full description.
58. Doctrine and Covenants 76:75.
59. Doctrine and Covenants 76:72.

"receive of his glory, but not of his fulness."[60] Of terrestrial beings, Elder Alvin R. Dyer, a former Apostle and member of the First Presidency,[61] taught, "These, for the most part, will be men [and women] who, during earth-life existence, sought the excellence of men; and some who gave of their time, talents and endeavor to the ways of [human]-made ideals of culture, science, and education, but thought not to include God and his ways in their search for a complete life."[62]

Terrestrial people who are "blinded by the craftiness of men" are *not* those who have never heard the gospel of Jesus Christ who "would have received it."[63] "Blinded" individuals had the choice to take the gospel path and had the full capability and knowledge to follow it but openly decided not to accept it and remain influenced by the world. They conscientiously chose to reject the rigorous gospel path and elected to accept the less stringent "honorable path."

Telestial kingdom

The telestial kingdom is the lowest kingdom of glory, where only the Holy Ghost is in operation. Its glory is compared to the brightness of the stars, which are dim and have significant differences in brightness. The luster of this kingdom of glory is far less brilliant than the

---

60. See Doctrine and Covenants 76:71–80, 91 for a full description of the terrestrial kingdom of glory and the persons who inherit it.
61. Elder Alvin R. Dyer was ordained an apostle in 1967, although he was not a member of the Quorum of the Twelve. He served in the First Presidency from 1968–1970. He was released when President McKay died in 1970, returning to serve as an assistant to the Twelve and later as a member of the First Quorum of Seventy. He was the only person in Church history to serve as a member of the First Quorum of Seventy after being ordained to the office of Apostle. (See "Elder Alvin R. Dyer Dies," *Ensign*, May 1977.)
62. Alvin R. Dyer, *Who Am I?* (Salt Lake City: Deseret Book, 1973), 553.
63. Doctrine and Covenants 137:7, 8. Those ignorant of gospel truths in this life will have an opportunity to choose later. If they fully accept gospel truth at this later time, they will be heirs of the celestial kingdom. If they do not, then they may receive terrestrial or telestial glory depending on the Lord's final judgment of their lives.

other two.[64] Telestial individuals will come forth in the last resurrection when the one thousand years of the Millennium end.

The individuals in this kingdom did not accept the gospel of Jesus Christ in this life or the world of spirits. They did not deny the Holy Ghost, but they rejected the influence of the light of Christ, choosing wrong over right in most cases. They were the worst of the worst in this life. "These are they who are liars, and sorcerers, and adulterers, and whoremongers, and whosoever loves and makes a lie."[65]

Telestial people purposely and knowingly murdered, robbed, stole, took advantage of, harmed, hurt, abused, and victimized others throughout their lives with little to no thought of repentance. They were the worst of the worst in mortality.

Despite their despicable character and nature, God in His mercy will still assign them to a final kingdom of glory, after they have passed through the "hell" of waiting for the final resurrection in spirit prison. Its glory is dim, but it still "surpasses all understanding" compared to what we now know.[66] Of these telestial individuals, Elder John A. Widtsoe, formerly of the Quorum of the Twelve, taught,

> The [Doctrine and Covenants] explains clearly that the lowest glory to which man is assigned is so glorious as to be beyond the understanding of man.

---

64. On the scientific "magnitude scale," the brightest star is 31,000 times weaker than the moon and 12.7 billion times weaker than the sun. The dimmest star is 30 million times weaker than the moon and 12.3 trillion times dimmer than the sun. The brightest star is Sirius in Canis major. On the magnitude scale, a logarithmic scale where lower numbers are brighter, the moon is -12.7 and Sirius is -1.46. To convert that magnitude scale to a power, it is $2.512^{(-1.46-(-12.7))} = 2.512^{11.24} = \sim 31,000$. The moon is -12.7 and the stars at the limit of our eyesight are +6.0. To convert that magnitude scale to a power, it is $2.512^{(+6.0-(-12.7))} = 2.512^{18.7} = \sim 30,000,000$. See Elizabeth Howell, "Brightest Stars: Luminosity and Magnitude," accessed January 4, 2021, https://www.space.com/21640-star-luminosity-and-magnitude.html for a full description of this scale.
65. Doctrine and Covenants 76:103.
66. See Doctrine and Covenants 76:81–90; 98–106; 109–112 for a full description of the telestial kingdom of glory and the persons who inherit it.

'The Gospel is a gospel of tremendous love. Love is at the bottom of it. The meanest child is loved so dearly that his reward will be beyond the understanding of mortal man.[67]

This final judgment for telestial beings is merciful, which may cause some to wonder why they are not consigned to suffer longer or more intensely. Make no mistake—they will sufficiently suffer because of their lives of debauchery. However, they will also receive a merciful end to their suffering. If we do not wish mercy on them, the very vilest of sinners, then we may not merit mercy for ourselves—a critical thought to ponder.

Outer darkness

Outer darkness is the only final destination without glory. It is reserved for (1) Lucifer and those cast out with him in the first estate and (2) those who committed the unpardonable sin of denying the Holy Ghost—who put the Savior to an open shame while in mortal-ity—thus becoming "sons [and daughters] of perdition."[68] These are the only ones for whom the Lord will provide no mercy.

We do not know much of this kingdom of darkness. To the few it has been shown, the vision is quickly "shut up again."[69] We know "they [who are thrust there] are vessels of wrath, doomed to suffer the wrath of God, with the devil and his angels in eternity,"[70] where "there is no forgiveness in this world nor in the world to come."[71] We are purposely kept from knowing much about their fate because it is so dreadful.

We know they are in a place "where their worm dieth not, and the fire is not quenched."[72] Those born into mortality and cast into outer darkness will be resurrected with a body devoid of glory. We could

---

67. John A. Widtsoe, *The Message of the Doctrine and Covenants* (Salt Lake City: Deseret Book, 1969), 167.
68. Doctrine and Covenants 76:32.
69. Doctrine and Covenants 76:47.
70. Doctrine and Covenants 76:33.
71. Doctrine and Covenants 76:34.
72. Doctrine and Covenants 76:44.

imagine an eternal physical body that experiences ongoing physical, mental, and emotional torment and decay without the merciful release of death—a truly horrific state. These are the only individuals who do not benefit from the infinite Atonement of the Lord Jesus Christ and who He forever consigns to "hell."[73]

Who are eligible for committing this most serious of all sins? These individuals are very few and can only include those who had been active members of The Church of Jesus Christ of Latter-day Saints with a personal witness of Christ and a sure testimony of the Holy Ghost.[74]

This final doom for the most rebellious and unrepentant of the Father's children is something we must be aware of, but we should not unduly dwell on it.

A final judgment will come to all humankind. The Lord will eventually judge all men and women on who they have become, which is a product of their thoughts, words, deeds, and intentions. This final judgment occurs after their resurrection, which consigns them to a kingdom of glory or outer darkness. This final reward is the last consequence for choices made during mortality or in the spirit world.

The tests of knowledge we experience in the temple are symbolic of this final time of judgment. They give us an intermediate experience that allows us to demonstrate if we have kept our covenants. These portrayals should always bring to our minds this final "great and dreadful day of the Lord."[75]

What makes that final day and all the days leading up to it either "great" or "dreadful" are not the events themselves but our choices, which enable us to become what we will have become. "They are their own

---

73. See Doctrine and Covenants 76:30–38, 44–49 for a full description of this kingdom of darkness and the persons who inherit it.

74. The prophet Joseph Fielding Smith taught, "It is only those who have the light through the priesthood and through the power of God and through their membership in the Church who will be banished forever from his influence into outer darkness to dwell with the devil and his angels" (Joseph Fielding Smith, Conference Report, October 1958, 21.)

75. Doctrine and Covenants 110:16.

judges, whether to [choose to] do good or do evil,"[76] meaning what we will have become will be a product of our choices. May we choose wisely!

QUESTIONS TO CONSIDER

1. What did you learn about the plan of salvation during your last visit to the temple? Why is that understanding important for you at this time?

2. How can an understanding of Jesus Christ's role in the Father's plan help you with a challenge you are currently facing? What insights does the temple provide about His ability and desire to help you?

3. How do your temple covenants help you qualify for exaltation in the celestial kingdom?

4. What can you do at this time in your life to help your ancestors receive the blessings of exaltation?

NOTES AND INSIGHTS

_____

_____

_____

_____

_____

_____

_____

_____

_____

76. Alma 41:7.

Section 2

The Children of God and Their Exaltation

In 2016, we completed a temple walk activity with the youth of our ward—the Frisco 9th Ward. We walked more than seventeen miles from Frisco, Texas, to the Dallas Texas Temple.

These outstanding youth endured the Texas heat, blisters on their feet, and sheer exhaustion to make the sacrifice and walk to the temple. They did it as a symbol of their commitment to the Savior and their love of His temple. We loved them for their willingness to do a hard thing, something that would challenge them to overcome and achieve.

The points of doctrine contained in this section of the book pertain to the children of God and their journey to become more like Him. They are not unique to the temple, but they are foundational to it. Like our temple walk, our journey through mortality can be challenging. These points of doctrine provide an understanding of who we are, why we are here, and how we might successfully navigate the difficulties of mortality. When we learn them and attend the temple, the Spirit will open our understanding of how to apply them in our lives.

The final chapter in this section pertains to the family—the fundamental organizing unit of eternity. It completes this section because of its eternal importance in enabling us to become more like our Heavenly Parents. As Elder Boyd K. Packer, formerly of the Quorum of the Twelve, taught, "Temple. One other word is equal in importance to a Latter-day Saint. Home. Put the words holy temple and home together, and you have described the house of the Lord!"[1] The temple is where we make covenants, and the home is where we learn to keep them.

As you study the doctrine in this section—many of which you may have heard repeatedly—we invite you to take a fresh look at

---

1. Boyd K. Packer, "The Temple, the Priesthood," Conference Report, April 1993; emphasis added.

them. When we did this ourselves and took that fresh view to the temple, new insights came to us, which enabled us to solve various challenges we have faced. So, perhaps, a renewed study of these points of doctrine will do the same for you as you seek to learn from the temple.

Chapter 6

Our Divine Nature and Potential

"All human beings—male and female—are created in the image of God. Each is a beloved spirit son or daughter of heavenly parents, and, as such, each has a divine nature and destiny."

—First Presidency and Quorum of the Twelve [1]

This chapter covers our progression and our potential as children of God. We include a discussion of how we help and bear with others on their individual journeys of spiritual progress. As we grow in the understanding and implications of how imperfect children progress towards perfection, we will be more open to insights from the temple regarding what we can do for ourselves and others in that process.

Personal Application: Aaron

Each of us needs help on our journey of spiritual progression in this life. We experienced the difference one young woman made in the life of one of her peers when she was patient with the

---

1. "The Family: A Proclamation to the World," *Ensign*, November 1995, 102.

spiritual progress of a friend.[2] I taught early-morning seminary for three years. As is the case with a class that happens so early in the morning, I did not always have all eligible seminary students regularly attending.

I felt impressed at the beginning of the year to challenge my students to reach out to someone who was not attending seminary and invite them to come. One of the students in the class named Jenni, a senior, took the challenge and decided to invite her friend Lisa to start coming to seminary. Lisa's mom was a single parent who did the best that she could for her daughter. However, due to various challenges, Lisa did not always make it to church activities or seminary.

Jenni began inviting Lisa to come to seminary, talking with her regularly about coming to class. At first, there was no change. Then, to everyone's delight, Lisa began to come. Her attendance was sporadic, but she began to attend. No one pressured her to do anything more than she could do.

Lisa's seminary attendance slowly spilled over to Sunday church meetings and Wednesday youth activities, where she also began to come more frequently. Given her family situation, she had to get herself up for seminary and attend church on her own, which meant that she still missed sometimes. However, little by little, we saw more and more of Lisa, which was miraculous, indeed.

When Jenni graduated, we wondered what would happen with Lisa. Would she continue to come, or would she fall back into her previous attendance patterns? To everyone's delight, she continued to attend both seminary and church, and she did so with more frequency than before. Her attendance was never perfect, but it was consistent.

We watched Lisa's progress over time. Eventually, years later, Lisa was married in the temple and became a mother in Zion, as did Jenni. All these blessings came about because of a series of simple, unwearied invitations made by a faithful young woman

---

2. Story used with permission.

*and because of the patience of all involved with the gradual prog-
ress of a precious daughter of God.*

*As we more consistently have patience with the spiritual prog-
ress of others, striving to be more curious and less judgmental, we
will see great miracles in our lives and theirs. The greatest miracle
is for us and them to become more like our Heavenly Parents.*

**All men and women have an eternal nature with a divine
origin, destiny, and purpose.** The temple teaches of the divine
nature of all God's children. Prophets and apostles have repeatedly
taught of our infinite potential. In a landmark statement on this subject, the First Presidency and Quorum of the Twelve jointly and unit-
edly taught, "All human beings—male and female—are created in
the image of God. Each is a beloved spirit son or daughter of heavenly
parents, and, as such, each has a divine nature and destiny."[3]

In the scriptures and the temple, we learn that men and women
are not accidents of nature. We were created premortally with individual identity, eternal purpose, and divine destiny. We were created in
the image of our Heavenly Parents, with the same physical attributes.
We are heirs of a Heavenly Father and King and a Heavenly Mother
and Queen with an eternal purpose and destiny.

In the restored gospel of Jesus Christ, we learn the role and divine
nature of men and women. We discover that men and women are
unique yet unified, distinct in approach and rationale yet aligned in
purpose and outcome. Sons and daughters are equally loved, accepted,
and appreciated by God. Individually, we each have work to do on the
earth, and if we are both faithful and true to our covenants, we receive
a sure promise in the temple that we will be protected until our work
is complete.

**The Father invites us to awaken and rise to our eternal poten-
tial.** In the temple, we are all invited to awaken to an improved

---

3. "The Family: A Proclamation to the World," *Ensign*, November 1995, 102.

understanding of the world and our role in it and arise to our eternal potential.[4] Each of us needs to spiritually "awaken" periodically.

To awaken spiritually is to become self-aware of our current spiritual condition and how it compares to our divine potential. When we understand our gaps—or at least part of them—then we can make changes to begin to close them, seeking the help of our Heavenly Father and our Savior to accomplish it. When we understand our strengths and talents, we can use them to carry out the Father's work more effectively.

The Lord invites the brethren to rise to Heavenly Father's glory and to the majesty of their wives. Likewise, He invites the sisters to rise to the grandeur of Heavenly Mother and the dignity of their husbands. He encourages children to rise and honor their parents and for parents to rise to the humility and submissiveness of their children. He invites all members to elevate to the sacredness of their covenants and their destiny as sons and daughters of God.

We can also awaken to the reality of God and His Son and their involvement in our lives, to the revelations of the Spirit, to the precious blessings we have received, to the importance of our spouse and family, and to a recognition of the negative influence of our humanity or the adversary in our lives.

Our eternal destiny to become like our perfect Heavenly Parents is realized along an imperfect mortal path. The purpose of the temple is to enable us to become like our Heavenly Parents and realize our eternal destiny as their sons and daughters. Their plan is for us to develop all Their traits and characteristics, which makes us like Them. To that end, the Savior invited us, "I would that ye should be perfect even as I, or your Father who is in heaven is perfect."[5]

Unfortunately, our journey on the path to perfection may seem daunting due to our imperfections. To help calm our anxieties, Elder Neal A. Maxwell, formerly of the Quorum of the Twelve, encouragingly taught,

---

4. See 2 Nephi 8:24–25.
5. 3 Nephi 12:48.

The Greek rendering for "perfect" is, by the way, "complete, finished, fully developed." . . . One of the problems we have in the Church is that we consider perfection in abstraction, and it becomes too intimidating. But when we think of it in terms of the specific, cardinal attributes, and we strive to develop these in a steady process of self-improvement, it is quite a different matter.[6]

The imperfect and sometimes challenging journey of mortal life enables us to slowly develop all the Father's godly traits. While here, our *progress* is likely more important than our *destination*.

The restored gospel of Jesus Christ is a gospel of spiritual progression. The scriptures and living prophets teach the doctrine and principles of progress. The temple portrays and illustrates the continuous development and improvement of God's children as they slowly become more like their Heavenly Parents—until the Savior eventually perfects them. In temples with multiple floors, the ascent from lower floors to higher floors is symbolic of this progression.

Individuals progress as they consistently gain more spiritual "knowledge and intelligence."[7] Knowledge is spiritual learning gained by study; intelligence is the application of spiritual learning by faith. "If a person gains more knowledge *and* intelligence in this life through his [or her] diligence and obedience than another, he [or she] will have so much the advantage in the world to come."[8]

This "principle of intelligence"—meaning the godly character that we develop as we strive to learn and then apply that learning—is the only thing that will "rise with us in the resurrection,"[9] for what we have become on the inside will be what we see on the outside at that day. Before that day, what we are outwardly radiates and affects those

---

6. Neal A. Maxwell, "In Him All Things Hold Together," *BYU Speeches* (Provo: Brigham Young University, March 31, 1991), accessed March 31, 2021, https://speeches.byu.edu/talks/neal-a-maxwell/in-him-all-things-hold-together/.

7. Doctrine and Covenants 130:19.

8. Ibid; s added.

9. Doctrine and Covenants 130:18.

around us.[10] With effort and progress, our character improves, as does our effect on others.

The process of perfection requires repeated, consistent action by the individual and by those who minister to him or her. Some of our imperfections can and should be changed now, others may need more time for us to change, and some imperfections may not change until after this life. It takes inspired discernment to know when to act diligently and when to wait on the pace of their individualized progress kindly and patiently.[11] None of us will become perfect in an instant or even in this life.

To assist us in having patience in the process of progression and perfection, Elder Bruce R. McConkie, formerly of the Quorum of the Twelve, wisely counseled,

> [You] don't need to get a complex or get a feeling that you have to be perfect to be saved. You don't. . . . What you have to do is get on the straight and narrow path—thus charting a course leading to eternal life—and then, being on that path, pass out of this life in full fellowship. I'm not saying that you don't have to keep the commandments. I'm saying you don't have to be perfect to be saved. If you did, no one would be saved. . . .
>
> If you're working zealously in this life—though you haven't fully overcome the world and you haven't done all you hoped you might do [or become all you might become]—you're still going to be saved. You don't have to do what Jacob said, 'Go beyond the mark.' You don't have to live a life that's truer than true. You don't have to have an excessive zeal that becomes fanatical and becomes unbalancing.

---

10. President David O. McKay taught, "Every man [or woman], every person radiates what he or she is. Every person is a recipient of radiation. The Savior was conscious of this fact. Whenever he came into the presence of an individual, he sensed that radiation. . . . Christ was ever conscious of the radiation from the individual, and, to a degree, so are you, and so am I. It is what we are and what we radiate that affects the people around us" (David O. McKay, Conference Report, April 1969, 150.)

11. We should have this same patience for our own progress!

What you have to do is stay in the mainstream of the Church and live as upright and decent people live in the Church. . . . If you're on that path when death comes . . . you'll never fall off from it, and, for all practical purposes, your calling and election is made sure.[12]

This statement should give us all hope and reassurance that our best—albeit imperfect—efforts are sufficient for salvation.

The gradual process of helping others progress requires kindness, compassion, and patience. The temple portrays the kindness, compassion, and patience of Heavenly Father, His Son, and Their servants in helping men and women progress. The spiritual change that occurs as we become more like our Heavenly Parents happens slowly and over time.

In the premortal realm, we learned that this world would be a fallen place, full of all manner of imperfections and injustices. Because of that condition, we, too, would be imperfect and subject to all types of issues, requiring time and effort to resolve.

We were admonished in the premortal world to love God and "walk after his commandments."[13] We were also admonished to love our neighbor. In the New Testament, John wrote, "This is the message that ye heard *from the beginning*, that we should love one another."[14] As the Savior taught during His mortal ministry, "A new commandment I give unto you, That ye love one another; as I have loved you, that ye also love one another. By this shall all men know that ye are my disciples, if ye have love one to another."[15]

When we love others, we see them as God sees them. Of this ability to see as He sees for true disciples of Christ, Sister Michelle D. Craig, a member of the Young Women General Presidency, taught,

---

12. Bruce R. McConkie, The Probationary Test of Mortality, address given at the University of Utah Institute of Religion, January 10, 1982, http://www.ldss-criptureteachings.org/2018/07/26/5867–2/. Accessed January 4, 2021.

13. 2 John 1:6.

14. 1 John 3:11; emphasis added.

15. John 13:34–35.

Understanding how God sees us prepares the way to help us
see others as He does. . . . Jesus Christ sees people deeply.
He sees individuals, their needs, and who they can become.
Where others saw fishermen, sinners, or publicans, Jesus saw
disciples; where others saw a man possessed by devils, Jesus
looked past the outward distress, acknowledged the man, and
healed him. Even in our busy lives, we can follow the example
of Jesus and see individuals—their needs, their faith, their
struggle, and who they can become.[16]

Like us, our neighbors do not keep the commandments perfectly
and are subject to all kinds of flaws. Ministering to them requires us
to have patience and compassion with their shortcomings and their
spiritual development, which can be terribly slow and even impercep-
tible in some cases. We can only do this when we see them as God
does.

In all our efforts to minister, we should treat people according to
their divine potential, not their current mortal position. We should
strive to absorb the bad and amplify the good in others. We should
be patient with progress, however small. We should preach truth but
always remember mercy. These acts are ones of compassion and reconciliation in the similitude of the Savior. [17]

We must have perfect love throughout mortality to not condemn
nor cast out any of Father's children who are genuinely—but slowly—
making progress. Even those who are currently openly rebelling may
eventually return and repent, and we could be the means of bringing
them back into the fold.[18] Ultimately, we must continue in love until

---

16. Michelle D. Craig, "Eyes to See," Conference Report, October 2020.
17. Sister Sharon Eubank of the Relief Society General Presidency provided a
unique insight that could help us remember mercy: "Jacob 2:17 reads, 'Think
of your [brothers and sisters] like unto yourselves, and be familiar with all and
free with your substance, that they may be rich like unto you.' Let's replace the
word *substance* with *mercy*—be free with your *mercy* that they may be rich like
unto you. We often think of *substance* in terms of *food* or *money*, but perhaps
what we all need more of in our ministering is *mercy*" (Sharon Eubank, "By
Union of Feeling We Obtain Power with God," Conference Report, October
2020; emphasis added.)
18. See 3 Nephi 18:30, 32.

a person meets "the measure of the stature of the fulness of Christ,"[19] which will likely only occur in the eternities.

The temple models the kindness, patience, love, and consistency of all involved in this process of progression. We are encouraged to emulate and embody those same godly traits when we leave and continue our ministering elsewhere. Living prophets have reinforced these principles. In a message to the Relief Society, but with principles applicable to all, Joseph Smith lovingly taught us how we should approach this most important work:

> We must be merciful to one another and overlook small things. . . . Nothing is so much calculated to lead people to forsake sin as to take them by the hand, and watch over them with tenderness. When persons manifest the least kindness and love to me, O what power it has over my mind, while the opposite course has a tendency to harrow up all the harsh feelings and depress the human mind. . . . God does not look on sin with allowance, but when men [and women] have sinned, there must be allowance made for them.[20]

Allowance by us for others' imperfections is a similitude of the Savior's mercy for our shortcomings. In our ministering, we must "remember the worth of souls is great,"[21] for that thought will properly guide our attitudes and actions.

We should avoid unrighteous judgment as we help others progress. As changes occur in our neighbors' lives, we may be tempted to make unrighteous judgments about them as we observe their progress. However, we—as imperfect mortals—are not to judge the ultimate, eternal outcome for any child of God.

We may warn, exhort, teach, and encourage, but we should stop short of making a final judgment. Our responsibility is simply to "speak the truth in love"[22] as we teach and to be "kind one to another

---

19. Ephesians 4:13.
20. Joseph Smith, *Teachings of the Prophet Joseph Smith*, 240–241.
21. Doctrine and Covenants 18:10.
22. Ephesians 4:15.

[and] tenderhearted"[23] as we minister and assist them in their progression. This action is tolerance for people and progress and not lenience for sin. We must avoid sin and lovingly forgive the sinner.

Personal Application: Aaron

On one occasion as bishop, I took a group of young men on a high adventure to Broken Bow, Oklahoma. At the state park, we saw water being released from a dam due to heavy rains that had occurred the week before. The water gushing through the dam's gates was impressive, evidence of the great power stored in the water being held back by the structure.

A mental model that may help us in our efforts to resist judging is to picture the mercy and forgiveness of the Savior as water being held back by a great dam. The sinner's willing repentance opens the gates of the dam and allows His mercy and forgiveness to flow freely.

The forgiveness was always there—it just needed the person to choose to open the gates for it to be unleashed in significant quantities. What a beautiful and joyous thought to contemplate that the Savior has an unlimited amount of forgiveness waiting for us all! What hope and what responsibility it gives us to know our part in receiving it.

When we understand that forgiveness of our sins and the sins of everyone else is merely a set of repentant choices away, then we will have a great love for others and ourselves. We will be more patient and kinder in our attitudes toward and our dealings with them. We will have a positive belief in them because we will earnestly hope that they will make choices that would allow mercy and forgiveness to flow freely in their lives. We will follow the admonition of Micah, who said, "[God] hath shewed thee, O man, what is good; and what doth the Lord require of thee, but to do justly, and to love mercy, and to walk humbly with thy God?"[24]

We should teach, minister, love, and then wait to allow the Perfect One to make the appropriate final judgment of how much of

---

23. Ephesians 4:32.
24. Micah 6:8; emphasis added.

His unlimited pool of forgiveness they have accessed. To us, the Lord says, "Leave judgment alone with me, for it is mine and I will repay."[25] Whatever remains of their development after a lifetime of progress can be mercifully acquitted by a loving Savior who perfectly knows every individual's spiritual trajectory and can perfectly see what the end of their course would have been if given sufficient time.

In an article entitled "You Love, He Saves," author Krista Rogers Mortensen encourages us to look at our own hearts and focus on love when we help others progress. She learned this lesson through personal experience with ministering to her adult children who had stopped participating in the Church. Said she,

> For a long time, I pleaded with the Lord to change their hearts, and finally the Lord answered my prayers. But not in the way I expected.
>
> Instead of simply changing my children's hearts, He showed me that I needed to start by changing my own heart. . . . He reminded me that my role isn't to judge or save them but to love them. Jesus Christ is their Savior and Judge. . . .
>
> As I turned to the Savior for healing, my heart began to soften toward my children. . . . It didn't mean giving up on trying to help them, but when loving them [instead of changing them] became the driving force behind my interactions with them, it changed *how* I interacted. . . .
>
> I listened more and talked less. I asked questions about their lives and their interests. Instead of judgment, I showed curiosity. I replaced criticism and disappointment with expressions of love, and my children could feel that it was genuine.[26]

"Be curious and not judgmental." What a lovely and inspired approach to working with others!

---

25. Doctrine and Covenants 82:23.
26. Krista Rogers Mortensen, "You Love, He Saves," *Ensign*, July 2020.

The prophet Alma taught, "Now the Spirit knows all things."[27] He knows and monitors the progress of each child of God. If we have the gift of discernment, we, too, can get a sense of their progress and for what we may do to assist in it. This gift will allow us to make the appropriate intermediate judgments and enable us to show love and compassion toward all God's children according to their individual needs.

Suppose someone feels the need to meet with a presiding Church authority to discuss something he or she is facing. In that case, the leader will judge whether any issues require his involvement, commensurate with God's laws and the Church's processes. In the role of "common judge," what is being judged by the priesthood leader with keys is *not* the person but rather what the person needs to *do* to progress. He is trying to judge how mercy can lift the person, *not* how justice can condemn them. In some specific cases, merciful limits may be placed on the individual by those with priesthood keys to allow spiritual healing to occur, like immobilizing an injured limb to reduce pain and encourage healing.

Even with any imposed limits, we who minister as friends, family, or fellow members have been instructed to do the following:

> Nevertheless, ye shall not cast [them] out from among you, but *ye shall minister unto [them]* and shall pray for [them] unto the Father . . . for ye know not but what they will return and repent, and come unto me with full purpose of heart, and I shall heal them; and ye shall be the means of bringing salvation unto them.[28]

As we continue to minister, we may see great miracles occur!

Personal Application: Aaron

Bearing with others in whatever situation they face enables us to be more like our Savior, who bears with us and whose arms are

---

27. Alma 7:13.
28. 3 Nephi 18:30, 32; emphasis added.

stretched out still.[29] *Allow me to share a personal experience that taught me this most important principle.*[30]

A sister in our ward has a daughter who is LGBTQ+. Her daughter went through a very dark time in her life, but with the effort and love of her mother and family, she successfully navigated those difficult times. This sister told me that her temple covenants helped her focus on the Savior and His love for her family.

When I was serving as this sister's bishop, a policy change was made regarding LGBTQ+ people. When the change was announced, she tried to understand what it would mean for others like her daughter. She and her husband had a difference of opinion about it. After Church, she went to her room to be alone and avoid an argument.

After a few hours, she came out to make cookies to help get her mind off her worries. Then, still wondering what to do, the doorbell rang. When she answered it, I was standing at the door.

I had been at Church, and as I was leaving to go home, I received a prompting to go and see this sister. I didn't know why, but I acted on the impression and went to her home. I arrived just as she had come into the kitchen.

We sat and talked for about an hour. We had previous discussions about her daughter. She helped me understand how she came to a place of acceptance and love for this precious child of God. On this day, we talked about how important it is to love and care for our LGBTQ+ brothers and sisters. I counseled her to continue to be accepting and focus on her relationship with her Heavenly Father and her daughter.

As we talked, she realized that my being at her home unannounced when she needed help was a message from God that He knew her and was aware of her situation. She also realized that God knew her daughter, too. Most importantly, her connection with God that day when He bore her burdens through me has made a lasting impact on her life.

---

29. See Isaiah 5:25; 9:12, 17, 21; 10:4; 2 Nephi 9:12, 17, 21; 15:25; 20:4.
30. Story shared with permission.

Author Tom Christofferson clarified what "acceptance" should mean for disciples of Christ:

> *I have used the term acceptance in conjunction with, and perhaps synonymously with, love. I mean it to convey the willingness to recognize reality. . . . Accepting others does not mean that we condone, agree with, or conform to their beliefs or choices, but simply that we allow the realities of their lives to be different from our own. Difference is not conformity; in fact, it is exactly the opposite. . . . A willingness to accept the realities of another's life conveys respect for agency, for maturity, for responsibility, for intelligence.[31]*

Because I did not allow judgment to get in the way of acceptance, I helped this sister find a positive path forward. Although her situation did not change, her capability to handle it in productive ways did because of my loving actions. Her temple covenants and faith in her Savior and His Atonement continue to sustain and enable her to move forward in faith and love.

The Father encourages and enhances the individuality and unity of all His children. The temple celebrates the identity and personality of each child of God. Each person has unique gifts and talents inherent in his or her divine nature. Heavenly Father celebrates and reinforces these differences and His children's diversity in the design of His plan of salvation.

All children of God have varying gifts and talents, which allows them to contribute to the Lord's work and to the world in unique ways. In the divinely organized institution of the family, each person has a different role. Similarly, in the Church, all members have opportunities to serve and contribute that are amplified and enhanced by their unique, divine attributes.

---

31. Thomas H. Christofferson, *That We May Be One: A Gay Mormon's Perspective on Faith and Family* (Salt Lake City: Deseret Book, 2017), 59–60.

Because of His desire to honor the inherent differences between His children, the Father does not view equality in the same way the world defines it. Instead, He defines equality in at least four ways in His plan:

First, references in the scriptures to equality involve giving all people equal opportunity to receive the gospel, partake in all its associated saving ordinances, and receive all the blessings of exaltation.

Second, modern-day prophets affirm that husbands and wives are to "help one another as equal partners" in leading their families, always respecting the differences in their divinely instituted roles. The joint and unified leadership of a man and a woman in the home is paramount in the Father's plan.

Third, Church callings and assignments bring equal blessings to all individuals, irrespective of the nature or scope of the role, if they magnify their duty. The heartfelt service of all men and women in the Church is equally valid and accepted by God irrespective of where they serve.

Finally, our Heavenly Father and His Son love all people regardless of race, gender, ethnicity, or any other defining mortal characteristic. "All are alike unto God."[32] All can find favor with Him if they keep His commandments. President Nelson affirmed,

> God does not love one race more than another. His doctrine on this matter is clear. He invites all to come unto Him, "black and white, bond and free, male and female." I assure you that your standing before God is not determined by the color of your skin. Favor or disfavor with God is dependent upon your devotion to God and His commandments and not the color of your skin.[33]

The world teaches that achieving equality means ensuring different individuals are precisely equivalent, with exactly the same roles, responsibilities, and rewards. On the other hand, Heavenly Father wants to enhance rather than erase the inherent differences and gifts of each of his children, so all benefit from that variety. Our Father wants

---

32. 2 Nephi 26:33.
33. Russell M. Nelson, "Let God Prevail," Conference Report, October 2020.

all His children to not only develop but to celebrate the divine differences each person brings to the family, the Church, and the world. Individuals are distinct but are all needed. They are like the different parts of the body—each of which is required but quite different.[34]

With great diversity between His children, the Father is concerned with unity. He asks His children to be unified in all their efforts. He wants them to have their "eye single to the glory of God"[35] and be one. Repeatedly in the scriptures, the Father puts a premium on unity in the Church and the family.[36]

If the Father were to reinforce His children's diverse qualities and talents without commanding us to be one, we could eventually grow apart. To prevent this unintended consequence from occurring, He gives us the strict command to be unified, which keeps us aligned with each other and with Him. When we seek unity amid diversity, we will achieve the equality that He desires. We will also feel the belonging we desire.

Zion was unified. However, unity is an *outcome*, not a *means* to an outcome. When we use unity as a *means*, then we can become overly accommodating, fearing to offend when correction is needed. We can fall prey to "group think" or fail to bring a variety of opinions and views to a decision. Worst of all, we can exclude anyone who doesn't look, act, or think like us or like the majority.

In the restored gospel of Jesus Christ, we can honor the variety of God's children and still be unified. Elder Quentin L. Cook of the Quorum of the Twelve taught, "With our all-inclusive doctrine, we can be an oasis of unity *and* celebrate diversity. Unity and diversity are not opposites. We can achieve greater unity as we foster an atmosphere of inclusion and respect for diversity."[37]

Collective unity can only come when we individually choose righteousness, humbly submit to the will of God, regularly repent, and

---

34. See 1 Corinthians 12:14–26.
35. Doctrine and Covenants 4:5.
36. See John 17:11, 21–22; 1 Corinthians 1:10; 2 Corinthians 13:11; Ephesians 4:3–5, 11–13, 16; Philip. 2:2; Doctrine and Covenants 31:5, 38:27; Moses 6:68, 7:8.
37. Quentin L. Cook, "Hearts Knit in Righteousness and Unity," Conference Report, October 2020; emphasis added.

lovingly accept the variety and beauty of all God's children. When unity is an *outcome* of righteous, loving choices, then it has the intent that the Father desires—to bring His people together in righteousness despite their diversity or variety.

Unity is not conformity. It is "having our hearts knit together . . . in love towards one another"[38] with all the beautiful variety we individually bring.

Personal Application: Julie

Our family is highly diverse. Aaron's mother is Filipino, and his father is Polish. They met at a Young Single Adult activity when his father was stationed in the Philippines during the Vietnam conflict. His sister is a full-blooded Korean, having been adopted when she was a young child. Living with diversity is an integral part of our family, and it has prepared us to embrace the differences we see in others around us.

One of those opportunities happened when we were living near Houston. The stake reorganized our English-speaking ward and combined it with a small, struggling Spanish branch. These good brothers and sisters came from various Spanish-speaking countries. Most held jobs as laborers, whereas many of our English-speaking members were professionals. So, the new ward was a cultural and socioeconomic mix.

On Sundays, we had interpreters translate the talks for us. When English speakers gave talks, the Spanish-speaking members would wear headphones, and when the Spanish speakers gave talks, the English speakers would wear headphones.

When fast Sundays occurred, we would break our fast together after the meeting. We would bring food to share, which was a mix of dishes from different cultures. For some of our members with the least means, that meal was sometimes their only one that day, even if they weren't fasting.

---

38. Mosiah 8:21

We learned to love and accept each other, despite our cultural and language differences. Aaron and I came to love these wonderful members. Aaron speaks Spanish, but I do not. Yet, I never felt that my language barrier prohibited me from being friends with everyone in our ward. I truly came to love our ward members, and I appreciated their backgrounds and cultures.

This little ward south of Houston taught me the importance of both diversity and unity. Things were never perfect in that unit, but we were happy. Our time in that ward was a lesson of how Zion and its temple bring different people together in Christ.

The human body is sacred, and the Lord desires that we guard it as such. Temple ordinances bless our bodies to function as designed and remind us to use them in the work of the Lord. The ordinances instruct us in the essential physical and spiritual functions of many of its limbs and organs. The scriptures likewise teach that our bodies are sacred, even a "temple of the Holy Ghost."[39] We require a physical body, which the Lord will perfect in the Resurrection, to become like our Heavenly Parents.

To enter the temple, we must accept and live the Lord's law of health, called the Word of Wisdom.[40] The Lord gave it to us in this last dispensation to protect our sacred physical bodies from harm. He has always had some type of health code for covenant sons and daughters. Under the Mosaic law, they were not to consume certain foods. The Word of Wisdom outlines our modern-day restrictions.

Why give us such health guidelines when our bodies eventually age and decay anyway? Several likely reasons exist.

First, the Lord wants to protect us from "evils and designs which do and will exist in the hearts of conspiring men [and women] in the last days." He warns and forewarns us of dangers related to our bodies.[41] The early Saints of Joseph Smith's time could never have imagined all the ways that evil men and women

---

39. 1 Corinthians 6:19.
40. See Doctrine and Covenants 89.
41. Doctrine and Covenants 89:4.

could damage our bodies, such as with illicit drugs or other harmful substances or habits.

Second, the Lord wants us to have good health so we can more effectively do His work and have joy in this life. When we can "run and not be weary," "walk and not faint," and have "wisdom" and "great treasures of knowledge," we will have a much more joyous and enjoyable life.[42] We will also be physically, mentally, and emotionally able to be effective instruments in His hand as He uses us to work for the salvation of all His children. Even when illnesses and declining health come, we will be in a more positive place than if we started with poor health.

Third, obeying the Word of Wisdom generates humility, meekness, and faith in us. Living this law is as much about faith as health. When we humbly accept and live this law—that can be trying for some—we learn submissiveness to Him, which will benefit us when other commands or instructions come. Taming the desire to partake of some of the pleasurable substances of life enables us to control the natural man and woman, enabling us to obey other commandments given for our benefit.

Finally, a healthy body is more prepared to receive inspired messages from the Lord. The poor health and addictions that come from not properly caring for or abusing our physical bodies block the sacred, subtle channels of revelation that the Lord uses to communicate with us. The adversary wants to cut us off from those messages, so he works tirelessly to attack our physical bodies. Given the eternal importance of hearing the Lord's voice to guide, comfort, and protect us, this aspect is perhaps the most important reason for living the Lord's law of health. Of this principle, Elder Boyd K. Packer, formerly of the Quorum of the Twelve, taught, "The Word of Wisdom is, I think, only incidentally to keep us healthy, if we will observe it. . . . It is not that you are going to be a healthy athlete all of your life, and it is not that you are going to avoid old age. It is that you *will* have the key

---

42. Doctrine and Covenants 89:19–20.

to revelation. When your body begins to deteriorate, the patterns of revelation will be augmented and magnified."[43]

Even when we obey the Word of Wisdom, we may face issues with our sacred mortal body. We cannot now fully understand how much joy it gave us in the premortal world to know we would have a body, even an imperfect and a fallen one. A son or daughter of God with a fallen, mortal body is developmentally far ahead of a being with no such body. Therefore, we should avoid murmuring when we or someone we know inherits or develops some defect or dysfunction.

Our Savior will resurrect us all, and He will restore us to our "perfect frame."[44] No part of our mortal frame—physical, mental, or emotional—will be lost. He will remove any barriers due to the Fall, and we and our loved ones will come forth gloriously renewed, "for all old things shall pass away, and all things [in our bodies and minds] shall become new."[45] Elder Jeffrey R. Holland of the Quorum of the Twelve lovingly taught,

> I bear witness of that day when loved ones whom we knew to have disabilities in mortality will stand before us glorified and grand, breathtakingly perfect in body and mind. What a thrilling moment that will be! I do not know whether we will be happier for ourselves that we have witnessed such a miracle or happier for them that they are fully perfect and finally 'free at last.' Until that hour when Christ's consummate gift is evident to us all, may we live by faith, hold fast to hope, and show 'compassion one of another' [see 1 Peter 3:7].[46]

Until that glorious time of renewal, we can have patience with our current physiological and psychological challenges by deeply pondering the function and purpose of our sacred body. This introspection will give us greater insight into what we should do with our talents,

---

43. Boyd K. Packer, "The Instrument of Your Mind and the Foundation of Your Character," *BYU Speeches* (Provo: Brigham Young University, February 2, 2003), accessed February 7, 2021, https://speeches.byu.edu/talks/boyd-k-packer/instrument-mind-foundation-character/.

44. See Alma 11:42–44. See also Doctrine and Covenants 29:25.

45. Doctrine and Covenants 29:24.

46. Jeffrey R. Holland, "Like a Broken Vessel," Conference Report, October 2013.

strengths, and gaps and how we can try to improve their function or shore up their dysfunction while in mortality. These efforts will more effectively forward our progress towards becoming more like our Father in Heaven.

QUESTIONS TO CONSIDER

1. What did you learn about your divine potential during your last temple visit? What does that mean to you at this point in your life?
2. What do you learn about ministering from the temple? With that understanding, how can you best minister to others to help them realize their divine potential?
3. What does the temple teach us about being "curious and not judgmental"? How can you show your love toward others by avoiding unrighteous judgment?
4. What have you learned about diversity and unity from the temple? In what ways can you celebrate the diversity of others and still find unity with them? How can you do that at Church? In your community? In your family?

NOTES AND INSIGHTS

_____

_____

_____

_____

_____

_____

_____

Chapter 7

Agency, Choice, and Accountability

*"Agency is the power to think, choose, and act for our-
selves. It comes with endless opportunities, accompanied
by responsibility and consequences."*

—Sharon G. Larsen[1]

This chapter covers the critical temple doctrines of agency, choice, and accountability, which are abundantly taught in our temple experience. Moral agency is our most fundamental right, and it comes with the responsibility of accepting the consequences of our choices. Our agency unlocks either opportunities or tragedies. It all depends on us and our choices.

Personal Application: Aaron

*Agency, choice, and accountability are fundamental tenets
of the gospel and the temple. I had a powerful experience that
reinforced them for me. As part of a regional leadership program,
I spent an entire day in Huntsville, Texas, touring two different*

---

1. Sharon G. Larsen, "Agency—A Blessing and a Burden," Conference Report, October 1999.

penitentiaries. Seeing the many men whose lives were broken due to their choices, which led them to maximum-security confinement, was a somber experience.

We also saw all the things that the state is trying to do to rehabilitate these men. They had job training, education, and entrepreneurship programs. Of course, not all the prisoners chose to take advantage of these opportunities, but those who did began to turn around their lives.

At the end of our visit, we heard from two ex-convicts who had successfully moved through the entrepreneurship program. I was amazed to see the change in their lives and their viewpoints on life. One of the men was incarcerated when he was fourteen years old, and he spent twenty years in prison. When he got out at age thirty-four, he felt lost. He had entered the entrepreneurship program while still in prison, and then he continued with their placement efforts when he left, which gave him purpose. He is now fully employed and contributing to society.

When he was asked about the difference between him and others who have not been successfully rehabilitated, he provided an insightful answer. He said he's moved on and doesn't see his past choices as a part of his life. He only looks forward to what will be and doesn't worry about what was.

In contrast, he related that many other men spend all their time in prison looking back to what they lost, and when they get out, they try to go back to that old life. He observed that they are the ones who aren't successfully rehabilitated and end up back in prison again.

Past choices caused these men to be punished. However, those who chose a different path forward—one that would lead them away from their troubled past and toward a positive future— were the ones who progressed. As bishop, I tried to teach our youth, "Let the consequences be your guide." Indeed, choices do determine destiny!

Our moral agency is infinitely important to our progress. The temple explains and amplifies the eternal importance of agency, which is "the ability and freedom God gives people to choose and to act for themselves."[2] The Father gave the great gift of moral agency to all His sons and daughters. Using our agency correctly is the key to becoming like our Heavenly Parents. Agency is our most powerful and eternally influential gift.

To enable and protect our freedom, Heavenly Father ensures we can know and understand good from evil. "For behold, ye are free; ye are permitted to act for yourselves; for behold, *God hath given unto you a knowledge* and he hath made you free. He hath given unto you that ye might *know* good from evil, and he hath given unto you that ye might *choose* life or death."[3]

"The power is in them," and this power is the agency of men and women, for "they are agents unto themselves."[4] This power to choose is the greatest weapon we have in the battle between good and evil because it unlocks the potential of Jesus Christ to redeem us through His infinite Atonement.

Moral agency is critical to our development into independent, noble beings as He is.[5] The reason for us having our moral agency is so we might "stand independent"[6] in the universe, being able to "act" and not be "acted upon"[7] and having conquered all through the gift and power of Christ.

Having to overcome through Christ eternally ties us to Him, which keeps us humble and submissive—two foundational requirements for becoming like God and using His infinite power on behalf of others for eternity. Therefore, all people must choose for themselves, for they are "free according to the flesh" to "choose liberty and eternal life" or "to choose captivity and death."[8]

The Father has a great reverence for our agency. Moral agency is among the Father's most fundamental points of doctrine and most

---

2. "Agency," *Guide to the Scriptures*, 2013.
3. Helaman 14:30–31; emphasis added.
4. Doctrine and Covenants 58:28.
5. See Doctrine and Covenants 29:35.
6. Doctrine and Covenants 78:14. This scripture speaks of the independence of the Church, but this principle applies to us as individuals.
7. 2 Nephi 2:13.
8. 2 Nephi 2:27.

precious gifts. As portrayed in the temple, He will never violate our agency, even when the choices made will cause pain and heartache to Him and His children because He knows our agency is the key to exaltation and the key to becoming like Him. To protect our agency, He always invites and persuades and never forces or coerces.[9]

Therefore, when making invitations, His Spirit and voice are still and small, not harsh and loud.[10] His approach is one of gentleness and lovingkindness.[11] His model of perfect persuasion and inspired invitation is described in the scriptures and portrayed in the temple. We must adopt it if we want to become like Him. Of God's approach in protecting agency, President Howard W. Hunter has said,

> To fully understand this gift of agency and its inestimable worth, it is imperative that we understand that God's chief way of acting is by persuasion and patience and long-suffering, not by coercion and stark confrontation. He acts by gentle solicitation and by sweet enticement.
>
> He always acts with unfailing respect for the freedom and independence that we possess. He wants to help us and pleads for the chance to assist us, but he will not do so in violation of our agency. He loves us too much to do that, and doing so would run counter to his divine character.[12]

We should intently strive to emulate this model in all our interactions with others. It will enable us to follow His example in protecting and respecting the agency of all.

Jesus Christ protects our agency through His infinite Atonement. The Savior enables our freedom to choose eternal life via His Atonement. Redemption is the freedom from bondage. As taught in the temple, because of His redemption, we are no longer

---

9. See Doctrine and Covenants 121:41–42.
10. See 1 Kings 19:12; 1 Nephi 17:45; Doctrine and Covenants 85:6.
11. See Psalm 63:3.
12. Howard W. Hunter, "The Golden Thread of Choice," Conference Report, October 1989, 21.

bound by the conditions of the Fall or the wrong choices we make because of it—if we repent. The Atonement allows us to have the freedom to learn from making mistakes because those mistakes will not eternally condemn us.

Without the potential for redemption, we would not have the freedom to choose it because one wrong choice would block our progress, making any other future right choices irrelevant. The Savior's Atonement makes correct future choices relevant to our salvation even when some of our past decisions have violated eternal law. Consequently, He is the ultimate protector of our agency.

We must proactively use our agency to act. With this great gift of agency, we are encouraged to be "anxiously engaged" and to "do many things of [our] own free will."[13] The temple and its ordinances give us many opportunities to act of our own free will. This mandate means we must act on the principles we know to be true, even when He does not give us specific guidance on the matter. This choice is the ultimate use of our agency and is an act of faith. Of this principle, President Ezra Taft Benson taught,

> Usually the Lord gives us the overall objectives to be accomplished and some guidelines to follow, but he expects us to work out most of the details and methods. . . . Those spiritually alert look at the objectives, check the guidelines laid down by the Lord and his prophets, and then prayerfully act—without having to be commanded 'in all things.' This attitude prepares men [and women] for godhood.[14]

The Father's deep respect for our agency does *not* mean men and women can veto His will. When He invites them to act in accordance with and submission to His will, He will not coerce them to accept or comply. However, He will move forward and find other ways or other people to accomplish His work if they choose not to engage, or worse, if they decide to become a barrier to Him and His servants.

---

13. Doctrine and Covenants 58:27.
14. Ezra Taft Benson, Conference Report, April 1965, 121.

The Lord warned, "I command and men [and women] obey not; [consequently] I revoke and they receive not the blessing."[15] The scriptures and our early Church history provide examples of such adjustments, which guard the individual's agency and still allow the Father to accomplish His work.[16]

To draw down the Lord's precious blessings, we should actively and willingly accept and act on His divine invitations. Otherwise, we risk losing our opportunities.

Personal Application: Aaron

I learned the blessings of acting and the consequences of not acting while on a high adventure activity as bishop. On one day of our trip, we took the boys on a kayaking expedition down the river near our camp. The guide who dropped us off at the river told us that the excursion would be about two hours long and that he would meet us at the stopping point. We just needed to look for him at the side of the river.

He paired us with another group of campers and asked us to stay together. We got in our yellow kayaks, and we headed off down the river, having fun with the boys and our new friends along the way.

After several hours, we realized that we had not seen our guide waiting for us by the river. We kept going, expecting to see him soon. When we were far past our time, we got worried that something had happened. I counseled with the other leaders, and we decided to pull over to the side of the river and look for help. We called to the other campers and told them what we were doing. Instead of coming with us, they chose to continue down the river.

I went with a few others up the embankment, and we found some houses in the remote area. I used a phone at one of the houses

---

15. Doctrine and Covenants 58:32.
16. For example, section 81 was originally given to Jesse Gause, who was called to be a counselor to Joseph Smith. When he failed to comply with the call, it was transferred to Frederick G. Williams. (See heading to Doctrine and Covenants 81.)

to call our guide, but he did not answer. The lovely elderly women who let us into their home offered to take us back to town for help. I went with them, and I left the boys with the other leaders.

Eventually, I found our guide. He didn't realize that the river would be running so fast because of water released from the dam upstream earlier that day. We had already passed by when he got to the ending spot due to the river's speed. He was distraught because he had no way of getting in touch with us because none of us had taken cell phones into the kayaks.

The other group who chose not to stop had to be rescued by park rangers, who found them many miles down the river. If we had not decided to stop, we might have suffered the same fate. We acted, and we avoided trouble. They did not act, and they ended up lost and exceptionally far from their intended destination.

Our agency gives us the ability to act in accordance with the Lord's will. When we choose that course, we will be kept safe and remain on the path He wants for us.

Accountability and capability are required for choice and consequence to operate properly. The prophet Mormon taught that repentance and baptism are "unto those who are accountable *and* capable of committing sin."[17] Little children—those who are under the age of eight—are not accountable, so they do not need to repent or be baptized.[18]

There also individuals whose capability is compromised due to various issues of mortality. Where people are not capable of understanding or choosing right from wrong, for whatever set of reasons, the consequences of their choices will mercifully be suspended or acquitted by a loving Savior, who has fully met the demands of justice for all.

Choice and consequence are eternally and inevitably tied together. The temple emphasizes choice *and* consequence. The gospel of Jesus Christ teaches we are free to act for ourselves. However, when we make a choice, we select "the way of everlasting death" or "the

---

17. Moroni 8:10; emphasis added.
18. See Moroni 8:8–16.

way of eternal life,"[19] meaning we choose the consequences of those actions. "Ye can do good and be restored unto that which is good, or have that which is good restored unto you; or ye can do evil, and have that which is evil restored unto you."[20]

The temple reinforces that God gave agency to men and women, but with our agency comes the inevitable consequences of our choices. We cannot avoid these repercussions except through sincere repentance, and even then, some consequences may remain or may take time to resolve. Blessings flow from good choices; penalties result from poor choices. Indeed, "every man [and woman] receiveth wages of him whom he [or she] listeth to obey."[21]

What are these wages? Ultimately, our character and our attributes are either enhanced or degraded by each choice we make. Each time we make good choices, we gain the attributes of godliness, and each time we make poor choices, we lose those attributes. Unrepentant choices allow these character injuries to remain; sincere repentance cleans our slate and enhances our character. Other wages of choices include myriad other blessings gained or lost, such as access to temples, covenant priesthood blessings, good physical health, or even financial stability.

Our words, our works, and our thoughts will bless us or will harm us because of the freedom He gave us to act on the knowledge we have received.[22]

Whosoever will believe might be saved, and that whosoever will not believe, a righteous judgment might come upon them; and also if they are condemned they bring upon themselves their own condemnation.

And now remember, remember, my brethren [and sisters], that whosoever perisheth, perisheth unto himself [or herself]; and whosoever doeth iniquity, doeth it unto himself [or herself]; for behold ye are free, ye are permitted to act for yourselves.[23]

19. 2 Nephi 10:23.
20. Helaman 14:31.
21. Alma 3:27.
22. See Alma 12:14–15.
23. Helaman 14:29–30.

Therefore, we should always let consequences guide our choices.

For those who are accountable and capable, the decision to repent can bring mercy and a restoration of blessings through the infinite and eternal Atonement of Jesus Christ. The choice to not repent restores evil for evil, corruption to incorruption. We cannot suppose that wickedness will be restored to happiness.[24]

Sadly, the fully accountable and capable who do not repent "shall be as though there had been no redemption made."[25] If we procrastinated the day of our repentance when we were fully knowledgeable and fully able to repent in this life, then we will face a situation "wherein no labor can be performed"[26] when we pass out of this life. As President Thomas S. Monson was prone to say, "Decisions determine destiny."[27]

We often face the difficulty of conflicting "right" choices as disciples of Christ. In the scriptural story of Adam, Eve, and their decision in Eden,[28] we learn that we must always keep the highest commandment when faced with a conflict between two commandments, both of which are from God and for our benefit. This decision is not the choice between good and evil; it is the even more refining choice between two "goods" that conflict. The higher "good" should always take precedence.

The Savior modeled this choice of priorities during His ministry. On one occasion, a Canaanite woman came to Him to heal her daughter.[29] Although His Father instructed Him not to go unto the Gentiles and only minister to Israel's lost sheep, He agreed to perform the miracle she sought. The *higher* spiritual law of generating faith unto salvation for this daughter of God took priority over the *lesser* administrative practice of not going to the Gentiles.

---

24. See Alma 41 for a full discussion of this principle.
25. Alma 12:18.
26. Alma 34:32–35.
27. Thomas S. Monson, "Decisions Determine Destiny," *BYU Speeches* (Provo: Brigham Young University, November 6, 2005), accessed January 4, 2021. https://speeches.byu.edu/talks/thomas-s-monson/decisions-determine-destiny/.
28. See Genesis 1–3, Moses 2–4.
29. See Matthew 15:22–28.

These types of conflicting "good" decisions are among the most stretching of all the choices we make. However, they accelerate our development more than almost any other. Due to His infinite Atonement, only the Savior can make all things right, especially the things that are—of no fault of our own—in conflict, where we cannot resolve the contradiction in mortality. The temple reinforces and enhances this understanding.

So, what are we to do when faced with such contradictions? We must do our best to make an inspired choice and then trust that the Savior will remedy any resulting consequences in the eternities. This process is an act of faith and is a chief reason "faith in the Lord Jesus Christ" is the first principle of the restored gospel.

God will not be mocked by those who violate covenants. The scriptures teach God will not be mocked,[30] and the temple repeats this warning. To "mock" is to take something lightly or to act as if it has no consequence. We "mock" God when we openly violate His commandments or willingly break our covenants.

The temple reinforces this great and terrible truth: Violations of sacred covenants bring severe eternal consequences. Even if people believe that they can violate covenants and experience no consequences, they will be sadly mistaken in the eternities. Their ultimate character will fully expose their unrepentant choices. Again, God will not be mocked.

To avoid mocking God, we must act with integrity. Speaking of the need to act with authenticity to receive promised blessings, President John Taylor taught, "It is not enough for us to embrace the Gospel . . . *if our hearts are not right*, if we are not pure in heart before God, if we have not pure hearts and pure consciences, fearing God and keeping His commandments, we shall not, unless we repent, participate in these blessings about which I have spoken, and of which the Prophets bear testimony."[31]

---

30. See Galatians 6:7; Doctrine and Covenants 63:53; 104:6; 124:71.
31. John Taylor, *Teachings of Presidents of the Church: John Taylor* (Salt Lake City: Deseret Book, 2001), 114–15; emphasis added.

A special case of mockery is feigned obedience and false outward goodness, which is called hypocrisy. Hypocrisy is "the practice of claiming or appearing outwardly to have moral standards or beliefs to which a person's actual or unseen behavior does not conform."[32] This pretense of virtue is a most serious sin and is a form of deception.[33] Hypocritically violating temple covenants while maintaining the appearance of goodness is solemn mockery.

Jesus Christ vehemently condemned the sin of hypocrisy. "Woe unto you . . . hypocrites!" was His cry.[34] He warned them, "Ye also outwardly appear righteous unto men, but within ye are full of hypocrisy and iniquity. . . . How can ye escape the damnation of hell."[35] Unrepentant hypocrisy will result in harsh punishments in time.

A person cannot hide sin or sacrilege from the Lord, even if he or she deceives other people for some time. It may appear that those who secretly choose wickedness succeed temporally in this life, even though spiritual blessings are withdrawn due to their unrighteous choices. Anytime people choose evil, they are "left to their own strength."[36] Because of their natural abilities or accumulated resources, this strength may allow them to have some measure of success for some time, even for a long time.

Hypocrites may even be given support by unsuspecting individuals, which further enhances their position. To us, they may appear "happy," "set up," and "even delivered."[37] Ultimately, the Lord will not justify or approve their choices. They will "become weak" and will "cease to [be] preserve[d]."[38]

The Prophet Joseph Smith taught, "Remember God sees the secret springs of human action, and knows the hearts of all living. . . . It is also useless to make great pretentions when the heart is not right

---

32. See "Hypocrisy," google.com dictionary.
33. See Doctrine and Covenants 50:6–9.
34. See Matthew 23:13–15, 23, 25, 27, 29 for the Savior's condemnation of hypocrites and hypocrisy.
35. Matthew 23:28, 33.
36. Helaman 4:13.
37. Malachi 3:15.
38. Helaman 4:24–25.

before God, for God looks at the heart."[39] Put simply, God's measuring rod is our character, and character cannot be hidden from God.

The Lord assures us that the hypocrites' eternal outcomes will align with His perfect knowledge of their fraud and deceit. He will "reveal the secret acts of men [and women]."[40] They will eventually have a "bright recollection of all [their] guilt" when they stand before God[41] because the record of their deeds embeds itself upon their very spirits by shaping their eternal character. They will have become precisely what they chose to become, even though it may have been hidden from the world at large during this life. President John Taylor taught the sobering truth:

> The spirit lives where the record of [people's] deeds is kept—that does not die—[people] cannot kill it; there is no decay associated with it, and it still retains in all its vividness the remembrance of that which transpired before the separation by death of the body and the ever-living spirit.
>
> [People] sleep for a time in the grave, and by-and-by [they] rise again and go to judgment; and then the secret thoughts [and acts] of all are revealed before Him. . . . When we get into the eternal world, into the presence of God our Heavenly Father, his eye can penetrate every one of us, and our own record of our lives here shall develop all.[42]

Hypocrisy is purposed deception; it is not human failure. We can strive to do good and yet fall short. None should feel bad about these failures, but we should strive to move forward and repeatedly try to improve the next time. In our consistent efforts to improve, the Lord does not condemn but encourages us. Elder Jeffrey R. Holland of the Quorum of the Twelve encouragingly taught,

> Brothers and sisters, every one of us aspires to a more Christlike life than we often succeed in living. If we admit that honestly

39. Joseph Smith, *The Personal Writings of Joseph Smith*, comp. D. Jessee (Salt Lake City: Deseret Book, 1984), 264.
40. Doctrine and Covenants 88:109.
41. See Alma 11:43.
42. John Taylor cited in *Journal of Discourses*, 11:78–79.

and are trying to improve, we are not hypocrites; we are human. . . . If we persevere, then somewhere in eternity our refinement will be finished and complete—which is the New Testament meaning of *perfection*.[43]

Therefore, let us sincerely—albeit imperfectly—continue to do our best to become like our Heavenly Parents. Then, and only then, will we eventually become perfected in Christ.

We have an infinite need to choose to "come unto Christ, and be perfected in Him."[44] The temple is a beacon that calls us to Christ. The scriptures also repeatedly invite us to come unto Christ. Using our agency to come to Him is the most important choice we can make in this life, for it gives us access to the blessings of His infinite Atonement. As Alma invited, "Come and fear not!"[45]

Jesus Christ is our Judge, but He is also our Advocate. As our Advocate, He is on our side. He is pleading our cause before the Father. He wants us to succeed. To us He implores,

Listen to him who is the advocate with the Father, who is pleading your cause before him—Saying:

Father, behold the sufferings and death of him who did no sin, in whom thou wast well pleased; behold the blood of thy Son which was shed, the blood of him whom thou gavest that thyself might be glorified;

Wherefore, Father, spare these my brethren that believe on my name, that they may come unto me and have everlasting life.[46]

The Savior begs us to choose to take advantage of His efforts on our behalf! Without Him, we are forever lost and fallen.[47] With Him

---

43. Jeffrey R. Holland, "Be Ye Therefore Perfect—Eventually," Conference Report, October 2017.
44. Moroni 10:32.
45. Alma 7:15.
46. Doctrine and Covenants 45:3–5.
47. See Alma 42:6.

and in Him, we can do all things.[48] When we believe this sacred and hopeful truth as much as He does and choose to use our agency to act upon it, we will see great blessings flow.

QUESTIONS TO CONSIDER

1. What did you learn about agency, choice, and accountability in your last visit to the temple? What application does it have in your life at this time?
2. How can your temple covenants enable you to make better choices? How can they keep you spiritually safe?
3. What are some consequences of not keeping your temple covenants? How can you avoid "mocking God?"
4. How can the temple and its covenants help you with a choice you are currently facing? What points of temple doctrine can help you make a choice that is aligned with Heavenly Father's will for you?

NOTES AND INSIGHTS

_____

_____

_____

_____

_____

_____

_____

---

48. See Philip. 4:13.

Chapter 8

Commandments and Covenants

"Divine covenants make strong Christians. . . . In times of distress, let your covenants be paramount and let your obedience be exact."

—D. Todd Christofferson[1]

This chapter covers covenants and commandments. Contrary to the world's view, they do not limit us, but they liberate us—making us free to receive all the Father has. They can propel us forward if we make and keep them, or they can hinder us if we don't. They are a powerful vehicle for spiritual power and blessings, should we humbly choose to take advantage of what they offer.

Personal Application: Julie

Commandments and covenants enable us to navigate life's rough waters. An experience from a girls' camp I attended serves as an example. I was the co-camp director for our ward's girls' camp in 2014. We decided to take the girls to a camping site in Tahlequah, Oklahoma, where we had great activities planned.

---

1. D. Todd Christofferson, "The Power of Covenants," Conference Report, April 2009.

One of the exciting activities was to go rafting. We took buses down to the river as a group. When we arrived, the staff had all the rafts lined up and ready to go. There was a large trailer full of life jackets and paddles. The girls were to grab a life jacket and a paddle, get with their friends in a raft, and set out down the river.

One group of highly excited, giggling girls ran to get their life jackets, and they bolted to get in a raft so they could be together with their friends. However, as we watched the current take them down the river, we realized that only one of the girls had a paddle! In their excitement, the rest of the girls had not grabbed one.

Aaron and one of his counselors jumped in a raft with some extra paddles and paddled furiously toward them before they got too far down the river. Fortunately, they were able to get the girls paddles, and they made it through the rest of the rafting trip without any issues.

Covenants and commandments are like these paddles. When going down the river of life, they enable us to propel forward, steer clear of trouble, and navigate ourselves to our desired eternal destination. Without them, we are adrift, and the currents of life will take us where they want us to go and may put us in dangerous situations. Fortunately, Heavenly Father gave us commandments and offered us covenants, which protect and guide us through life.

Eternal laws are outwardly expressed through God's commandments. The temple affirms that eternal law exists, and it is outwardly expressed in the commandments of God. Commandments are those everlasting boundaries that outline the pathway of holiness.

Commandments do not violate agency; they enable it. They provide the blessings or consequences for the wise or poor use of agency. With commandments, we understand how our agency can bless or harm ourselves or others. Keeping them enables us to develop the character of Christ; breaking them limits our progress and cause others to fail in theirs.

Without commandments, our agency would be frustrated because the choice between what is eternally right and wrong would not exist. Blessings and punishments would not exist, and justice and mercy would cease to function. Lehi taught this sublime truth to his righteous son Jacob,[2] just as Alma taught it to his rebellious son Corianton.[3]

Without commandments to guide us, there would be no potential for happiness. Real joy can only come where a boundary *is* set and when we *willingly* stay within it. Blessings and cursings, which are the withholding of blessings, accompany obedience and disobedience to commandments. "If ye will keep my commandments ye shall prosper in the land—but if ye keep not [my] commandments ye shall be cut off from [my] presence."[4]

The Father gave us commandments from the beginning because He loves us. He gave them to us for our eternal benefit. Of this great truth, President Spencer W. Kimball taught,

> Long before this world was created, all of the spirits of the men and women who were assigned to this earth lived in a spiritual existence. And one day a great conference was held, . . . And He who presided at this meeting said to all of us who were assembled: . . . "The world is for you, and everything that is in it. I want you to be happy and have every necessity and luxury, and all I ask is that . . . you will do certain things that I specify. . . . Now, when you go down to the earth I expect you to follow these rules and live the commandments strictly."[5]

Ultimately, God gives us commandments to help us understand the conditions that gave Him His divine characteristics and enable us to develop those same divine attributes. Yes, commandments are the boundaries on the pathway to exaltation—to becoming like our Heavenly Parents.

Elder Dallin H. Oaks, current President of the Quorum of the Twelve, has taught, "The Final Judgment is not just an evaluation of a sum total of good and evil acts—*what we have done*. It is an acknowledgment of the final effect of our acts and thoughts—*what we have*

---

2. See 2 Nephi 2:13.
3. See Alma 42:17–26.
4. Alma 37:13.
5. Spencer W. Kimball, *Teachings of Spencer W. Kimball* (Salt Lake City: Deseret Book, 1982), 30–31; emphasis added.

become. It is not enough for anyone just to go through the motions. The commandments, ordinances, and covenants of the gospel are not a list of deposits required to be made in some heavenly account. The gospel of Jesus Christ is a plan that shows us how to become what our Heavenly Father desires us to become."[6]

Covenants are eternally important and individually made. The temple is a house of covenants. Each person must make and keep sacred covenants to qualify for eternal life and become like our Heavenly Parents. A covenant is a two-way agreement that establishes a new relationship. In the case of gospel covenants, the agreement is between the Savior and us, His children. He gives the conditions, we agree to the terms, and if we keep our commitments, He delivers His promised blessings.

The most fundamental tenet of all covenants made with the Lord is contained in this phrase: "I will be your God, and ye shall be my people."[7] It expresses the personal nature of the covenant relationship between God and us—His people. If we willingly choose to be His, He is bound to always be there for us.

The Father sets the conditions of our covenants. The Savior offers us the covenants, and the Church houses those covenants. Those with priesthood authority deliver covenants via ordinances, which are sacred ceremonies. The Holy Ghost ratifies our covenants. People activate their covenants and receive the power that flows from them through their agency.

Covenants extend our faith beyond just a belief—they prompt us to action. They allow God to recognize our willing actions as the keys to unlock specific blessings, thus reconciling us to Him. Covenants also encourage us to develop humility and meekness—two foundational traits of godliness—because they are enabled and reinforced through our willing submission to them.

---

6. Dallin H. Oaks, "The Challenge to Become," Conference Report, October 2000; emphasis added.
7. Jeremiah 7:23. See also Leviticus 26:12; Jeremiah 11:4, 24:7, 30:22, 31:1, 32:38; Ezekiel 11:20, 14:11, 36:28, 37:23; Zechariah, 8:8; 2 Corinthians 6:16; Doctrine and Covenants 42:9.

Ultimately, the receipt and keeping of all covenants lead to the assurance of eternal life because, through them, we will qualify for the redemptive actions of the Savior, who will sanctify and acquit us of all sin. We can sufficiently develop all the traits and characteristics required to become like our Heavenly Parents through them.

Each person must *individually* choose to make and then keep covenants. We do not make "group covenants" because the act of "becoming" requires individual progress. Even in the marriage covenant between a man and a woman, each person must individually agree to make and then seek to keep that most precious of all covenants. If one person fails to live up to it, the other person's covenants are still intact if he or she remains faithful. So, each of us must remain faithful and true to our covenants to realize the promised blessings.

Ordinances are the rites—exercised by one holding priesthood authority, presided over and authorized by one with the keys of the priesthood, willingly accepted by the person receiving them, and revealed by God—in which we make covenants with Him. Ordinances are an intersection of God, His children, and His power. They are the vehicle through which He delivers sacred covenants, which we willingly accept.

All God's children should seek out and receive saving ordinances, keeping their associated covenants and commandments.

Covenants and agency are eternally tied together. We may ask, "Why does the Father use covenants as His primary means for blessing His children?" Among the many reasons, one connects to their agency and His deep reverence for it. *Covenants guard our agency.* They must be willingly entered into and kept for the promised blessings to flow.

From the beginning, our Heavenly Father has always protected the agency of men and women. Agency is the innate ability for His children to choose their course of thought and action. Covenants require that both parties who enter them do so of their own free will. We must *choose* to make covenants, and we must *choose* to keep covenants.

Covenants also outline the explicit terms and conditions for blessings to flow, which enable the use of our agency to receive them. If we make those righteous choices, then the Savior can pour down blessings onto us and offer us the protection of His Atonement. He is bound to do so. If we do not choose to accept or to keep covenants, we have "no promise."[8] Without the willing acceptance and keeping of covenants and their associated commandments, the very delivery of blessings could violate agency. For, blessings should not be delivered without their commensurate voluntary actions.[9]

Why would the Father use the covenant path as the way to bless His children? After all, so many would be unable to receive them because a person holding priesthood authority must perform sacred ordinances. Logistically, fewer priesthood holders exist than the total number of human beings at any given time on earth. Although this aspect of the plan's design may have several potential purposes, we suggest that the tie between covenants and agency may be the most important.

The Father protects our agency fully and wholly. He provided a Savior to activate our covenants and protect those who may not receive them in this life due to legitimate barriers. Their ability to receive covenants later because of the Atonement of Jesus Christ is an example of how the Father both protects agency and corrects any injustices or unfairness that may occur due to circumstances in this life. It further points all humankind to the Savior, who will mercifully resolve all barriers to accepting and living truth in this life.

God be praised for Christ's eternal love in respecting agency and His infinite mercy in correcting all unfairness that may come from it!

The covenant path is our secure way back to the Father. We make and keep covenants in an increasing succession, culminating in the temple's covenants, called the "covenant path." The first covenant we make on the covenant path occurs in the waters of baptism. It is the gateway to the path of exaltation.

Baptism is the "first fruits" of repentance"[10] and is part of the new and everlasting covenant.[11] When we accept this first covenant of baptism, we formally agree to willingly follow all the words and commandments our Savior has given us, as documented in holy writ, as spoken by living prophets, or as communicated directly via the Holy Ghost.

---

8. Doctrine and Covenants 82:10.
9. See Doctrine and Covenants 130:20–21.
10. Moroni 8:25.
11. See Doctrine and Covenants 22:1.

Thus, after baptism, the scriptures' verses become more than just a historical record; living prophets' words become more than just a pleasant discourse; and the Spirit's promptings become more than just a good feeling. These directions become covenant language we are now bound to follow. The iron rod is the word of God, and, to covenant sons and daughters, the words of God are the terms of their agreement with Him.

Baptism also joins us to Abraham's family, giving us access to the Abrahamic covenant's blessings as adopted sons and daughters.[12] Our patriarchal blessings inform us of which tribe of Abraham we joined upon our baptism. Chief among our responsibilities as a member of this extraordinary family is bearing "this ministry and Priesthood unto all nations,"[13] a call to missionary work and to ministering.

After baptism, other subsequent covenant "fruits" follow, including priesthood ordinations and temple ordinances. As we walk down the covenant path, moving from baptism, to the receipt of priesthood ordinations for the brethren, to the sacred endowment with its conferral of priesthood power on brothers and sisters, and, finally, to the new and everlasting covenant of marriage, we make more significant and sacred covenants with our Heavenly Father. Bonnie D. Parkin, a former member of the Young Women General Presidency, taught,

Covenants—or binding promises between us and Heavenly Father—are essential for our eternal progression. Step by step, he tutors us to become like him by enlisting us in his work. . . .

Forged through priesthood authority, our kept covenants bring blessings to fill our cups to overflowing. How often do you reflect that your covenants reach beyond mortality and connect you to the Divine? Making covenants is the expression of a willing heart; keeping covenants, the expression of a faithful heart.[14]

---

12. See Abraham 2:8–12.
13. Abraham 2:9.
14. Bonnie D. Parkin, "With Holiness of Heart," Conference Report, October 2002.

In each covenant, we make more significant commitments, which open to us greater blessings based on the use of our agency, until we reach the greatest blessing of them all—eternal life. We become more like our Heavenly Parents each step of the way.

The new and everlasting covenant is a light, a standard, and a messenger for us. Covenants are the tangible expression of God's promises to His children. Through them, we have the assurance that our faith and our agency will qualify us for Christ's saving grace. In the temple, we receive the fulness of the new and everlasting covenant.

The everlasting covenant is the covenant that the Father made with Adam, wherein He promised Adam and Eve that they could be saved through the merits and mercy of Jesus Christ, if they hearkened to His doctrine.[15] God gave the everlasting covenant to all subsequent prophets and all people who joined the fold by baptism. To Abraham, it was called the Abrahamic covenant.

When the Lord restored the covenant in our day, he called it the *new* and everlasting covenant. The covenant is new because it was given anew in our dispensation. It is everlasting because the Savior never forgets or breaks it.

Of covenants, the Lord has said, "I have sent mine everlasting covenant into the world, to be a light to the world, and to be a standard for my people, and for the Gentiles to seek to it, and to be a messenger before my face to prepare the way before me. Wherefore, *come ye unto it*."[16] The new and everlasting covenant is the light, the standard, and the messenger that we hold up and to which we freely come. It encompasses all covenants made along the covenant path.

As a *light*, the new and everlasting covenant guides us through the Holy Ghost, and it disperses the powers of darkness for us. As a *standard*, it is the foundation upon which the Lord established His Church. It holds the boundaries of our conduct and is the measuring rod for our receipt of blessings. As a *messenger*, it conveys the will of

---

15. See Moses 5:9.
16. Doctrine and Covenants 45:9; emphasis added.

God for us, and it communicates all the blessings and requirements for us to become like our Heavenly Parents.

Because the new and everlasting covenant is the same as the Abrahamic covenant,[17] it provides us access to all the blessings promised to Abraham, Isaac, and Jacob as we become members of this unique family, which we join when we are baptized. The temple's ordinances articulate the blessings and responsibilities that come from membership in this family.

Its chief benefit is eternal life with our posterity as we become heirs of God. As rulers in the House of Israel, its chief duty is that we "bear this ministry and Priesthood unto all nations,"[18] meaning we will strive to bring the covenant to the entire world. This duty continues with God for eternity.

Our efforts to make and keep the new and everlasting covenant will guide, bless, and protect us on our journey of mortality.

We must strive for exactness and precision in keeping commandments and covenants. The temple encourages us to be precise in our efforts to become like our Heavenly Parents. The scriptures record examples of exact obedience in the lives of valiant men and women.[19] They are examples of individuals who did everything in their ability to perform the work the Lord gave them without deviation.

To this end, Elder Bruce R. McConkie taught, "Obedience is the first law of heaven, the cornerstone upon which all righteousness and progression rest. It consists in *compliance* with divine law, in *conformity* to the mind and will of Deity, in *complete subjection* to God and his commands."[20]

Exact obedience is synonymous with perfect submissiveness—not necessarily with perfect compliance—because our humanity often

---

17. See Genesis 12:1–3; 17:1–8; Abraham 2:8–12.
18. Abraham 2:9.
19. See Genesis 6–8 for the story of Noah; see Daniel 1–3 for the story of Shadrach, Meshach, and Abed-nego. See 1 Nephi for multiple stories of Nephi being obedient. See Alma 57 for the story of Helaman's stripling sons.
20. Bruce R. McConkie, *Mormon Doctrine* (Salt Lake City: Deseret Book, 1966), 539; emphasis added.

leads to imperfect execution. However, we can always strive to be perfect in our submission, willingness, and intent.

By striving to obey commandments and keep covenants with exactness, we demonstrate our complete, voluntary willingness to "submit to all things which the Lord seeth fit to inflict upon [us], even as a child doth submit to his [or her] father."[21] These actions show forth deep and sincere humility and meekness—two foundational godly attributes.

In the Doctrine and Covenants we learn, "When we obtain any blessing from God, it is by obedience to the law upon which it is predicated."[22] Ultimately, through perfect submission and increasing precision, we draw down the power of heaven, including the power to become like our Heavenly Parents. President Russell M. Nelson taught, "We . . . increase the Savior's power in our lives when we make sacred covenants and keep those covenants with precision. Our covenants bind us to Him and give us godly power" which he called "power sufficient to deal with the burdens, obstacles, and temptations of our day."[23]

Personal Application: Aaron

An example from the animal world may help us understand how to keep the commandments and our covenants with greater exactness. Of all the predators in the world, the most efficient is somewhat surprising. While lions only capture about 25 percent of their prey, and sharks only about 50 percent, the dragonfly captures 90–95 percent of its prey. So how does it hunt with such high efficiency?

The dragonfly's anatomy allows it to fly forward, backward, up, down, and side to side. In addition, its brain has a rapid neural pathway that allows it to track a single target efficiently. It has the ability for selective attention, focusing on a single insect

---

21. Mosiah 3:19.
22. Doctrine and Covenants 130:21.
23. Russell M. Nelson, "Drawing the Power of Jesus Christ Into Our Lives," Conference Report, April 2017.

from a swarm. Dragonflies use a simple rule to intercept mosquitoes, flies, and other small flying insects, which are also moving.

The dragonfly keeps its prey in one of the facets of its eye. It adjusts its flight trajectory and speed to maintain the image on that same spot of its retina, which keeps its angle of approach constant. This technique results in a nearly perfect hit rate.[24]

Similarly, keeping our eye on the Savior will result in greater exactness in keeping His commandments and our covenants. If we focus on Him, we will make selective choices from among the many options available to us about what we will think, do, and say. We will never be perfect, but our exactness will improve as we focus on Him.

Disciples of Christ can find harmony in keeping the first and the second great commandments. The temple encourages us to keep all commandments. All commandments given to the children of God via covenants are encompassed by and contained within the two great commandments, as articulated by the Savior: Love God and love your neighbor.[25] His summary can simplify our approach to obedience. Unfortunately, there can be a divine tension in them, which encourages us to develop faith in and dependence on the Lord to live them both.

The first great commandment is to love the Lord with all our heart, might, mind, and strength.[26] The Savior clarified how we can show our love to Him when He said, "If ye love me, keep my commandments."[27] Loving the Lord is equivalent to obedience to His will and His commandments. The first great commandment describes our commitment toward our Heavenly Father.

---

24. Mihai Andrei, "Article suggests dragonflies are the most effective predators in the animal world—95% success rate," *ZME Science*, October 9, 2020, accessed June 4, 2021, https://www.zmescience.com/ecology/animals-ecology/article-suggests-dragonflies-are-the-most-effective-predators-in-the-animal-world-95–success-rate/.
25. See Matthew 22:37–39.
26. Ibid.
27. John 14:15.

The second great commandment is "like unto the first," meaning it is equally as important to recognize and obey. The second commandment is to "love thy neighbor as thyself."[28] Love of neighbor is manifested in our treatment of them—having compassion, demonstrating patience and forbearance, being gentle and kind in our words, chastening with sincerity, and so on. The second great commandment describes our commitment toward our neighbor.

Exact obedience in these two great commandments—to love God and love neighbor—is essential, but it can be challenging to do consistently. Nevertheless, sincerely striving to find harmony in keeping the two great commandments can accelerate our efforts to become like our Heavenly Parents. By so doing, we learn by personal experience how they must eternally harmonize law and love or justice and mercy.

The world has a different approach to law and love.[29] The world often strives to destroy or to homogenize norms of behavior and standards of obedience to help with the acceptance of and compassion for individuals whose situation falls outside of eternal boundaries. They mistakenly believe the boundary creates a barrier to love.

However, the temple demonstrates that disciples of Christ follow a simultaneously rigorous and inclusive path. They must accept and adhere to commandments *and* reach out in love to anyone who falls outside the Lord's standards. Disciples must sincerely minister to them with love unfeigned, accepting them as fellow children of God without reservation and inviting them to "come unto Christ and be perfected in him."[30]

The first great commandment is about our relationship with God, and the second great commandment is about our relationship with our neighbor. Problems generally arise when we mistakenly switch that focus.

When we apply the first great commandment to our relationship with our neighbor, we can become judgmental, for we could begin to focus on their imperfections and could even begin to coerce them

28. Matthew 22:39.
29. See Dallin H. Oaks, "Love and Law," Conference Report, October 2009 for an excellent discourse on this topic.
30. Moroni 10:32.

into obeying the commandments. When we apply the second great commandment to our relationship with God, we can become overly tolerant, justifying sins out of an abundance of love for the individual.

If we genuinely love God, we will focus on our *own* imperfections and our *own* need for sincere repentance and perfect submission to Him. We will strive to do His will in all things, and at all times, and in all places. The focus will be on *us* and *our* relationship with Him.

If we genuinely love our neighbors, we will minister to *them* in every way, having compassion for *any* trouble, adversity, or imperfection they face. We will celebrate their gifts and talents and appreciate the diversity they offer. We will encourage, teach, and invite them to accept and live divine law, and we will do so out of love and concern for *them*.

We will also simultaneously love, accept, and help everyone—including ourselves—who falls short for whatever reason. We will especially love and support anyone who is a victim of abuse and sin by another. In all our efforts, we will continue to love and minister with authenticity and compassion despite any situation the person faces—of his or her making or not. The focus will be on *others* and our relationship with *them*.

When we have legitimately done everything possible to keep and harmonize both commandments authentically, He will accept our offering and declare our efforts as sufficient or "good." The Savior will resolve in eternity any conflicts that appear to exist between these two great commandments. And He will mercifully forgive us for any honest mistakes we make in finding that harmony along the course of our lives if we have sought His will in all things.

We must map out and take an undeviating path back to the Father. The scriptures teach that the Savior's path is "straight" and not "crooked."[31] The temple encourages us to willingly chart a course that remains on His route and to stay within the bounds set by the Lord. We pave this path by our exact obedience, our perfect willingness, and by our selfless service to all God's children. Disobedience,

---

31. See Alma 7:20; 37:12.

rebellion, and apostasy of any sort lead us off the path to our eternal inheritance. We should run to repentance anytime we need to make a course correction and return to the covenant path.

QUESTIONS TO CONSIDER

1. What new understanding did you have about keeping commandments with exactness during your last temple visit? What blessings can come to you through your exact obedience?
2. What covenants in the temple most impressed you during your last visit? What did you learn about them? How can you best keep them?
3. How can your temple covenants help you navigate a difficult situation you are currently experiencing?
4. In what way can the temple and its doctrine help you keep the first and the second great commandments?

NOTES AND INSIGHTS

_____

_____

_____

_____

_____

_____

_____

_____

_____

Chapter 9

The Fall and Its Effects

"Mortality and death came into the world through the Fall of Adam [and Eve]. Immortality and the possibility of eternal life were provided by the Atonement of Jesus Christ."

—Russell M. Nelson[1]

This chapter covers the core doctrine of the Fall. Understanding it can allow us to navigate the difficulties of mortality with greater hope and purpose. This comprehension also helps us see the joys and positive progress that can come from life's challenges, as a "lily out of the ooze"[2] or peace amid the "peals of thunder"[3] loudly sounding around us.

Personal Application: Aaron

When my father, Ken Bujnowski, passed away in April of 2021 of a sudden heart attack, the loss was a blow to our entire

---

1. Russell M. Nelson, "The Creation," Conference Report, April 2000.
2. Karen Lynn Davidson, *Our Latter-day Hymns: The Stories and the Messages* (Salt Lake City: Deseret Book, 2009), 35.
3. Joseph Smith, *The Words of Joseph Smith* (Orem: Grandin Book Company, 1991), 196.

family and all his close friends. It happened so quickly that I was the only one who could say goodbye in person because only I was with him at the hospital when he was treated.

My angel mother took it the hardest. She and my father were married for nearly fifty-two years. They were always together. When he passed away, it left a massive hole in her life. He had done all the administrative tasks of the home—paying bills, making repairs, maintaining their cars. So, she acutely felt his absence.

Mom shed many tears for a long period as she dealt with the grief of losing Dad. His death was extremely hard on her. However, out of that pain, we witnessed miracles occur in her life. Already a sweet and service-oriented person, she became more endearing and service-minded.

The opposition eventually gave her strength she would not have otherwise had. In time, she received "beauty for ashes, the oil of joy for mourning, [and] the garment of praise for the spirit of heaviness."[4] We have learned through this experience what it means that "Adam [and Eve] fell that man [and woman] might be; and men [and women] are, that they might have joy."[5]

The Fall was necessary for our progression. The temple clearly teaches the doctrine of the Fall. The story of Adam and Eve is the story of the Fall. It recounts the actions of two real people—our first parents. The account is also a symbolic allegory that we can apply to ourselves, who are contemporary "Adams" and "Eves."

When Adam and Eve partook of the fruit of the tree of knowledge of good and evil in the Garden of Eden, they initiated what is termed "the Fall."[6] The Fall is the separation of men and women from God due to their sin and humanity. It precipitated the phase of the plan of salvation called mortality, which enabled the formation of families with children and posterity.

---

4. Isaiah 61:3.
5. 2 Nephi 2:24.
6. Doctrine and Covenants 20:20.

The Father first commanded Adam and Eve to multiply and replenish the earth.[7] He then commanded them not to partake of the fruit of the tree of knowledge of good and evil.[8] As they considered how to keep both commandments, the adversary came, tempting them.

The adversary beguiled or charmed Adam and Eve by lying about the consequences of their choice and by shading why they needed to eat the fruit of the tree of knowledge of good and evil. He told them, "You shall not surely die; For God doth know in the day ye eat thereof, then your eyes shall be opened, and ye shall be as gods, knowing good and evil."[9]

The adversary's temptation caused Eve to think deeply about whether to eat of the tree. Of this influence and its effect on Eve, author Beverly Campbell has written the following:

> The Hebrew word which has come to be translated *beguiled* is a rare verb form of unusual depth and richness. Because it is a form no longer in use, it is almost impossible to translate. "It is safe to say that it indicates an intense multilevel experience which evokes great emotional, psychological, and/or spiritual trauma." . . . This intense, multilevel experience caused Eve to step back, reevaluate, reassess, and ponder the tree of knowledge of good and evil.[10]

Struggling through this decision, Eve came to understand that eating the fruit was necessary for their progression. Transgressing the second command would allow her to keep the first. She partook of the fruit, and then she offered it to her husband, Adam. He also freely partook.[11] By doing so, they *both* voluntarily accepted the positive and negative consequences of their actions.

---

7. See Genesis 1:28; Moses 2:28.
8. See Genesis 2:16–17; Moses 3:16–17.
9. Moses 4:10–11.
10. Beverly Campbell, *Eve and the Choice Made in Eden* (Salt Lake City: Deseret Book, 2003), 71.
11. See Moses 4:12.

In whatever way they were influenced and came to their decision, Adam and Eve's willing Fall was necessary for God's plan to move ahead. The Book of Mormon provides additional insight on this topic:

> If Adam had not transgressed he would not have fallen, but he would have remained in the garden of Eden. And all things which were created must have remained in the same state in which they were after they were created; and they must have remained forever, and had no end.
>
> And they would have had no children; wherefore they would have remained in a state of innocence, having no joy, for they knew no misery; doing no good, for they knew no sin.[12]

What a dire consequence that would have thwarted the plan of Heavenly Father! What a blessing that our valiant first parents made this courageous and faith-filled choice!

Adam and Eve fell that men and women might exist as mortals, which would enable them to have a family and have the opposing experiences that would develop godly attributes. They also fell that we might eventually become like the Father.

They fell that we might progress to be faithful, kind, merciful, loving, charitable, tried, stretched, edified, tempted, strengthened, loyal, trusted, and at peace. Ultimately, they fell that we "might have joy."[13]

The Fall's effects are pervasive. As taught in the temple, the Fall was necessary for our progression, and its consequences are far-reaching. It affects every aspect of our mortal existence. It influences all physiological, psychological, inter-relational, societal, or environmental aspects of mortality. It even affects the restoration of the gospel as imperfect, fallen people try to carry out God's perfect work.

We witness and experience myriad issues related to the Fall during mortality. These experiences may include pains, sicknesses,

---

12. 2 Nephi 2:22–23.
13. 2 Nephi 2:25.

and infirmities (physical, emotional, or mental); rejection and abuse at the hands or the words of another; mischaracterizations, lies, betrayals, or intrigue by supposed friends; contradictory, unfair, or unjust actions, circumstances, or happenstances; broad-based environmental calamities or human-made devastations; doubts, misgivings, or a lack of knowledge, facts, and data; or any other painful and heartbreaking event.

The Fall is so ubiquitous to our mortal life that we may not always be fully aware of its effects, much like a person who scuba dives in a dirty lake eventually acclimatizes to the cloudy water. The limited representations in the temple about specific issues and difficulties of a fallen world should expand in our minds to represent every challenging and unresolvable issue we deal with in mortality.

The Fall creates variation in people, situations, and circumstances. Each of us has an aspect of our lives that deviates from the Lord's eternal standard or the perceived "norm." Therefore, because of the Fall, we would suggest that variants are the *norm* rather than the *exception* in mortality. So, we must be as patient with others' variations as they are with ours. Our empathy is an expression of the Savior's love for the heartbreaking issues brought about by the Fall.

As mortal beings, we do not fully comprehend the nature of the Fall with its *imperfection* because we cannot fully grasp the nature of Eden and its *perfection*. Opposition provides perspective. Only in the temple do we get a glimpse of both to provide the proper opposing perspective between imperfection and perfection. This perspective enables us to "endure [the Fall] well"[14] by having a grounded hope in Christ, both for ourselves and for others.

Experience is the great enabler and enhancer of becoming like our Heavenly Parents during mortality. The temple affirms that we live in a fallen world to have both positive and negative experiences. These experiences teach us and develop in us the characteristics of godliness. Every experience we have in this life is part of the Father's method of molding us in His eternal image.

---

14. Doctrine and Covenants 121:8.

Therefore, experience, not time, is the measure by which heaven delineates our mortal progress. Of this truth, Elder Neal A. Maxwell, formerly of the Quorum of the Twelve, taught,

> This life is not lineal. It is experiential. It is not really chronological, though we use clocks and calendars and wristwatches. It is essentially experiential. . . . We should . . . see life as being comprised of clusters of soul-stretching experiences. Even when these are overlain by seeming ordinariness or are wrapped in routine. Some who are very young chronologically can be Methuselah's as to their maturity in spiritual things.[15]

Temple ordinances encourage us to learn from our experiences. When good or bad experiences happen to us in this life—whether due to our choices, the choices of others, or the incidental and uncontrollable circumstances of mortal life—we often ask, "Why this?," "Why me?," or "Why now?"[16]

However, to take full advantage of our blessings or our trials, we should more often ask, "What am I meant to learn from this?," "What godly traits will this enable me to develop?," "How will this help me to become more like my Heavenly Father?," or "How can I endure this well?"

We should ask these questions during positive experiences *and* during negative experiences. If we do not ponder the positive, blessings can lead to pride[17] and ingratitude.[18] However, if we remember the source of our blessings, we will become humble and grateful.[19] If we do not ponder the negative, we can become bitter and frustrated.

---

15. Neal A. Maxwell, "If Thou Endure It Well," *BYU Speeches* (Provo: Brigham Young University, December 2, 1984), accessed February 6, 2021, https://speeches.byu.edu/talks/neal-a-maxwell/if-thou-endure-well/.
16. We tend to ask these questions more often during negative experiences than positive ones.
17. Pride can be defined as enmity toward God, enmity toward humankind, and as a self-centered nature.
18. Ingratitude can be defined as a lack of recognition of the external sources of blessings.
19. See Alma 62:48–49.

During a time of war in the Book of Mormon, some people became hardened because of their afflictions, while others became softened.[20] Those who softened "did remember how great things the Lord had done for them"[21] amid their afflictions, while those who were hardened did not.

This understanding will help us appreciate and take advantage of all the experiences of life—the good and the bad, the joyous and the painful.

Opposition—with its divine blessings and inherent difficulties—is an integral part of the mortal experience. The scriptures teach that "there is an opposition in *all* things."[22] The temple portrays both sides of opposition: the easy and the challenging, the good and the bad.

The blessings and good times in life provide peace, joy, and happiness. The challenges and adversities of life cause sorrow and strife. However, both provide the necessary experiences for God to refine and perfect us. As Elder Jeffrey R. Holland of the Quorum of the Twelve observed, "Man's extremity is God's opportunity."[23]

Paradoxically, the imperfections and difficulties of mortality are both barriers to and facilitators of the peace, joy, and happiness promised to us in this life and of our ultimate destiny as heirs of godliness in the eternities. This dichotomy is the great mystery of godliness: We must choose to experience imperfection to receive our final exaltation.

Opposing choices allow us to be agents unto ourselves. In the Book of Mormon, Lehi taught, "It must needs be that there was an opposition . . . the one [choice] being sweet and the other bitter. Wherefore, the Lord God gave unto [His children] that [they] should act for [themselves]. Wherefore, [people] could not act for [themselves]

---

20. See Alma 62:41.
21. Alma 62:50.
22. 2 Nephi 2:11; emphasis added.
23. Jeffrey R. Holland, "Lessons from Liberty Jail," CES Fireside (Provo: Brigham Young University, September 7, 2008), accessed February 6, 2021, https://speeches.byu.edu/talks/jeffrey-r-holland/lessons-liberty-jail/.

save it should be that [they were] enticed by the one or the other."[24] Thus, without opposing choices, our agency would be compromised.

For everything we observe or experience in mortality, there exists an opposing idea, issue, or experience. Every gospel doctrine, principle, and practice must have an opposing ideology. Every circumstance must also have its opposite, which may neither be good nor bad but simply contrasting. For example,

- If someone teaches God exists, then there must be a person who teaches God does not exist.
- If we observe an inactive or struggling member, then we will also find a valiant member.
- If truth exists, then error must also exist;.
- If we discover a bad, slothful, or dwindling person, then there must exist a good, striving, and seeking person.
- If a functional, thriving two-parent family exists, a single parent family or a dysfunctional or struggling family must also exist.
- If we observe a married couple, we must also find a divorced person or someone who has never married.
- If we experience sadness, we will also experience happiness;
- If someone is straight, someone else must be LGBTQ+.
- If someone has a healthy body, then someone must have a broken body.
- If we find a person with a healthy mind, there must exist emotional or mental illness in another person.

Likewise, we cannot understand and experience joy without experiencing sorrow. We cannot understand patience without having to wait. We cannot enjoy the sweet without tasting the bitter. We cannot be faithful without being tempted.[25]

These contradictory experiences may not be proportional in terms of number, but they are generally comparable in their depth and reality. We often experience sorrow followed by joy or vice versa. In these opposing experiences, we can grow into men and women of godliness

---

24. 2 Nephi 2:15–16.
25. See Doctrine and Covenants 29:39.

by exerting faith in God and His timing. As Elder Jeffrey R. Holland of the Quorum of the Twelve taught,

> For every infirm man healed instantly as he waits to enter the Pool of Bethesda, someone else will spend 40 years in the desert waiting to enter the promised land. For every Nephi and Lehi divinely protected by an encircling flame of fire for their faith, we have an Abinadi burned at a stake of flaming fire for his. . . . The point? The point is that faith means trusting God in good times and bad, even if that includes some suffering until we see His arm revealed in our behalf.[26]

The need for this divine experiential symmetry is a profound and sublime truth that we must ponder and understand, or we risk misunderstanding many of the things that occur in this life. We must trust that "all things have been done in the wisdom of him who knoweth all things."[27]

A deeper understanding of the principle of opposition provides gratitude and encourages preparation in times of peace and ease, and it provides hope and encourages endurance in times of adversity and challenge. Elder Richard G. Scott, formerly of the Quorum of the Twelve, taught,

> Just when all seems to be going right, challenges often come in multiple doses applied simultaneously. When those trials are not consequences of your disobedience, they are evidence that the Lord feels you are prepared to grow more (see Proverbs 3:11–12).
>
> He therefore gives you experiences that stimulate growth, understanding, and compassion which polish you for your everlasting benefit. To get you from where you are to where He wants you to be requires a lot of stretching, and that generally entails discomfort and pain.[28]

---

26. Jeffrey R. Holland, "Waiting on the Lord," Conference Report, October 2020.
27. 2 Nephi 2:24.
28. Richard G. Scott, "Trust in the Lord," Conference Report, October 1995, 18.

We should not be surprised when something happens that seems counter to the Lord's plan of happiness for us. We should recognize it as part of that plan. This understanding does not mean we have to like what has happened, but we must comprehend that its existence should not be unexpected. If we properly understand opposition, we can be disappointed by it but not in despair, challenged but not overcome. As Paul eloquently said, "We are troubled on every side, yet not distressed; we are perplexed, but not in despair; Persecuted, but not forsaken; cast down, but not destroyed." [29]

The adverse effects of difficulty and trial are unavoidable. Temple ordinances reinforce that mortality would be difficult. None can avoid these difficulties. The scriptures affirm we will all have pains, afflictions, sicknesses, infirmities, and temptations of every kind.[30] This realization is not a statement of fatalism but of realism.

Unfortunately, pains, afflictions, sicknesses, and infirmities— although unwanted and unfair—can result in conditions that cause physical and mental anguish and cause spiritual lapses and sin in the same way direct temptations might. So, we must be ever watchful and vigilant for any source of iniquity.

The Savior warned us that difficulties of every sort would "beat upon" us in this life as do floods and winds in the storm.[31] This visual imagery is instructive.

Trials and adversity pound away at our testimonies, at our gospel knowledge, at our spiritual reservoirs. They can come from those closest to us and can happen when we are most vulnerable. They can occur after we have experienced a spiritual high or before we experience a spiritual high. They can come when we are at our lowest of lows. The beating is real and personalized to each of us. It can be intense and can last for years.

Therefore, we must stay close to our Savior and assist others to come to Him so that we can receive the healing, protection, and deliverance only He can provide. He is the firm foundation—the

---

29. 2 Corinthians 4:8–9.
30. See Alma 7:11–12.
31. See 3 Nephi 11:39–40.

rock—upon which we should build to avoid sinking into the shifting sands of adversity.[32] When "sore trials come upon [us],"[33] they can be a reminder of our need for Christ.

Adversity—although difficult—accelerates our spiritual development and progression. Many great blessings come from our mortal experiences, the chief of which is the ability to become like our Heavenly Parents. The design of mortality helps us in our eternal progress by providing refining experiences needed to develop the attributes and character of godliness. The temple portrays this progress.

The experience of adversity enormously accelerates our development. The Lord designed mortality to be challenging, but it is difficult for our benefit. As with the children of Israel in the days of Moses, "the more they afflicted them, the more they multiplied and grew."[34]

During times of adversity, we can accelerate the development of a godly character and more clearly see our gaps so we can be aware of them and seek the Father's help and His Spirit to improve. It may seem counterintuitive that adversity can both push against us and move us forward, but it works in this way.

Of the seeming contradiction that the headwinds of adversity can move us forward, Elder Orson F. Whitney, formerly of the Quorum of the Twelve, said,

> No pain that we suffer, no trial that we experience is wasted. It ministers to our education, to the development of such qualities as patience, faith, fortitude and humility. All that we suffer and all that we endure, especially when we endure it patiently, builds up our characters, purifies our hearts, expands our souls, and makes us more tender and charitable, more worthy to be called the children of God . . . and it is through sorrow and suffering, toil and tribulation, that we

---

32. Ibid.
33. "Did You Think to Pray?" *Hymns*, no. 140.
34. Exodus 1:12.

gain the education that we come here to acquire and which will make us more like our Father and Mother in heaven. [35]

Although blessings may be challenging to recognize, they do and will come out of adversity, but only if we found ourselves on Jesus Christ and His restored gospel. We must trust and find comfort in this eternal truth. Sister Linda S. Reeves, a former member of the Relief Society General Presidency, taught,

> I do not know why we have the many trials that we have, but it is my personal feeling that the reward is so great, so eternal and everlasting, so joyful and beyond our understanding that in that day of reward, we may feel to say to our merciful, loving Father, "Was that *all* that was required?" . . .
>
> What will it matter . . . what we suffered here if, in the end, those trials are the very things which qualify us for eternal life and exaltation in the kingdom of God with our Father and Savior? [36]

As the Lord lovingly reminded us, "Ye cannot behold with your natural eyes, for the present time, the designs of your God concerning those things which shall come hereafter, and the glory which shall follow after much tribulation. *For after much tribulation come*

---

35. Orson F. Whitney, cited in Spencer W. Kimball, *Faith Precedes the Miracle* (Salt Lake City: Deseret Book, 1972), 98. President George Q. Cannon, formerly of the First Presidency, further taught, "The Saints should always remember that God sees not as man sees; that he does not willingly afflict his children, and that if he requires them to endure present privation and trial, it is that they may escape greater tribulations which would otherwise inevitably overtake them. If He deprives them of any present blessing, it is that he may bestow upon them greater and more glorious ones by and by" (George Q. Cannon, "Beneficial Results of Continued Obedience to the Teachings of God's Servants," *Millennial Star* [Manchester, England: The Church of Jesus Christ of Latter-day saints, 3 Oct. 1863], 634, cited in Daniel H. Ludlow, *Companion to Your Study of the Doctrine and Covenants, Vol. 1* [Salt Lake City: Deseret Book, 1978], 310).

36. Linda S. Reeves, "Worthy of Our Promised Blessings," Conference Report, October 2015; emphasis original.

the blessings!"[37] This perspective can help us retain a "brightness of hope"[38] amid the darkness of life.

Personal Application: Aaron

While on a sailing trip in San Francisco on a large sailboat in August of 2008, I asked the captain what happens if the winds turn against the boat's course. She told me that sailors learned long ago that they could sail into adverse winds. Ships can "beat" into the wind by "tacking." Tacking is the process by which the ship is steered at a slight angle to the oncoming wind for a while. Then, the sails are shifted such that the angle is changed. The ship sails along in this zig-zag pattern of alternating angles toward its destination.

During the trip against the wind, the captain does not take a direct course, but by repeatedly adjusting the angles toward the desired direction, the ship can reach its final port. Although the course in adverse winds is indirect, the actual speed while tacking is often faster than the wind itself.[39]

We can follow the same principle as we head into the winds of adversity in our lives. Usually, trials force us to follow a set of indirect pathways toward our destination. This pattern is the correct way to navigate difficulty. However, we must be attentive and patient while we navigate ourselves and our families in this way. If we stay in a single direction for too long, we will end up far off course. Frequent course corrections are needed while navigating adverse winds.

Tacking is possible while sailing because the sailboat has both a rudder to steer and a keel—a large fin under the water—that prevents the ship from being pushed to one side by the wind.

---

37. Doctrine and Covenants 58:3–4; emphasis added.
38. 2 Nephi 31:20.
39. Interview by the author with the captain and crew of a 51–foot Morgan Ketch sailboat while sailing in San Francisco Bay in 2008. See also www.physicsbuzz-physicscentral, The American Physical Society, "The Physics of Sailing: How Does a Sailboat Move Upwind?" May 12, 2015, accessed February 20, 2021, http://physicsbuzz.physicscentral.com/2015/05/the-physics-of-sailing-how-does.html.

Likewise, our faith in Jesus Christ is our stabilizing "keel" in the storms of life, and our testimonies of His restored gospel and our covenants are our guiding "rudder." Both are necessary to navigate adversity successfully.

Both the wicked and the righteous will experience suffering while in mortality. The adversity of the fallen world spoken of in the temple applies to all—both the wicked and the righteous. We can classify the sources of adversity in this life into several categories. They include (1) our own choices due to our agency; (2) the choices of others due to their agency, which the Lord will not interfere with but from which He may find ways to protect us; (3) the will of God in preparing and proving us by experiences He specifically designed; and (4) events merely incident to the fallen nature of mortality. All children of God will experience adversity due to one or more of these sources.

The scriptures teach that those who choose wickedness will experience an extra measure of suffering in this life—for judgments shall surely come upon them—while the righteous will surely be preserved.[40] Our righteous efforts enable us to avoid the heartache and destruction that come upon those who do not keep the commandments of God.

However, prophets have also taught that the difficulties of this life will affect the righteous as well as the wicked. So, no one will be immune to their influence. As the Savior taught, "[God] maketh his sun to rise on the evil and on the good, and sendeth rain on the just and on the unjust."[41] Of this alarming fact, Joseph Smith taught,

I explained . . . that it is a false idea that the Saints will escape all the judgments, whilst the wicked suffer; for all flesh is subject to suffer, and "the righteous shall hardly escape" [D&C 63:34]. . . . So that it is an unhallowed principle to say that such and such have transgressed because they have

40. See 1 Nephi 22:14–19, 28.
41. See Matthew 5:45; 3 Nephi 12:45.

been preyed upon by disease or death, for all flesh is subject to death; and the Savior has said, "Judge not, lest ye be judged."[42]

This teaching was not meant to be discouraging. Joseph meant for it to help those who are trying to do good but who still suffer to "be not weary in well-doing."[43]

Understanding that all will suffer can give us faith to find healing and, perhaps more importantly, the "faith *not* to be healed" when the Lord does not will it.[44] It can enable us to see hope amid trial. It can also help us avoid the adversary's temptation or our mortal tendency to feel shame, self-loathing, and discouragement when trials come because they are not always our fault.

This realization should enable us to remain resolute in the face of difficulty as we lean on the Lord for help, support, and eventual deliverance. It will help us remember "out of small [trials] proceedeth that which is great."[45]

The difference between the wicked and the righteous who suffer is this: The wicked grow bitter, angry, and hateful, while the righteous become more humble, kind, and loving. The righteous become like their Heavenly Parents, and the wicked do not. Over time, life's challenging experiences continually refine the righteous and deteriorate the wicked until the separation of the two is clear. Their final character traits will be their ultimate differentiator and separator.[46]

At times, the Father, Son, and Holy Ghost will withdraw their presence from us, which can be a trial for our benefit. The scriptures teach, "For my Spirit will not always strive with man [and woman]."[47] The temple also portrays this situation. The Godhead withdraw their

42. Joseph Smith, *History of the Church*, 4:11.
43. Doctrine and Covenants 64:33.
44. David A. Bednar, "Accepting the Lord's Will and Timing," *Ensign*, August 2016.
45. Ibid.
46. See Matthew 13:24–43 for the parable of the wheat and tares, Matthew 13:47–50 for the parable of the net, and Matthew 25:32–33 for the parable of the sheep and goats.
47. Doctrine and Covenants 1:33.

divine presence for at least two reasons: (1) to allow us to gain experience and to learn for ourselves essential principles we must discover on our own and (2) to remove Themselves when we are unworthy of Their holy presence, which encourages us to repent and return to Them. This withdrawal is part of the opposition of life.

In either case, they withdraw because they love us and because they want us to grow and to progress. "For a small moment have I forsaken thee, but with great mercies will I gather thee."[48] Their withdrawal is intended to develop the faith and hope that they will return to teach and comfort us, either personally or via their authorized ministers.

We must minister to one another with love and without judgment to help alleviate the effects of the Fall. The temple teaches us to minister to others in this fallen world. The effects of the Fall are growing in scope and intensity as we move toward the Second Coming of our Savior. Time only amplifies its effects. Therefore, we must have an increasing amount of charity for all those who suffer either personally or collectively from this increasingly fallen world. Many are broken because of the Fall, but we can be a means of help, support, love, and service as we minister to and sustain them during their difficult times.

We are *all* "fallen and are lost."[49] We *all* experience trials and difficulties. We have *all* "sinned, and come short of the glory of God."[50] We *all* have imperfections and weaknesses. This understanding should encourage us to have great compassion and mercy on others who, like us, are making their way imperfectly back to the Father in a fallen world.

To paraphrase Jacob, we must "administer of our [*mercy*] to them that standeth in need"[51] for any reason, even when those needs are caused by sin. Elder Dale G. Renlund of the Quorum of the Twelve lovingly taught,

> In our lifelong quest to follow Jesus Christ, His example of kindness to those who sin is particularly instructive. We, who

---

48. 3 Nephi 22:7.
49. Alma 34:9.
50. Romans 3:23.
51. Jacob 2:17.

are sinners, must, like the Savior, reach out to others with compassion and love. Our role is also to help and bless, lift and edify, and replace fear and despair with hope and joy. The Savior rebuked individuals who recoiled from others they viewed as unclean and who self-righteously judged others as more sinful than they. . . . In doing so, Jesus Christ also set the example for us to follow—to show respect to all and hatred toward none.[52]

Even if we have been the recipients of the sins, mistakes, or mistreatments by our "enemies," our mandate is the same. The Savior encouraged, "I say unto you, Love your enemies, bless them that curse you, do good to them that hate you, and pray for them which despitefully use you, and persecute you; That ye may be the children of your Father which is in heaven; for he maketh his sun to rise on the evil and on the good, and *[He] sendeth rain on the just and on the unjust.*"[53]

We may someday experience "rain" and need the help of another's umbrella. Why deny that same help to others? Who knows—we might even need help from our legitimate or supposed enemies.

What is more important than the extent of anyone's fall or the cause of his or her suffering is that person's willingness to overcome the Fall's effects using the blood of the Lamb. We must, therefore, simply minister to everyone—providing spiritual, emotional, or physical comfort, help, and mercy—as they are willing to allow and until final deliverance comes.

We can experience peace, joy, and happiness in mortality and receive exaltation and eternal joy in eternity, despite the effects of the Fall. The restored gospel of Jesus Christ, including our temple experience, shows us the entirety of the plan. The Father designed His plan to provide us peace, joy, and happiness, regardless of anything that may occur to us or because of us due to life in a fallen world. We are that we might have joy![54]

---

52. Dale G. Renlund, "Our Good Shepherd," Conference Report, April 2017.
53. Matthew 5:44–45; emphasis added.
54. Russell M. Nelson, "Joy and Spiritual Survival," Conference Report, October 2016.

Joseph Smith taught, "Happiness is the object and design of our existence; and will be the end thereof, if we pursue the path that leads to it; and this path is virtue, uprightness, faithfulness, holiness, and keeping all the commandments of God."[55]

The gospel of Jesus Christ enables us to find joy amidst adversity and trouble. Sister Sheri L. Dew, a former counselor in the Relief Society General Presidency, taught,

> I was thinking about [the difficulties of life] on one occasion as I sat through a meeting where the speaker seemed preoccupied with focusing on "how hard it is to live the gospel." . . . *It's not living the gospel that's hard. It's life that's hard.* . . . The gospel is the Good News that provides us with the tools to cope with the mistakes and miscalculations, the heartaches and heartbreaks, the pressures and disappointments we can expect to experience here in mortality.[56]

Our joy can and should come now and in the future, irrespective of what has happened, what is happening, and what will happen to us. As President Russell M. Nelson has taught, "The joy we feel has little to do with the circumstances of our lives and everything to do with the focus of our lives. When the focus of our lives is on God's plan of salvation . . . and Jesus Christ and His gospel, we can feel joy regardless of what is happening—or not happening— in our lives. Joy comes from and because of Him. He is the source of all joy."[57]

Personal Application: Julie

I will share my own personal trial of grief and heartache, which has been made light because of the gospel of Jesus Christ. My challenge is losing my physical health to cancer. In 2017, I was diagnosed with stage 2 breast cancer. It shocked my family and me

---

55. Joseph Smith, *Teachings of the Prophet Joseph Smith*, 255–56.
56. Sheri L. Dew, *No Doubt About It* (Salt Lake City: Deseret Book, 2001), 106; emphasis added.
57. Russell M. Nelson, "Joy and Spiritual Survival," Conference Report, October 2016.

because I don't have a family history of breast cancer. In addition, the results of genetic testing showed that I did not carry the BRCA gene. So, the reason this affliction had come upon me was a mystery.

At that time, I had so many things going on in my life. My daughter had just gotten married a month before, and I had gone back to school to finish my degree. I had my whole grad plan worked out, which would allow me to graduate in just a couple of years. Little did I know that my plans were going to change dramatically.

I went through my cancer treatments, which included several surgeries, thirty-one rounds of radiation, and ongoing medication that I must take for a total of ten years. Because of all these interventions, my body is not the same. I don't think it ever will be. I mourn for how my body used to be—fit and strong—every day.

Breast cancer has changed my whole life. The many side effects of my medication can make some days a terrible struggle. One thing I have learned through this challenging experience is that I am not alone. I know that my Savior experienced my pain and frustration during His Atonement. He knows what I feel on my worst days. I also know that when I pray and ask for peace, it is given to me.

I am still in the middle of my cancer journey. Its end is yet to be written. However, the gospel and my temple covenants have sustained me and provided me with comfort and hope. Life is hard. Cancer is hard. But the gospel is joyous, despite and especially during those hard things. Because of the Fall, I have experienced anguish, but because of my Savior and His gospel, I have experienced joy that has transcended my pain.

The Savior has the capability to personally understand and infinitely succor us in our adversity, however extreme. Fortunately, we know from the scriptures and the temple that Jesus Christ "will take upon him the pains and the sicknesses of his people," their "infirmities," and any other things which "bind" them.[58]

---

58. Alma 7:11–12.

He knows by personal experience the pain and the suffering each child of God has felt. He knows our pains individually and very personally because He felt those exact pains at Gethsemane and on the cross at Calvary. He knows and understands us completely. Therefore, He knows "how to succor" us[59]—meaning how to help and comfort us—even as we pass through the challenging but refining experiences of life.

If we ever feel like no one understands, we can rest assured that we have a Holy One who does. Even when we experience trials that are the most extreme imaginable—ones that pierce us to the core and perhaps also lead us into temptation—we can know He comprehends what we feel, and He will have compassion on us.

Feelings of comfort and compassion will come via His Spirit directly to us if we turn to the Savior. They may not come immediately, but they will come "in process of time,"[60] undoubtedly coming in the eternities. We must trust that He can grant mercy, comfort, and healing to any whose fallen mortal bodies create seemingly insurmountable and unfair barriers or whose situation is heartbreakingly out of their control for any reason. In this faith, peace will eventually come, despite the adversity and heartbreak of the moment.

We can overcome the effects of the Fall through the Atonement of Jesus Christ. The temple teaches that we overcome the Fall's spiritual impact via repentance, which is a sacred gift given through the Atonement of the Savior Jesus Christ. We overcome the temporal and physical effects of the fall in that same way—by our faith in Him.

For those things that we can change, repentance and effort are necessary, but they can be difficult. Some are early in that process of change and only have a "desire to believe"[61] that it will happen. For others, they are further along in their progress. For all, we should look for the desire—the willingness—to repent and change as our primary measuring rod of progress.

---

59. Ibid.
60. Moses 7:21.
61. Alma 32:27.

For those things that cannot change and are not our fault—such as physical or mental disabilities or disease—we must have patience and compassion. As we thoughtfully observe willingness and desire to progress and just do their best in very tough circumstances, we will more readily see the grandeur in even significantly "fallen" people.

The physical, mental, and emotional effects of the Fall will all be resolved in the resurrection because everyone will resurrect in their perfect form due to the Atonement of Jesus Christ.[62] Everything broken in our bodies and minds will be repaired and renewed on that glorious future day. Until then, our struggles or the struggles of those we love and serve may be so severe that hope begins to wane.

To encourage us to look forward to that long-hoped-for day when all our troubles, trials, and sins—all the effects of the Fall—are healed by a compassionate Savior, Elder Jeffery R. Holland of the Quorum of the Twelve has lovingly taught,

> Whatever your struggle, my brothers and sisters—mental or emotional or physical or otherwise—do not [give up]! Trust in God. Hold on in His love. Know that one day the dawn will break brightly and all shadows of mortality will flee. Though we may feel we are 'like a broken vessel,' [see Ps. 31:12] as the Psalmist says, we must remember, that vessel is in the hands of the divine potter.
>
> Broken minds can be healed just the way broken bones and broken hearts are healed. While God is at work making those repairs, the rest of us can help by being merciful, nonjudgmental, and kind. I testify of the holy Resurrection, that unspeakable cornerstone gift in the Atonement of the Lord Jesus Christ![63]

May we all retain the hope of that glorious, longed-for day, when the Savior will give us "beauty for ashes, the oil of joy for mourning, [and] the garment of praise for the spirit of heaviness!"[64]

---

62. See Alma 11:42.
63. Jeffrey R. Holland, "Like a Broken Vessel," Conference Report, October 2013.
64. Isaiah 61:3.

QUESTIONS TO CONSIDER

1. What did you learn about the Fall during your last temple visit? How does that understanding apply at this time in your life?
2. How can your temple covenants enable you to endure adversity well? What can you do to draw spiritual strength from them?
3. How can the temple and its covenants help you with a current trial you are facing? What temple doctrine might best apply to your situation?
4. In what ways can you minister to someone in need of support during their trials?

NOTES AND INSIGHTS

_____

_____

_____

_____

_____

_____

_____

_____

Chapter 10

Justice and Mercy

"All [humankind] can be protected by the law of
justice, and at once each of us individually may be
extended the redeeming and healing blessing of mercy
[by our Mediator, Jesus Christ]."

—Boyd K. Packer[1]

This chapter covers the perfect justice and mercy that the Savior offers all God's children. When we understand these interconnected points of doctrine, we will be open to the temple's sublime yet powerful message regarding them. We might suggest that mercy is the central theme of the temple. Here, God offers all His children on both sides of the veil the merciful gift of saving ordinances. Through the temple and its ordinances, we will come to understand Jesus Christ's pivotal role in harmonizing justice and mercy and our role in accessing His power to deliver.

Personal Application: Aaron

I learned a poignant lesson about justice and mercy when I was in high school. At the end of my freshman year, a friend told me about an open spot in the drumline of our state championship

---

1. Boyd K, Packer, "The Mediator," Conference Report, April 1977.

high school marching band. He said they would be going to the Rose Bowl that year, an exciting prospect.

I decided to join, and I turned in the paperwork. Because marching band is always in the fall, I thought I had no more obligations until the next school year. I did not realize that I was supposed to have attended many music events over the summer, including percussion and band camp. Unfortunately, I did not attend any of them.

At the beginning of the next school year, I naively went into the band directors' offices to begin with the band, thinking I would be warmly received by them. Nothing was further from the truth. To achieve the success they enjoyed with a large organization of more than three hundred teenagers, they had a strict set of rules about attendance and practice.

I can still vividly remember the scolding I received that day! They expected me to have attended all the practice sessions and band camps to learn the music and the marching. Because of my absence, they would not allow me to march that season. They were justified in telling me I would not be able to participate at all that year.

I felt terrible! I told them that I wanted to be a part of the marching band and that I would do anything to make it up. Mercifully, they told me that if I wanted to be part of the band, I would have to be a band manager. Band managers were the equipment crew that hauled equipment before and after practices and performances and loaded the truck. They told me that I could still learn the drums, but I would have to do it independently. If I learned how to play well enough, they would allow me to march bass drum in the Rose Bowl Parade in January.

Although disappointed, I humbled myself and accepted their offer. I worked diligently that year to learn the drums. The process wasn't easy. Fortunately, I learned to play well enough to march in the 1987 Rose Bowl Parade.

I continued to work, and I earned a spot playing snare in the drumline the following year. In my senior year, those same band directors appointed me as drumline co-captain, and my peers elected me as band president. Eventually, I went on to march in the BYU marching band, earning a music scholarship for my participation.

How grateful I am for those band directors who were both just and merciful with me. I deserved to be cut from the drumline because of my poor decisions. However, they were merciful in giving me a second chance—one that I took advantage of by doing my part to correct what I had done wrong. Many wonderful things occurred because of that mercy, including meeting my future wife, Julie, in the marching band.

Justice and mercy are in perfect harmony in the plan of salvation because of Jesus Christ and His Atonement. Justice and mercy are two fundamental doctrines taught in the temple. "Justice is an eternal law that requires a penalty each time a law of God is broken."[2] Mercy is the suspension of that penalty, even when we deserve it.

The Father has a great love for His children. Nevertheless, He must administer perfect justice, delivering consequences for choices made. Sins and transgressions must result in punishments according to the requirements of the perfect law. This law dictates that He only gives eternal blessings to the perfect.

Unfortunately, all men and women have sinned, "and thus we see that all mankind were fallen, and they were in the grasp of justice; yea, the justice of God, which consigned them forever to be cut off from his presence."[3] As imperfect mortals, our default position is to be in the unyielding grasp of justice.

Fortunately, Jesus Christ provides the path to perfect mercy because He fully met all the demands of justice required by the perfect law via His infinite and eternal Atonement. The Savior stands in place of the perfect law—having met its requirements fully—and issues the gospel law, a substitute law of which He is the author and finisher.[4]

The Savior's alternative law allows Him to grant us mercy if we use our agency and willingly choose to abide by its principles, precepts, ordinances, and covenants. In this way, "justice exerciseth all his demands, and also mercy claimed all which is her own."[5] He is the Mediator who

2. "Justice," *Guide to the Scriptures*, 2013.
3. Alma 42:14.
4. See Hebrews 12:2.
5. Alma 42:24.

harmonizes both.[6] The scriptures and the temple repeatedly teach this perfect harmony provided by the Savior. Alma taught,

> Do ye suppose that mercy can rob justice? I say unto you, Nay; not one whit.[7] . . . [Jesus Christ] shall bring salvation to all those who shall believe on his name; this being the intent of this last sacrifice, to bring about the bowels of mercy, which overpowereth justice, and bringeth about means unto men that they may have faith unto repentance.
>
> And thus mercy can satisfy the demands of justice, and encircles them in the arms of safety, while he that exercises no faith unto repentance is exposed to the whole law of the demands of justice; therefore only unto him that has faith unto repentance is brought about the great and eternal plan of redemption.[8]

In the second verse above, "mercy" could be treated as a proper noun. Who is mercy? *Jesus Christ is Mercy.* What a beautiful and comforting thought! *He* encircles us in His loving arms, protecting us from the consequences of death and sin. Elder Neal A. Maxwell, formerly of the Quorum of the Twelve, further taught of the intimate and personal nature of our Savior's mercy:

> If there is any imagery upon which I would focus . . . it is two scriptures from the Book of Mormon. The one in which we are reminded that Jesus himself is the gatekeeper and that 'he employeth no servant there.' (2 Nephi 9:41). . . . I will tell you . . . out of the conviction of my soul . . . what I think the major reason is [why he 'employeth no servant there'], as contained in another Book of Mormon scripture which says he waits for you 'with open arms.' (Mormon 6:17.)
>
> That's why he's there! He waits for you 'with open arms.' That imagery is too powerful to brush aside. . . . It is imagery

---

6. 1 Timothy 2:5.
7. Alma 42:25.
8. Alma 34:15–16.

that should work itself into the very center core of one's mind—a rendezvous impending, a moment in time and space, the likes of which there is none other. And that rendezvous is a reality. I certify that to you. He does wait for us with open arms, because his love of us is perfect.[9]

Those who do not repent and continue in sin "shall be *as though* there had been no redemption made; for they *cannot* be redeemed according to God's justice."[10] In the end, the Savior will deliver perfect justice and a commensurate consequence in these unfortunate cases.

So, we should not "procrastinate the day of [our] repentance to the end . . . wherein there can be no labor performed,"[11] "for that same spirit which doth possess your bodies at the time that ye go out of this life will have power to possess your body in that eternal world."[12] Elder Melvin J. Ballard, formerly of the Quorum of the Twelve, warned,

This life is the time in which men [and women] are to repent. Do not let any of us imagine that we can go down to the grave not having overcome the corruptions of the flesh [through repentance] and then lose in the grave all our sins and evil tendencies. They will be with us. They will be with the spirit when separated from the body [if we do not repent].[13]

Fortunately, the sublime and hopeful truth is that "mercy claimeth the penitent, and mercy cometh because of the atonement."[14] "Therefore, may God grant unto you, my [beloved] brethren [and sisters], that ye may begin to exercise your faith unto repentance [now], that ye begin to call upon his holy name, that he would have mercy upon you!"[15] Yes, repentance unlocks mercy!

---

9. Neal A. Maxwell, "But a Few Days," address to CES Religious Educators, September 10, 1982, Salt Lake Palace Assembly Room, 7.
10. Alma 12:18; emphasis added.
11. Alma 34:33.
12. Alma 34:34.
13. Melvin J. Ballard, "The Three Glories," cited in Duane S. Crowther, *Life Everlasting* (Salt Lake City: Horizon Publishers, 2017), 39.
14. Alma 42:23.
15. Alma 34:17.

Just consequences eventually come with open rebellion to God.
The temple teaches that individuals who choose not to repent nor come
unto Christ—the rebellious—will face the consequences of their willing choices. One of these consequences is the forfeiture of blessings.
The scriptures call this forfeiture a "curse,"[16] which includes the loss
of the Spirit, the priesthood and priesthood power, the ordinances of
salvation, certain privileges of membership,[17] or even the person's full
membership in the kingdom. Ultimately, the lack of godly characteristics and traits "curses" us, for we fail to *become* like our Heavenly
Father.

Unfortunately, those who choose not to repent will eventually face
exquisite pain in the eternities. The Lord warned us,

> Therefore I command you to repent—repent, lest I smite you
> by the rod of my mouth, and by my wrath, and by my anger,
> and your sufferings be sore—*how sore you know not, how
> exquisite you know not, yea, how hard to bear you know not.*
>
> For behold, I, God, have suffered these things for all, that
> they might not suffer if they would repent;
>
> But if they would not repent they must suffer even as I.[18]

What a dreadful consequence for those who do not repent! This
consequence can be avoided through the willing choice to repent.

We receive our final reward or punishment in the Savior's last
judgment. He judges what we have become, not just what we have
done. He judges how much of His infinite mercy we have qualified
for. Nephi taught,

> Wherefore, they stand in the presence of him, to be judged of him
> according to the truth and holiness *which is in him.* Wherefore,
> the ends of the law which the Holy One hath given, unto the
> inflicting of the *punishment* which is affixed, which punishment

---

16. 1 Nephi 2:23.
17. Such as taking the sacrament, holding a calling, having a temple recommend,
    and so on.
18. Doctrine and Covenants 19:15–17; emphasis added.

that is affixed is in opposition to that of the *happiness* which is affixed, to answer the ends of the atonement. [19]

Punishment is not the Savior pushing the unrepentant down. Punishment is His inability to lift them up due to their own choices and lack of repentance. Because they did not freely act on the invitation to repent, they will be "acted upon . . . by the punishment of the law at the great and last day, according to the commandments which God hath given."[20] They will be left without the full measure of mercy that could be offered to them.

Some people may have trouble with the law of justice and reciprocity because they misunderstand the need for such punishment or justice. They are like Alma's son Corianton, who saw injustice in God's punishment of the unrepentant sinner.[21] They have great compassion for those who have heart-wrenching issues that sometimes lead them away from commandments and covenants. Likely, they cannot resolve the seeming dichotomy between the love the Savior has for us and His need to withhold His mercy from us or punish us if we choose to rebel.

The Savior does not relish having to exercise justice, but He must do it to maintain His integrity and honor, which is His power.[22] If He were not perfectly just, He would compromise His divine role in the universe. Alma taught, "Now the work of justice could not be destroyed; if so, God would cease to be God."[23] The merciful fact is that He only executes justice after giving us multiple opportunities to repent and return. When we continue in our disobedience and rebellion despite these invitations, He must be perfectly just.

Those who struggle with the justice of God sometimes mistakenly seek to invalidate eternal laws as an act of mercy. However, this desire is a misapplication of the concept of mercy. The actual law of mercy does not destroy justice, but mercy supersedes or overcomes justice in those cases where it is warranted, as judged by the Perfect One who

19. 2 Nephi 2:10; emphasis added.
20. 2 Nephi 2:26.
21. See Alma 42:1.
22. See Doctrine and Covenants 29:26.
23. Alma 42:13.

already met the full demands of justice for all of us. Invalidation of eternal law would have a cascade of negative consequences.[24]

Instead of invalidating eternal law, we must recognize the eternal nature of God's laws, respect the consequences when they are violated and left unrepented, and look to the Savior as the perfect purveyor of merciful help and healing if we repent and seek His forgiveness sincerely and regularly. This approach keeps us focused on Him and gives us the proper, balanced perspective when we observe sin in the lives of others or experience it in our lives.

Our Savior, Jesus Christ, has the overwhelming desire to be merciful. In the temple, we learn that Jesus Christ is both our Advocate and Judge and that He has perfect discernment to know when justice and mercy are needed. We must trust in Him to make His perfect judgment. Although He must be perfectly just, multiple scriptures clarify that He relishes mercy and is frustrated when we do not understand His mercy.[25] Jesus Christ *is* mercy![26]

The resurrected Savior told the Nephites, "I have compassion for you; my bowels are filled with mercy."[27] In the Hebrew tradition, the "bowels" were the seat of feelings, whereas, in western culture, the heart is the seat of emotions.[28] The scriptures often speak of the Lord's compassion using this somewhat unusual phrase.[29]

Therefore, the imagery in the phrase "the bowels of mercy" conveys the deep compassion and love the Savior has toward all those to

---

24. 2 Nephi 2:13.
25. Alma 33:16 reads, "Thou art angry, O Lord, with this people, because they will not understand thy mercies which thou hast bestowed upon them because of thy Son." The word "angry" can be read "frustrated."
26. See Alma 34:16, where mercy is treated as a proper noun.
27. 3 Nephi 17:7.
28. See John Durham Peters, "Bowels of Mercy," *BYU Studies Quarterly* (Provo, UT: Brigham Young University 1999), Volume 38, Issue 4, Article 2, October 1, 1999. See also *New Testament Seminary Teacher Manual* (Salt Lake: The Church of Jesus Christ of Latter-day Saints), Lesson 134: Philemon, accessed February 6, 2021, https://www.churchofjesuschrist.org/study/manual/new-testament-seminary-teacher-manual/introduction-to-the-epistle-of-paul-to-philemon/lesson-134–philemon?lang=eng.
29. See Mosiah 15:9; Alma 7:12; 34:15; Doctrine and Covenants 101:9.

whom He offers mercy, which includes all who have sinned, fallen short, but have returned and repented. Mercy is the heartfelt benevolent act of a loving Savior.

In the Old Testament, the Hebrew word often translated into English as "mercy" is *hesed*. More accurately, this word means "faithful and intimate, redemptive love."[30] It could also be translated as "unfailing, faithful, steadfast, or loyal love." The word is "not merely an emotion or feeling but involves action on behalf of someone who is in need."[31]

Accordingly, when we speak of the "mercy" of Jesus Christ, it should bring into our minds His great act of atonement, His unfailing actions to faithfully invite us to partake of His protection, and His loving kindness in extending redemption, deliverance, healing, and strength to us despite our weaknesses.

The scriptures describe the Savior "encircling [His people] in the arms of safety."[32] This phrase is the visual representation of "atonement," which is a reconciliation to the Father whereby the Savior protects us from the full consequences of our sins.

The Savior figuratively wraps His protecting arms around us. He protects us from the consequences of our sins and transgressions to the fullest extent possible, based on our choices which allow that mercy to be extended. Indeed, Jesus Christ and His infinite Atonement are where "justice, love, and mercy meet in harmony divine."[33]

Unfortunately, there still may be some short-term, unreconcilable consequences that result from our choices despite the mercy that will eventually come to us.[34] However, over an eternity, they will all be

---

30. Edwin Brown Firmage, "Violence and the Gospel: The Teachings of the Old Testament, the New Testament, and the Book of Mormon," *BYU Studies Quarterly*, Vol. 25 No. 1 (Provo, UT: Brigham Young University 1985), 6. See also footnote 14, accessed February 14, 2021. https://byustudies.byu.edu/wp-content/uploads/2020/02/25.1FirmageViolence-ab148ed3–6a69–49aa-9d3c-858130e81b3a.pdf.

31. www.gotquestions.org, "What is the meaning of the Hebrew word *hesed*?" accessed February 14, 2021, https://www.gotquestions.org/meaning-of-hesed.html.

32. Alma 34:16.

33. "How Great the Wisdom and the Love," *Hymns*, no. 195.

34. See Doctrine and Covenants 138:59.

resolved, and the lasting effects of any unfortunate or unfair issues will all be eternally "swallowed up in Christ,"[35] and all will be restored to their "proper order"[36] by Him.

Elder J. Ruben Clark, formerly of the Quorum of the Twelve, beautifully taught about the bounteous mercy of the Savior when He stands to make His final judgment and reconciliation:

> In his mercy, in his tenderness, in his love, in his experience which came to him as mortal being, out of all of this there will come his judgment. We shall have all of the reward that love and mercy and tenderness and divine relationship can give for our services here on earth. We shall receive the punishments, and those only, which infinite justice require as they are tempered by the love and by the mercy and by the charity and by the experience not only of the Christ, but of the Father who, if we understand correctly, passed through those experiences which Christ, himself, lived through.[37]

This bounteous mercy is individually available to all who willingly seek it. Let us willingly seek it!

The grace of the Lord Jesus Christ is offered to all people as they qualify for it. The temple and the scriptures repeatedly testify that Jesus Christ "is full of grace and truth."[38] What is grace? The Bible Dictionary defines grace as a "divine means of help or strength, given through the bounteous mercy and love of Jesus Christ."[39] We

---

35. See Mosiah 3:11, 16:8.
36. Alma 41:4.
37. J. Reuben Clark Jr., *Behold the Lamb of God* (Salt Lake City: Deseret Book, 1962), 98. He further taught, "I believe that his juridical concept of his dealings with his children could be expressed in this way: I believe that in his justice and mercy he will give us the maximum reward for our acts, give us all that he can give, and in the reverse, I believe that he will impose upon us the minimum penalty which it is possible for him to impose" (J. Reuben Clark, Conference Report, October 1953, 84).
38. See John 1:14; 2 Nephi 2:6; Doctrine and Covenants 66:12; 93:11; Moses 1:6, 32, 52; 7:11. Grace is synonymous with mercy; truth is synonymous with justice.
39. "Grace," Bible Dictionary.

can also define grace as a blessing or gift we receive that we don't entirely deserve.

Every blessing we receive from our Father in Heaven is an act of grace, for we never *fully* merit any of them due to our imperfections. Therefore, when we qualify for—but not earn—blessings through these imperfect efforts and understand they came to us anyway, we should have a deep sense of gratitude for blessings received. These feelings will help us remain humble—even amid prosperous times—because we will be acutely aware of the divine source of all our blessings.

How are grace and mercy related? Grace is an unearned gift. Mercy is compassion or forgiveness toward someone who deserves punishment. Grace offers us a blessing we don't fully merit; mercy waives a punishment we fully deserve. Thus, the extension of mercy is an act of grace.

In an offering of grace to us despite our imperfect condition, Christ can extend mercy by forgiving us and acquitting us of the punishments we justly deserve if we have repented and have come unto Him. He can do this because He already paid the full price for all our sins and mistakes.

As a perfect Judge, He can decide who has complied with His gospel law's requirements and deliver blessings according to His grace. We reconcile to God[40] through Christ, who traded His perfect life for our imperfect life. His grace is a free, unmerited, unearned gift.

This "unearned" offering does not mean we have no part to play in our redemption. He asks us to do certain things to receive blessings and, eventually, to be reconciled to Him. Our effort is what the scriptures mean by the phrase "work out your *own* salvation with fear and trembling."[41]

However, because we will always do what He asks imperfectly, any blessings we receive are merely qualified for, not earned. The word "earned" would suggest blessings are fully gained through our efforts alone, whereas the term "qualified for" implies we have done what is

---

40. "Reconciled" means to be atoned or redeemed.
41. Mormon 9:27; emphasis added. See also Philippians 2:12.

sufficient, and the Lord, through His grace, grants the full measure of blessings which we could not gain on our own.

When we live the doctrine of Christ with a sincere heart[42] and with perfect willingness,[43] we will move forward on the covenant path to the best of our ability. For, as we "love God with all [our] might, mind and strength, *then* is his grace sufficient for [us], that by his grace [we] may be perfect in Christ."[44]

Indeed, our perfect willingness or eagerness will qualify us for the grace of Christ and His abundant mercy toward us, despite our imperfect thoughts, words, and deeds. His grace will slowly perfect us into becoming the men and women He wants us to become. Therefore, grace blesses us and saves us "after [meaning 'despite' or 'regardless of,' not 'because of'] all we can do."[45] This grace comes to us along the entire path of discipleship in mortality, including at its very conclusion in eternity.

Gracious and merciful blessings come with voluntary submission to the will of God. In the temple, we accept our covenants of our own free will. Each time we *willingly* accept and make a covenant with God and *willingly* renew our covenant, we demonstrate our submission to Him. Each time we *willingly* keep a commandment, follow counsel, or adhere to norms and standards, we also show our submission to Him. *Willingness* is an enabler of action by us and an activator of mercy on our behalf.

Willingness means being ready, eager, and prepared to do something, or it is something given or done readily.[46] It means to be excited and energetic in trying our best to do the things He asks. The scriptural phrases that capture this concept of spiritual willingness are "easy to be entreated"[47] and "quick to observe."[48]

---

42. A sincere heart is the same as having "real intent."
43. We can have perfect willingness without having perfect actions. Our genuine willingness will compensate for our imperfect actions.
44. Moroni 10:32; emphasis added.
45. 2 Nephi 25:23.
46. "Willing," *Oxford Dictionary of English*, 2030.
47. See Alma 7:23; Helaman 7:7.
48. Mormon 1:2.

Perfect willingness, not perfect action, is the key to the receipt of blessings because we can never be perfect in our thoughts, words, and deeds. Perfect willingness is what the scriptures call "full purpose of heart,"[49] which is required by the Savior. We would suggest that the "probationary state"[50] of this life is often a trial of willingness, not necessarily just of performance or capability.

The desires of our hearts drive our willingness, and our willingness drives our actions. Of these desires, Beverly Campbell, a former director of international affairs for The Church of Jesus Christ of Latter-day saints, wrote, "Desire is active, not passive. It has to do with more than wishing; it's about heartfelt longing, and it's about a real craving. Desire by its very nature places priority of one thing over another. . . . Desires, like all things in our lives, must be directed, managed, and controlled."[51]

When we participate in temple ordinances, they remind us of the principle of willingness or voluntary acceptance. Other ordinances have this same reminder. The Book of Mormon teaches us that after baptism, we should be "*willing* to bear one another's burdens, that they may be light," "*willing* to mourn with those that mourn," and be *willing* "to stand as witnesses at all times and in all things, and in all places."[52] The sacrament prayers also remind us that at baptism, we witness we are *willing* to take upon us the name of Jesus Christ, always remember Him, and keep His commandments.[53]

Our willing submission brings us all the enabling and redeeming powers of Jesus Christ, which come because of His infinite Atonement. "The Lord requireth the heart and a *willing* mind; and the *willing and obedient* shall eat the good of the land of Zion in these last days. And the rebellious [those who are unwilling and disobedient] shall be cut off."[54]

---

49. 2 Nephi 31:13.
50. Alma 42:13.
51. Beverly Campbell, *Eve and the Mortal Journey* (Salt Lake City: Deseret Book, 2005), 12.
52. Mosiah 18:8–9; emphasis added.
53. See Doctrine and Covenants 20:76.
54. Doctrine and Covenants 64:34–35; emphasis added.

At one point in the Book of Mormon, the Spirit of the Lord withdrew from the Nephites because of "the wickedness and hardness of their hearts," but His Spirit was poured out upon the Lamanites "because of their easiness and *willingness* to believe."[55] Therefore, actions *and* willingness or desires will be judged by the Savior in His assessment of us, for these things together determine what we will have become.

Alma wrote, "Whosoever *will come* may come and partake of the waters of life freely; and whosoever will not come the same is not compelled to come, but in the last day it shall be restored unto him *according to his deeds*" [56] and "if their *works* were good in this life, *and the desires of their hearts were good* . . . they should . . . be restored unto that which is good."[57] The rebellious will only "enjoy that which they are *willing to receive*, because they were *not willing to enjoy* that which they might have received."[58]

Thus, our sincere submissiveness and its accompanying actions will result in our sanctification, "which sanctification cometh because of [our] *yielding* our hearts unto God."[59] Willing submission develops within us the godly traits of meekness and humility, two foundational, eternal characteristics.

Willing submission to God is something uniquely ours to give, a deeply personal offering. Elder Neal A. Maxwell, formerly of the Quorum of the Twelve, taught,

> The submission of one's will is really the only uniquely personal thing we have to place on God's altar. The many other things we "give," brothers and sisters, are actually the things He has already given or loaned to us. However, when you and I finally submit ourselves, by letting our individual wills be swallowed up in God's will, then we are really giving something to Him! It is the only possession which is truly ours to give![60]

---

55. Helaman 6:35–36; emphasis added.
56. Alma 42:27; emphasis added.
57. Alma 41:3; emphasis added.
58. Doctrine and Covenants 88:33; emphasis added.
59. Helaman 3:35; emphasis added.
60. Neal A. Maxwell, "Swallowed Up in the Will of the Father," Conference Report, October 1995.

Willingness is also synonymous with a sincere desire, which is of utmost importance because without "real intent" even outwardly good actions will not be counted for our good.[61]

The need for real intent is especially important when legitimate barriers prevent the full expression of a heartfelt desire. Elder Dallin H. Oaks, current President of the Quorum of the Twelve, taught, "When someone wanted to do something for my father-in-law but was prevented by circumstances, he would say, 'Thank you. I will take the good will for the deed.' Similarly, I believe that our Father in Heaven will receive the true desires of our hearts as a substitute for genuinely impossible actions."[62]

Thus, perfectly sincere desire, coupled with willing and eager actions—however imperfect—are the activator of all blessings from God.

Hope and joy come from sincere repentance. We learn in the temple, and we read in the scriptures, about the pain and guilt that come from sin and transgression, which is the breaking of divine law. Indeed, "wickedness never was happiness"[63] and always was sorrow or sadness. Due to life in a fallen world, no one can live all the laws of God perfectly. "All have sinned, and come short of the glory of God."[64] Therefore, we all have a reason to have some measure of unhappiness in this life because of sin.

Unfortunately, these negative feelings often lead us to hide our sins rather than confess them, which only amplifies our sorrow. For this reason, "despair cometh of [unrepentant] iniquity."[65]

Fortunately, we can alleviate our pain as we confess what we have done and seek restitution and redemption through the great gift of repentance. "By this ye may know if a man [or a woman] repenteth of his [or her] sins—behold, he [or she] will confess them and forsake

---

61. See Moroni 7:6–7.
62. Dallin H. Oaks, "The Desires of Our Hearts," *BYU Speeches* (Provo, UT: Brigham Young University, October 8, 1985), accessed February 6, 2021, https://speeches.byu.edu/talks/dallin-h-oaks/desires-hearts/. See also *Ensign*, June 1986.
63. Alma 41:10.
64. Romans 3:23.
65. Moroni 10:22.

them."[66] When we become repentant, the mercy of Jesus Christ pours down upon us.

Repenting is an act. *Becoming repentant* is a state of being. One is a process; the other is an outcome. The Lord wants us to become repentant and not just repent. We become repentant when we have a sincere and thorough "change of heart,"[67] meaning we have a whole new outlook on life and eternity.[68] When our actions have "wrought a mighty change in us,"[69] and we have become humble, meek, and submissive, then the healing forgiveness of the Savior will flow freely to us, and He will redeem us from our former sinful state. "Mercy claimeth the penitent!"[70]

Therefore, we should run to repentance by confessing and forsaking sin and run to our Savior, who alone can cleanse and acquit us. We might suggest that the command to "repent . . . forevermore"[71] is one we can live perfectly because to do so we simply repeat it. Each time a child of God pursues repentance of sins sincerely and consistently—becoming humble and submissive in the process—the Savior promises, "The same is forgiven, and I, the Lord, remember [the sins] no more."[72] What a merciful promise by our Savior and Redeemer!

When we demonstrate our faith in Jesus Christ and His infinite and eternal Atonement by becoming repentant, we can have a sure and lasting hope of "good things to come."[73] When our faith is exercised consistently, even in the face of temptation and difficulty, we will "abound in hope" as "the God of hope fill [us] with all joy and peace in believing."[74] Indeed, we are "saved by hope" in Him.[75]

---

66. Doctrine and Covenants 58:43.
67. See Helaman 15:7; Alma 5:7.
68. "The Greek word of which ["repentance"] is the translation denotes a change of mind, a fresh view about God, about oneself, and about the world" ("Repentance," The Bible Dictionary).
69. Mosiah 5:7.
70. Alma 42:23.
71. Moses 5:8.
72. Doctrine and Covenants 58:42.
73. Hebrews 9:11.
74. Romans 15:13.
75. Romans 8:24.

The temple portrays the exquisite joy of repentance, and it enables us to achieve it. We can find joy in repentance! "Men [and women] are that they might have joy."[76] This joy comes through Christ. Indeed, through repentance, the sorrow of sin is "swallowed up in the joy of Christ."[77]

Personal Application: Aaron

When we were in college, Julie and I went to Texas so I could work as a summer intern. We lived in a one-bedroom apartment with a small kitchen. During that summer, Julie spent a few weeks in Tennessee while I stayed in Texas.

Shortly after Julie left, I noticed a problem in our apartment—fruit flies. These small, annoying bugs began showing up in our kitchen and soon spread to other parts of our apartment. I threw out all of the fruit on the kitchen counter and sprayed bug killer every place within view. But my efforts were to no avail— the fruit flies just kept coming back!

I lived in this predicament for the few weeks that Julie was gone. At the end of her vacation, Julie returned and immediately noticed our growing fruit fly problem. She quickly began searching the kitchen, and within minutes, she found a bag of old, rotting potatoes in the back of our pantry.

What did I do wrong in handling this problem? My first mistake was not fixing the problem quickly; I let the potatoes rot. My second mistake was not dealing with the source of the problem; I just took care of the symptoms. Finally, I ignored all the continuing signs that there was a problem and just learned to live with the consequences.

The process of repentance is similar. When we act quickly, remove the source of the sin, and do not ignore it, we can find joy. If we do not, our problems will grow. Becoming repentant will give us the character to deal with sin consistently and effectively. Repentance is our path to peace.

---

76. 2 Nephi 2:25.
77. Alma 31:38.

Forgiving others brings us healing, peace, and mercy. The temple enables us to experience the joy of forgiving others. The Savior can heal our hearts both as we seek repentance and as we extend forgiveness to others. We should extend mercy to them in the same way the Savior extends mercy to us. Because we all will want maximum mercy for ourselves on the final day of judgment, we should also extend the utmost mercy to others. During the Sermon the Mount, the Savior taught, "Blessed are the merciful: for they shall obtain mercy."[78]

Jennie Brimhall Knight, who served five years as the president of the Young Ladies' MIA in the early 1900s, taught of the relationship between forgiveness and mercy:

> To those who have been sorely tried and bitterly offended, remember it requires a prayerful, generous, and merciful heart coupled with a strong will to forgive, but remember also, an unforgiving heart places a barrier between itself and God's forgiveness. . . .
>
> So let us each and all bury our grievances whether they pertain to our immediate family, our church, or our neighbor, and cover this pitfall that deprives us of happiness with a slab of forgetfulness and forgive as we hope to be forgiven.[79]

The temple shows us a model of repentance and forgiveness. We should actively and sincerely forgive anyone who has sinned against us in any way, whether those offenses are real or perceived. Those who withhold this forgiveness of others remain with the "greater condemnation."[80]

Included in this pattern are the "blood and sins of this wicked generation,"[81] which are those habits, traits, and anything else inherited

---

78. Matthew 5:7.
79. Jennie Brimhall Knight, "Forgiveness Is Like Mercy," Discourse, Apr. 3, 1924, Afternoon Session, in "General Meetings," *Relief Society Magazine* 11, no. 6 (June 1924): 307–309. As recorded in *At the Pulpit: 185 Years of Discourses by Latter-day Saint* Women, 125. Title supplied by the editors.
80. Doctrine and Covenants 64:9–11.
81. Doctrine and Covenants 88:75.

or learned that negatively affect the choices we make. They include the "traditions of our fathers"[82] and other structural biases[83] that we may not even be aware of. We can forgive anyone who passed these things on to us, just as we seek forgiveness for the many improper actions we have, of our own accord, chosen.

It can be painful to forgive, especially in the most egregiously abusive circumstances. Much time and effort may be required to find the strength to forgive in these severe cases. However, our healing will come through the mercy of Jesus Christ, and He can give us the strength to extend mercy to others and allow Him as the perfect Judge to bear the weight of judgment. "Judgment is mine . . . and vengeance is mine also, and I will repay." [84] We can cast our burdens upon Him and, thus, find ultimate healing for ourselves.[85]

When considering our attitude toward forgiving others, we must understand the negative impact withholding forgiveness has on us. Elder Marion D. Hanks, a former member of the Quorum of Seventy, taught,

What is our response when we are offended, misunderstood, unfairly or unkindly treated, or sinned against, made an offender for a word, falsely accused, passed over, hurt by those we love, our offerings rejected? Do we resent, become bitter, hold a grudge? Or do we resolve the problem if we can, forgive, and rid ourselves of the burden? The nature of our response to such situations may well determine the nature and quality of our lives, here and eternally. . . .

But not only our eternal salvation depends upon our willingness and capacity to forgive wrongs committed against us. Our joy and satisfaction in this life, and our true freedom, depend upon our doing so.[86]

---

82. Enos 1:14.
83. These structural biases may include social, cultural, or familial biases embedded in our upbringing.
84. Moroni 8:20.
85. See Psalm 55:22.
86. Marion D. Hanks, "Forgiveness: The Ultimate Form of Love," Conference Report, October 1973, 15–16.

Indeed, we should strive to purge ourselves of the burden of hate and offense to truly be free.

The Savior offers mercy when accountability or capability are compromised. The restored gospel of Jesus Christ teaches us the expansiveness of the Savior's mercy and grace. He extends mercy to children of God who face extenuating circumstances or legitimate barriers while in mortality, which do not allow them to receive, understand, or comply fully with gospel law. This concept is core to temple doctrine.

First, some individuals never reach the age of accountability in this life, unfortunately dying before turning the age of eight. The plain and precious truth is that the Savior redeems these priceless children completely.[87]

Second, through the temple the Savior offers vicarious access to redemptive ordinances for any person who did not receive the fulness of the gospel in this life, who were without access to gospel law, or who "ignorantly sinned" because they never received truth.[88] These individuals will have the ability to accept the gospel when they hear it in the world of spirits after the day of this life is complete. If they accept it, the Lord will grant a full measure of mercy, and He will redeem them.

Third, there may exist legitimate and persistent barriers to achieving a full understanding of gospel law or to the full and willing expression of moral agency due to the unforeseen, uncontrollable, and unwanted circumstances of mortality, even when the fulness of the gospel *is* available in this life. As the prophet Mormon taught, individuals must be "accountable *and* capable"[89] to repent and be baptized.

In these unfortunate and unjust cases where accountability and capability are compromised, the Savior—with His perfect discernment and knowledge—can extend mercy at some point based on His perfect judgment. As Elder James R. Rasband of the Quorum

---

87. See Moroni 8:8–12, 22; Doctrine and Covenants 18:42.
88. See Mosiah 3:11; 15:24–25; Moroni 8:22; Doctrine and Covenants 45:54.
89. Moroni 8:10.

of Seventy taught, "Accountability for sin depends on the light we receive and hinges on our ability to exercise our agency."[90]

In any difficult or unfair cases, the Savior stands alone to make the final judgment of what will be done. The Savior has said, "And, again, I say unto you, that whoso having knowledge, have I not commanded to repent? And *he that hath no und*erstanding, *it remaineth in me* to do according as it is written."[91] *He alone* makes the decision as to what to do in complex cases that compromise capability. He will deliver mercy "according as [His] will, suiting his mercies *according to the conditions of the children of men.*"[92]

The Savior will apply His own judgment in any unjust or unfair mortal circumstances that legitimately warrant mercy from a loving and merciful Redeemer. Only *His* judgment counts; no one else stands at the gate. We can be assured that "His grace [is] sufficient"[93] to absorb every wrong, injustice, inequity, or disparity that occurs to us or to those whom we love and minister. As Joseph Smith taught,

> We need not doubt the wisdom and intelligence of the Great Jehovah; He will award judgment or mercy to [people of] all nations *according to their several deserts, their means of obtaining intelligence, the laws by which they are governed, the facilities afforded them of obtaining correct information*, and when the designs of God shall be made manifest, and the curtain of futurity be withdrawn, we shall all of us eventually have to confess that the Judge of all the earth has done right.[94]

For those who suffer from the most unwanted and heartbreaking issues, we must trust they will all be healed and be made whole by the grace of a merciful Savior "in process of time,"[95] and any resulting long-term consequences will be made right at some point. Understanding

---

90. James R. Rasband, "Ensuring a Righteous Judgment," Conference Report, April 2020.

91. Doctrine and Covenants 29:49–50; emphasis added.

92. Doctrine and Covenants 46:15; emphasis added.

93. Moroni 10:32.

94. Joseph Smith, *Teachings of Presidents of the Church: Joseph Smith* (Salt Lake City: Deseret Book, 2007), 404; emphasis added.

95. Moses 7:21.

this sublime truth, we can truly have hope in even seemingly hopeless situations, where the imperfect day of this life and the consequences of the Fall are in full effect.

No one is ever entirely lost or permanently broken, for the eye of the Savior is always upon them. Through His grace, He will make right those wrongs which we freely chose but for which we willingly repented, and He will make right anything unfair, which we did not freely choose. This action is reconciliation or atonement in its highest form. It is mercy and grace sufficiently and lovingly delivered.

As Elder Richard G. Scott, formerly of the Quorum of the Twelve, taught, "The Atonement will not only help us overcome our transgressions and mistakes, but in His time, it will resolve all inequities of life—those things that are unfair which are the consequences of circumstance or others' acts and not our own decisions."[96]

Dale G. Renlund of the Quorum of the Twelve further amplified this idea when he taught, "In the eternities, Heavenly Father and Jesus Christ will resolve all unfairness. We understandably want to know *how* and *when*. *How* are They going to do that? *When* are They going to do it? To my knowledge, They have not revealed *how* or *when*. What I do know is that *They will*."[97]

What a hope-filled promise for us all!

Every knee shall bow and tongue confess the living reality of Christ and the truthfulness of His gospel. The scriptures teach, "Every knee shall bow and every tongue confess" that Jesus is the Christ and His judgments are just and merciful.[98] The temple and its ordinances reinforce this concept. This phrase is a promise of hope to all disciples of Christ who have willingly chosen to bow their knees and confess the name of Christ with their mouth.[99] When persecutions

96. Richard G. Scott, "Jesus Christ, Our Redeemer," Conference Report, April 1997.
97. Dale G. Renlund, "Infuriating Unfairness," Conference Report, April 2021; emphasis original.
98. See Isaiah 45:23; Romans 14:11–12; Mosiah 27:31; Doctrine and Covenants 88:104.
99. See Romans 10:9–10.

from enemies or apostates come, this promise is the assurance that their current attacks will give way to future recognition. This promise provides strength and hope amid the opposition to truth for all faithful disciples of Christ.

This phrase also means that all men and women will not only understand, but they will agree with or "confess" the accuracy of the final, perfect judgments of Jesus Christ. When He assesses our desires, thoughts, words, and actions, we will agree that He is correct. We will not argue or disagree when we experience justice or mercy for ourselves or when we witness them for others.

We will all know, understand, and agree with His perfect judgment when He gives out our final reward according to His justice and mercy. We will "be constrained to exclaim: Holy, holy are thy judgments, O Lord God Almighty—but I know my guilt; I transgressed thy law, and my transgressions are mine." [100] At that day, we will know without a doubt that Jesus is the Christ, His judgments are just, His mercy is complete, and His lovingkindness is eternal.

QUESTIONS TO CONSIDER

1. What did you learn about justice and mercy during your last visit to the temple? How can you apply this new understanding in your life at this time?
2. In what ways does the temple and its ordinances help you qualify for Jesus Christ's mercy? What is your part in qualifying for it?
3. What does the temple teach you about repentance? How can you become more repentant in your life?
4. How can your temple covenants help you be more forgiving of others? Why is forgiving others essential to your happiness?
5. How can you apply the doctrine of mercy to a heartbreaking or unfair situation in your life or in the life of someone you love? How can that knowledge sustain you?

---

100. 2 Nephi 9:46.

NOTES AND INSIGHTS

Chapter 11

Sacrifice and Consecration

"A religion that does not require the sacrifice of all things never has power sufficient to produce the faith necessary [to lead] unto life and salvation."

—Joseph Smith[1]

This chapter covers the sacred doctrine of sacrifice, taught so powerfully in the temple. We will all have opportunities to live this doctrine, which sanctifies us and prepares us to become more like the Savior, who sacrificed everything for us. As we make our own sacrifices, we will learn more of Him and become more like Him.

Personal Application: Julie

I am a convert to The Church of Jesus Christ of Latter-day Saints. I joined the Church in Tennessee when I was just eighteen years old and was the only member of my family to accept baptism. Although my family members did not share my belief in the restored gospel, they generally supported my Church activity following my baptism.

---

1. Joseph Smith, *Lectures on Faith*, 58.

When Aaron returned from his mission in 1992, we decided to get married. Both of us wanted to have a temple wedding, even though this decision would mean that my family would not be able to attend the temple ceremony.[2] This sacrifice was difficult for me to make. My mother was a single mom for many years, so I had grown close to her and my sister. I had always wanted them to be a part of my wedding.

I did not struggle with the correctness of the decision—I knew it was the right thing to do both for myself and my future family. However, I struggled with the emotional loss of not having my family participate in one of the most important events in my life. My choice was a very real and emotionally taxing sacrifice. Despite the difficulty, I remained fully committed to my decision to be married for time and all eternity in the House of the Lord, which occurred in 1992, in the Atlanta Georgia Temple. This joyous event was the culmination of my spiritual aspirations to that point, which started as a non-member youth walking around the grounds of this same temple.

My sacrifice has brought our family untold blessings. First, my early commitment to the temple and its ordinances has fully blossomed into a firm testimony of the gospel, which has carried me through many other severe trials in my life. Second, my commitment to the temple has led to me completing much temple work for my family.

Finally, this simple yet profound decision we made thirty years ago has become the foundation upon which Aaron and I have been able to teach our children the eternal importance of the gospel and its covenants. They cannot question where our commitments and our loyalties align because we have demonstrated our allegiance to the Lord through this and other subsequent sacrifices. Indeed, we do not doubt that "sacrifice brings forth the

---

2. At this time, couples in the United States who did not marry in the temple had to wait one year to be sealed. Now, couples can be married outside the temple and immediately go to the temple to be sealed.

blessings of heaven."[3] *It has been true for us, and it will be true for you.*

Sacrifice is an eternal principle required of all disciples.
Sacrifice is a core doctrine of the temple. It has been part of the plan of salvation from the beginning. Sacrifice is "an act of offering to deity something precious,"[4] giving of the best we have. The Lord commanded Adam to sacrifice, even though he did not know why. Eventually, an angel taught him that his sacrifice was in "similitude of the sacrifice of the only begotten."[5] Therefore, Adam and all his posterity continued observing the law of sacrifice. It has continued down to our day, although we no longer observe the command to sacrifice animals.

Bruce R. McConkie taught, "The law of sacrifice is that we are willing to sacrifice all that we have for the truth's sake—our character and reputation; our honor and applause; our good name among men; our houses, lands, and families; all things, even our very lives if need be."[6]

Sacrifice connects closely to sanctification. "In ancient days, sacrifice meant to make something or someone holy."[7] Anciently, covenant people performed animal sacrifices to sanctify both the individual and the community. These animal sacrifices were "a type and a shadow" of things that were to come.[8] They pointed to Jesus Christ and His infinite and eternal sacrifice for us, which can sanctify and save us.

Following the infinite and eternal sacrifice performed by Jesus Christ, the Savior now asks us to make the sacrifice of a "broken heart and a contrite spirit."[9] This humble attitude allows us to make every other sacrifice required for our benefit or the good of others.

---

3. "Praise to the Man," *Hymns*, no. 27.
4. "Sacrifice," accessed January 7, 2021, www.merriam-webster.com.
5. Moses 5:6–8.
6. Bruce R. McConkie, "Obedience, Consecration, and Sacrifice," Conference Report, April 1975, 74–76.
7. "Sacrifice," *The Guide to the Scriptures*, 2013.
8. Mosiah 13:10.
9. 3 Nephi 9:19–20.

Why is sacrifice still necessary, given what Jesus Christ did vicariously for us? Joseph Smith taught, "A religion that does not require the sacrifice of all things never has the power sufficient to produce the faith necessary unto life and salvation."[10] Therefore, sacrifice enables us to develop the traits and characteristics of godliness more powerfully.

The covenant to sacrifice is implicit in the baptismal covenant, wherein we covenant "to mourn with those that mourn; yea, and comfort those that stand in need of comfort, and to stand as witnesses of God at all times and in all things, and in all places."[11] These acts require us to sacrifice our time and talents on behalf of others. Service and sacrifice are linked.

In the temple, we explicitly covenant that we are willing to sacrifice our will, sins, biases, opinions, and our very lives, if necessary, to advocate the cause of truth. The altars in the temple are symbolic of those sacrifices and remind us to make them when required.

"Sacrifice brings forth the blessings of heaven"[12] because it is the means of developing and demonstrating humility and submission to God's will and developing and showing meekness as we follow the direction given through God's servants. The meek and lowly who sacrifice are whom the Lord accepts. Said He, "Verily I say unto you, all among [the Saints] who know their hearts are honest, and are broken, and their spirits contrite, and are willing to observe their covenants by sacrifice—yea, every sacrifice which I, the Lord, shall command—they are accepted of me."[13]

The miracle witnessed in the selfless lives of Latter-day Saints is evidence of our covenant to sacrifice. In the temple, we sacrifice ourselves when we perform vicarious ordinances, standing as "saviors . . . on mount Zion" for our kindred dead.[14] We slowly perfect our sacrifices through our work in the temple.

Outside the temple, our covenant to sacrifice leads us to lives of selfless service for the benefit of others. We freely give of our time,

10. Joseph Smith, *Lectures on Faith,* 58.
11. Mosiah 18:8.
12. "Praise to the Man," *Hymns,* no. 27.
13. Doctrine and Covenants 97:8.
14. Obadiah 1:21.

talents, and resources with no expectation of compensation for providing relief and aid to others and helping build the kingdom of God. All these sacrifices sanctify us as a people, allowing us to become more like our Heavenly Parents.

We will all experience an intense "Abrahamic sacrifice" in our lives. Of all the sacrifices we covenant in the temple to make, one particular type stands out among the rest. An "Abrahamic sacrifice" is a term used for an extraordinary and intense sacrifice required of the people of God, His most elect and valiant sons and daughters. The Lord required Abraham to sacrifice Isaac—his only covenant son—on an altar,[15] a similitude of the sacrifice of the Only Begotten. This event is called the "Abrahamic sacrifice."

Two aspects define this extraordinarily intense sacrifice. From the *Old Testament Student Manual* we learn, "First, [Abraham] was asked to give up something very precious to him. . . . [Second,] an equally difficult, if not greater, test was what could be described as the question of the integrity of God."[16]

Soberingly, the Lord taught us that all Saints "must needs be chastened and tried, even as Abraham, who was commanded to offer up his only son. For all those who will not endure chastening, but deny me, cannot be sanctified."[17]

Why would our Father put us through such intense difficulties and chastening, ones that even cause us to question His divine motives? He does it to sanctify us and help us become more like Him. The Lord said to us, His Saints, "Verily, thus saith the Lord unto you whom I love, and whom I love I also chasten that their sins may be forgiven, for with the chastisement I prepare a way for their deliverance in all things out of temptation, and I have loved you."[18]

---

15. See Genesis 22:1–18.

16. See *Old Testament Student Manual: Genesis—2 Samuel* (Salt Lake City: The Church of Jesus Christ of Latter-day Saints, 1981), Section 6–12: "Genesis 22:1. Did God 'Tempt' Abraham?" 78.

17. Doctrine and Covenants 101:4–5.

18. Doctrine and Covenants 95:1; see also Helaman 15:3.

If you find yourself asking, "Why are *you* doing this to me?" during a particularly intense trial, and you are looking for meaning in it all, remember these words that Joseph Smith taught the early Quorum of the Twelve: "God will feel after you, and He will take hold of you and wrench your very heart strings, and, if you cannot stand it you will not be fit for an inheritance in the Celestial Kingdom of God."[19]

Furthermore, Elder. D. Todd Christofferson of the Quorum of the Twelve has taught, "Divine chastening has at least three purposes: (1) to persuade us to repent, (2) to refine and sanctify us, and (3) at times to redirect our course in life to what God knows is a better path. . . . Let us pray for His love-inspired correction."[20]

The only way we can become the men and women—the sons and daughters—Heavenly Father wants us to become is through the intense "valley of sorrow"[21] found in the rigorous chastisement of the sanctifying law of sacrifice.

The law of consecration is a companion to the law of sacrifice. We learn of the concept of consecration in the temple and in the scriptures of the Restoration. To consecrate is to dedicate something to a specific purpose. Elder Bruce R. McConkie taught,

> The law of consecration is that we consecrate [or dedicate] our time, our talents, and our money and property to the cause of the Church; such are to be available to the extent they are needed to further the Lord's interests on earth. . . .
>
> We are not always called upon to live the whole law of consecration and give all of our time, talents, and means to the building up of the Lord's earthly kingdom. . . . [W]hat the scriptural account means is that to gain salvation we must

19. Joseph Smith as recorded by John Taylor and cited in *Journal of Discourses*, 24:197.
20. D. Todd Christofferson, "As Many as I Love, I Rebuke and Chasten," Conference Report, April 2011.
21. 2 Nephi 4:26.

be able to live these laws to the full if we are called upon to do so.[22]

Consecration, then, is promising to give something to the Lord, and *sacrifice* is the fulfillment of our promise whenever He asks. For example, a Relief Society president consecrates a significant portion of her time to the ministry when she accepts her calling. She must be willing to give up time when required to serve the members of her ward. When she meets with the sisters and takes time away from her family, she is fulfilling her consecration by sacrificing that time.

Consecration engenders humility and meekness and is evidence of gratitude for blessings received. It sanctifies us and makes us holy. Sister Virginia H. Pearce, a former member of the Young Women General Presidency, taught,

> I find the word *consecration* intriguing. It means "to make holy and sacred . . . to sanctify." Consecration means that we dedicate our thoughts, our actions—our very lives to God. And in turn, he can consecrate our experiences—sanctify them, make them holy—no matter how difficult, foolish, or destructive. [23]

Ultimately, consecration is an accelerator to our becoming more like our Father in Heaven, and it provides the resources to allow the Lord's work to progress.

We are to be faithful and wise in the oversight of our stewardships. Closely tied to the principle of consecration as taught in the temple is the principle of stewardship. Stewardship is the responsible oversight of a resource, talent, or assignment. Upon consecrating

---

22. Bruce R. McConkie, "Obedience, Consecration, and Sacrifice," Conference Report, April 1975, 74–76.
23. Virginia H. Pearce, "Prayer: A Small and Simple Thing," address given at Brigham Young University Women's Conference, Marriott Center, Brigham Young University, Provo, Utah, April 28, 2011, cited in *At the Pulpit: 185 Years of Discourses by Latter-day Saint Women*, 289.

time, talents, or resources to the Lord, we are to oversee or care for those items until the Lord or His servants ask to use them.

We are always stewards of our resources.[24] The scriptures of the Restoration teach us how to be wise stewards, and the temple shows us an inspired pattern of proper stewardship. The Lord commands us to be "faithful, just and wise" stewards[25] to maximize the outcomes and output from our stewardships.

We are to magnify our callings and assignments. We are also to magnify our roles in the family. We are to magnify our efforts in whatever profession we choose and be wise stewards over our income so we can be self-reliant, have the means to bless others, and support the Lord's work by the full payment of tithes and generous payment of offerings.[26]

In speaking of magnifying our efforts, President Thomas S. Monson taught, "What does it mean to magnify a calling? It means to build it up in dignity and importance, to make it honorable and commendable in the eyes of all men [and women], to enlarge and strengthen it, to let the light of heaven shine through it to the view of other [people]. And how does one magnify a calling? Simply by performing the service that pertains to it."[27]

Likewise, President John Taylor taught, "If you do not magnify your calling, God will hold you responsible for those you might have saved, had you done your duty."[28]

At some point, we will give an account or report of all our stewardships.[29] President David O. McKay taught us about the priority order in that final report to the Savior:

---

24. See Doctrine and Covenants 42:32.
25. See Doctrine and Covenants 51:19; 72:22.
26. Part of the wise stewardship of income is the full payment of tithing, which is defined by the Lord as 10 percent of our income and interest annually (see Doctrine and Covenants 89). The payment of a full tithe is a requirement for entering the temple.
27. Thomas S. Monson, "The Call of Duty," Conference Report, April 1986.
28. John Taylor, *Teachings of the Presidents of the Church: John Taylor*, 164.
29. See Doctrine and Covenants 72:3, 16.

Let me assure you, Brethren [and Sisters], that some day you will have a personal . . . interview with the Savior, Himself. If you are interested, I will tell you the order in which He will ask you to account for your earthly responsibilities.

First, He will request an accountability report about your relationship with your wife [or husband]. Have you actively been engaged in making her [or him] happy and ensuring that her [or his] needs have been met as an individual?

Second, He will want an accountability report about each of your children individually. He will not attempt to have this for simply a family stewardship but will request information about your relationship to each and every child.

Third, He will want to know what you personally have done with the talents you were given in the pre-existence.

Fourth, He will want a summary of your activity in your Church assignments. He will not be necessarily interested in what assignments you have had, for in his eyes the [ministering brother or sister] and a mission president [and spouse] are probably equals, but He will request a summary of how you have been of service to your fellowmen [and women] in your Church assignments.

Fifth, He will have no interest in how you earned your living, but if you were honest in all your dealings.

Sixth, He will ask for an accountability on what you have done to contribute in a positive manner to your community, state, country and the world.[30]

President Nelson recently gave us additional insight as to the priorities we will be judged against in that final interaction with the Lord. He said in an interview at the age of ninety-six,

Judgment Day is coming for me pretty soon. . . . [In my final interview with the Savior], I doubt if I'll be judged by

30. David O. McKay from Notes of Fred A. Baker, Managing Director, Department of Physical Facilities of The Church of Jesus Christ of Latter-day Saints as shared by Robert D. Hales, "Understandings of the Heart," *BYU Speeches*, March 15, 1988.

the number of operations I did, or the number of scientific publications I had. I doubt if I'll even be judged by the growth of the Church during my presidency. I don't think it'll be a quantitative experience. I think he'll want to know: What about your faith? What about virtue? What about your knowledge? Were you temperate? Were you kind to people? Did you have charity, humility?[31]

Some individuals may struggle with managing the priorities described by President McKay and President Nelson as urgent needs arise in one given area. They either focus too much on one area of their life for long periods, or they haphazardly move from crisis to crisis, with little management over the level of effort expended across all areas.

In contrast, wise stewards have a long-term view of how to harmonize their stewardships. They understand the appropriate place of each of their stewardships—temporal and spiritual—and purposefully respond to the needs of each as required.

They are aware of the eternal importance of each stewardship. They also understand that any given stewardship may demand more attention in the present moment due to some immediate need. They always attempt to keep the overall priority in the long-term while meeting any short-term needs that may arise.

Thus, they are truly faithful and wise stewards. Because of this harmony, they are prepared to sacrifice any of their resources, which will have been well cared for, wisely managed, thoughtfully prioritized, and fully consecrated to the work of the Lord.

Personal Application: Julie

When Aaron was called as bishop, it surprised us both. It was a call we never anticipated. On the way home from the stake

---

31. Russell M. Nelson, cited in McKay Coppins, "The Most American Religion," *The Atlantic*, January/February 2021 Issue, published online December 16, 2020, https://www.theatlantic.com/magazine/archive/2021/01/the-most-american-religion/617263/.

president's office, we sat in silence for a bit. Concerned about the time commitment this call would have and its impact on our family, I told Aaron, "Don't you forget us when you are serving."

He looked at me and said, "I won't forget you. But I'll need you to let me serve when the Lord calls on me." We both agreed to these terms.

Many times, he would receive a text or a call, and he would immediately leave to help someone in need. He often couldn't share with us what the need was or who was being served.

Aaron also made sure to spend time with our family. Our children were teenagers when he served, and they had various activities and performances we were invited to attend. He always made time to attend these important events, and he made sure we just had personal time at home.

Some weeks, he was gone many nights, and other weeks he was home many nights. During his almost six years of service across two wards, we never felt slighted or shortchanged. We were blessed by our sacrifice of his time and our efforts to have personal and family time. Our choices were never perfect, but they were always right for us.

We must all find that "right place" for service in our lives amid all our competing demands. Inspiration, sacrifice, and love are the principles that will help us find it.

QUESTIONS TO CONSIDER

1. What did you learn about sacrifice and consecration during your last visit to the temple? How can you apply that learning in your life at this time?

2. What sacrifices do you find most difficult to make? What temple doctrine can help you be more willing to make that sacrifice the next time you are asked to make it?

3. How can your temple covenants help you better harmonize the competing stewardships in your life? What can you do to regularly re-harmonize them?

NOTES AND INSIGHTS

_____

_____

_____

_____

_____

_____

_____

_____

_____

Chapter 12

The Creation and Destiny of the Earth

"Grand as it is, planet Earth is part of something even grander—that great plan of God. Simply summarized, the earth was created that families might be."

—Russell M. Nelson[1]

This chapter covers doctrine related to the Creation and the earth. The temple celebrates God's creations and reminds us that they are His and that He made them for us. As we experience the earth and its beauty in mortality, we will come to see God's majesty and power in His creations in our daily lives.

Personal Application: Aaron

This world is beautiful! One morning while at a conference in Park City, Utah, I went for an early morning run to the top of the mountain near our hotel. On the run, I passed a moose and enjoyed the splendid views of nature. When I got to the top, I noticed that the sun was just beginning to come up over the distant mountains.

---

1. Russell M. Nelson, "The Creation," Conference Report, April 2000.

The scene was serene and magnificent. I couldn't help but think of our loving Heavenly Father, who wanted His children to have such a marvelous place to live during their mortal sojourn. With all the difficult things this life would bring, He surely wanted to give us glorious things to enjoy, such as the view I witnessed on that cool June morning.

Heavenly Father designed this world for us and our families. It provides us with all the experiences and opportunities to help us progress and find joy in the process.

We learn the centrality of the Creation to God's plan for His children. The Creation account portrayed in the temple focuses on the ascending order of importance in the Creation, which culminates in the most important thing God created. This pinnacle is the creation of a family, with Adam and Eve being joined by God in an eternal union. Following this event, the rest of the endowment and all the sealing ordinances teach us (1) how this family deals with temptations and the difficulties of a fallen world, (2) how God prepares and protects this family via covenants and divine direction, either personally or through authorized ministers, and (3) how the adversary seeks to destroy it. Central to the Creation account is the Father providing a Savior, who will deliver this family from death and sin through their faithfulness and His atoning sacrifice.

We find order and beauty in the world God created for us. The temple affirms the divine creation of the world and its eternal purpose. The Father carefully designed this world, and He meticulously built it through His Son, Jesus Christ.[2] This world was not an accident of nature. He created it spiritually before He created it physically,[3] and He patterned it after other worlds previously formed.[4] Although we do not know the exact mechanisms and processes by which He created it, we know the Lord will reveal these things at some point.[5] All its

---

2. See Genesis 1; Moses 2; Abraham 4.
3. See Moses 3:5.
4. See Moses 1:33–38; Abraham 3:12,17.
5. See Doctrine and Covenants 101:32–34.

elements (the mountains, hills, rivers, streams, oceans, and so on) are here for our benefit. They are beautiful and meant to be enjoyed and to give us joy!

All living things have the injunction to "fill the measure of their creation." In the temple, we learn that the Lord created each living thing in this mortal world for a specific purpose, and the Father wants them all to achieve that purpose. Men and women have a divine destiny. They are individuals with God-given talents and abilities.[6] They, too, must fulfill their ultimate purpose. The admonition to "fill the measure of their creation"[7] is also an invitation to develop and use our specific gifts and talents to their fullest.

Children of God have the delegated responsibility to take care of the earth. In the temple, we learn that the Father charges each of us with the responsibility to keep this world beautiful, wisely use its resources, and do nothing to damage it or anything in it. We received the role of lead stewards over the entire earth. It is ours to subdue and to care for.[8] Regarding available resources, we have the promise that "the earth is full, and there is enough and to spare"[9] if we faithfully discharge these duties.

We must work to subdue mortality. We can only overcome the adverse effects of the Fall by hard work and diligence. This statement is true temporally and spiritually. Both the Father and the Son model for us the need to work. Said the Savior, "The Father worketh hitherto, and I work."[10] The temple models the need for work through the efforts of patrons and ordinance workers. The scriptures abundantly teach the value of and need for work to accomplish our eternal objectives while living in a fallen, mortal world. The Lord commands,

---

6. See Romans 12:4–8.
7. Doctrine and Covenants 88:19.
8. See Genesis 1:26–28; 2:15.
9. Doctrine and Covenants 104:17.
10. John 5:17.

"Cease to be idle," [11] and "Thou shalt not idle away thy time." [12] In the temple, we also learn the value and blessing of work and effort. As President Nelson has taught, "The Lord loves effort." [13]

The Sabbath is an eternally important day of rest. In the scriptures and the temple, we learn that the Father and Son set a precedent for allocating a period of rest when they completed the creation and organization of the world. [14]

The word for this period in Hebrew was *shabat* and in English *sabbath*, meaning "to rest from labor." The record says He "sanctified it." [15] The Hebrew word translated in English as "sanctified" is *qadash*, meaning "to set apart as holy." Thus, this day of rest was considered sanctified and holy—a day set apart from the rest.

The Lord codified this need to sanctify the Sabbath when He included the command to "remember the Sabbath day, to keep it holy" [16] as part of the original Ten Commandments. In the latter days, He renewed this command to "offer up [our] sacraments upon my holy day," "with thanksgiving, with cheerful hearts and countenances." [17]

Ultimately, the Sabbath will become a "delight" [18] if we keep it faithfully. We will receive precious blessings from its observance. We will remain "unspotted from the world" [19] and will receive "the fulness of the earth." [20]

Why would the Lord provide us a Sabbath and then command us to keep it? We learn the Sabbath was "made for man, and not man for the sabbath." [21] Why is it made for us?

---

11. Doctrine and Covenants 88:124.
12. Doctrine and Covenants 60:13.
13. Joy D. Jones, "An Especially Noble Calling," Conference Report, April 2020.
14. See Genesis 2:2; Abraham 5:2.
15. Genesis 2:3 Abraham 5:3.
16. Exodus 20:8.
17. Doctrine and Covenants 59:9–16.
18. See Isaiah 58:13–14.
19. Doctrine and Covenants 59:9.
20. Doctrine and Covenants 59:16.
21. Mark 2:27.

First, in its most practical sense, the Sabbath provides spiritual, physical, and mental rest and respite because the Lord knew we would need it. The rigors of the world would tire us out, and the Sabbath gives us a day of rest and renewal.

Second, it establishes a sign of His covenant relationship with His people.[22] Through covenants, He can bless us if we choose to make and then keep them. In this way, He could bless us and still preserve our agency.

Third, keeping the Sabbath day holy is a test of our agency because we must interpret this commandment for ourselves. The Mosaic law dictated specific actions. However, the higher gospel law is less prescriptive and more descriptive, enabling agency and opening greater blessings.

Fourth, the Sabbath breeds meekness and humility as we prayerfully consider how we might faithfully keep it. These traits come as we willfully submit our will to His on this sacred day and put aside our wants and needs.

How do we keep the Sabbath day holy? To simplify our approach, President Russell M. Nelson has taught,

> How do we hallow the Sabbath day? In my much younger years, I studied the work of others who had compiled lists of things to do and things not to do on the Sabbath. It wasn't until later that I learned from the scriptures that my conduct and my attitude on the Sabbath constituted a sign between me and my Heavenly Father. With that understanding, I no longer needed lists of dos and don'ts. When I had to make a decision whether or not an activity was appropriate for the Sabbath, I simply asked myself, 'What sign do I want to give to God?' That question made my choices about the Sabbath day crystal clear..[23]

Our Sabbath day observance is a simple yet powerful way to bring the Spirit into our lives and to draw closer to and become like our Heavenly Parents.

---

22. See Ex. 31:13–17.
23. Russell M. Nelson, "The Sabbath Is a Delight," Conference Report, April 2015.

The Lord and His servants perform important saving work in each geography and each age of the earth. In the temple, we are shown the progress of men and women through the early periods of this earth and their progression during that time. The scriptures also document the Father's dealings with His children across multiple geographies and across time, from the beginning until now.[24] Through the temple's portrayal, we learn principles that can be used at any time but are most especially needed when we meet to give an accounting to the Savior. Temple ordinances symbolize the progression of an individual as he or she grows and matures spiritually.

Heaven and earth will eventually come together when this earth is renewed. The temple is a place where heaven and earth come together. As scholar Hugh W. Nibley explained, "[In the temple] all time and space come together; barriers vanish between this world and the next; between past, present, and future."[25] The temple is also considered the "navel," where heaven brings nutrition to earth.[26] The temple feeds us individually and feeds the Church more broadly each time we attend. Therefore, the temple is a great symbol of what will eventually occur when the Lord converts the earth into a celestial sphere. It is also a symbol of what will happen to us when He finally resurrects, renews, and grants us celestial glory.

QUESTIONS TO CONSIDER

1. What did you learn about the divine creation of this world during your last temple visit? How does that understanding help you appreciate and care for the earth?

---

24. See Doctrine and Covenants 20:11–12.
25. Hugh W. Nibley, *Mormonism and Early Christianity* (Salt Lake City: Deseret Book, 1987), 368.
26. "The Jews speak of the temple as the navel, the emphallos, of the earth, the very place that heaven brings nutriment to earth" (Truman G. Madsen, *The Temple: Where Heaven Meets Earth* [Salt Lake City: Deseret Book, 2008], 36–37.)

2. In what way does the temple and its ordinances teach you about work and effort? How can these principles bless you and others?

3. How can your temple covenants help you keep the Sabbath day holy? How can keeping this commandment help you grow spiritually?

NOTES AND INSIGHTS

_____

_____

_____

_____

_____

_____

_____

_____

_____

_____

Chapter 13

The Eternal Family

"When you come to the temple you will love your
family with a deeper love than you have ever felt
before. The temple is about families."

—Richard H. Winkel[1]

This chapter covers the doctrine of the family, which is core to the purpose of the temple and is embedded in all its teachings. The family unit is the eternal unit. Together with family members, we receive blessings, navigate difficulties, and support and love each other on our eternal journey.

Personal Application: Aaron and Julie

We love our little family. We have two wonderful children who bless our lives immensely. Because Aaron and I were married in the temple, we know that these two precious children will be with us for eternity. We genuinely believe in that promise.

Our marriage is the key to continuing our family unit throughout the eternities. We are not perfect, but we are progressing. In our marriage and relationship, we have become better disciples of Christ. We show love, kindness, and forgiveness one

---

1. Richard H. Winkel, "The Temple Is About Families," Conference Report, October 2006.

to another. Our covenant marriage has given us the strength to endure hard things and the ability to become more like our Heavenly Parents.

Our family has been crucial to navigating our life's difficulties. Whenever someone in our family faces hard things, we come together to support and love one another. When we experience successes, we all rejoice together. Our covenant family relationship has been the tie that binds us together and connects us to God.

The family's role is central to the plan of salvation, and marriage is central to the family. The restored gospel of Jesus Christ teaches that the family is the central organizing unit of eternity. The family is the vehicle through which the Father's choicest blessings are delivered to all His children. It is here that we develop godly characteristics; it is here that we learn to live covenants; it is here that we build eternal companionships and relationships.

The significant problems in life are not just solved *by* the family; they are solved *through* the family. It is the means by which we navigate the troubled waters of this fallen mortal world. The Lord knew that we would face myriad opposition, challenges, difficulties, and heartbreaks in mortality. Our families and their imperfect members are the perfect way to endure those problems well. Founded on love, patience, and understanding, families are our means of mercy, healing, and support.

The temple's ordinances confirm marriage between a man and a woman is ordained of God according to His law and is the center point of the family. Sister Julie B. Beck, a former Relief Society General President, has taught,

> The Creation of the earth was the creation of an earth where a family could live. It was a creation of a man and a woman who were the two essential halves of a family. It was not about a creation of a man and a woman who happened to have a family. It was intentional all along that Adam and Eve form an eternal

family. It was part of the plan that these two be sealed and form an eternal family unit. That was the plan of happiness.[2]

A healthy marriage leads to a healthy family. The temple shows us the importance of and the proper approach to joint decision-making and equal partnership between a husband and wife in the family. A husband and wife are indeed to "cleave" to one another and become one.[3] They are to do all things and make all decisions together. We also learn their specific and individual roles in the family, each of which is customized to his or her divine nature and destiny.

The sacred marriage relationship teaches us about the eternal relationship of our Heavenly Parents. It prepares us to become like them as we willingly trade our individual lives for our married and family lives. Thus, marriage is the highest, most developmentally significant step in our eternal progression while in mortality.

We need a binding action by the sealing keys of the holy priesthood for marriage and family relationships to persist into eternity. The temple ordinance of eternal marriage specifically promises us via the priesthood keys that the sacred marriage relationship and the divine family relationship will persist beyond the grave if both participants keep their covenants.

We learn the eternal truth that the emotional connection spouses feel toward each other or the emotional connection parents feel toward children will not be enough to create an eternal family unit. A sealing ordinance by keys of the priesthood followed by a lifetime of righteously living those covenants creates this eternal bond. Moreover, daily acts of love, kindness, and courage by individual family members deliver the practical blessings that the sealing ordinance offers.

Our emotive family connections are necessary but insufficient to have an eternal family. Why? Anything in mortality not ordained and

---

2. Julie B. Beck, "Teaching the Doctrine of the Family," Seminaries and Institutes of Religion Broadcast, August 4, 2009, accessed February 6, 2021, https://www.theredheadedhostess.com/assets/uploads/2010/08/2009–beck-teaching-the-doctrine-of-the-family__eng.pdf.

3. Genesis 2:24.

ratified by God or His authorized servants cannot persist, however much we as humans would want it to last.[4]

Without the sealing authority, we may feel the same *emotions* for our family on the other side, but we will not have the same *obligations*. We cannot fully understand the limitations that will prevent us from progressing together if we are not sealed together as an eternal family.

Does this mean that family members who have not been sealed by the holy priesthood will not love each other or care for each other in the next life? No! However, it means without the sealing covenant of eternal marriage, the commitment, commandment, and compulsion to sire and to rear a righteous posterity is no longer in force when the day of this life is over.

This commandment was the first law given to Adam and Eve: to multiply and replenish the earth. Without the binding power of the sealing ordinance, this law is no longer in force after this life, and this situation limits our eternal progression.

Unfortunately, some people experience barriers related to receiving the eternally binding covenant of marriage in this life. We learn they will be denied no blessings, despite these imperfections. On this topic, Elder D. Todd Christofferson of the Quorum of the Twelve has taught,

> Some of you are denied the blessing of marriage for reasons including a lack of viable prospects, same-sex attraction, physical or mental impairments, or simply a fear of failure that, for the moment at least, overshadows faith. Or you may have married, but that marriage ended, and you are left to manage alone what two together can barely sustain. Some of you who are married cannot bear children despite overwhelming desires and pleading prayers. . . . With confidence we testify that the Atonement of Jesus Christ has anticipated and, in the end, will compensate all deprivation and loss for those who turn to Him. No one is predestined to receive less than all that the Father has for His children.[5]

---

4. See Doctrine and Covenants 132:7.
5. D. Todd Christofferson, "Why Marriage, Why Family," Conference Report, April 2015.

Specifically, to sisters who are denied marriage or who have experienced divorce, Joseph Fielding Smith encouragingly taught,

> You good sisters, who are single and alone, do not fear, do not feel that blessings are going to be withheld from you. . . . If in your hearts you feel that the Gospel is true, and would under proper conditions receive these ordinances and sealing blessings in the temple of the Lord, and that is your faith and your hope and your desire, and that does not come to you now, the Lord will make it up, and you shall be blessed— for no blessing shall be withheld. The Lord will judge you according to the desires of your hearts when blessings are withheld, and He is not going to condemn you for that which you cannot help.[6]

Finally, for those parents who have wayward children—whose hearts are broken because their children have departed from the right way—we are promised that the sealing ordinances will have the power to draw them back at some point. Elder Orson F. Whitney taught,

> You parents of the wilful and the wayward! Don't give them up. Don't cast them off. They are not utterly lost. The Shepherd will find his sheep. They were his before they were yours— long before he entrusted them to your care; and you cannot begin to love them as he loves them.
>
> They have but strayed in ignorance from the Path of Right, and God is merciful to ignorance. Only the fulness of knowledge brings the fulness of accountability. Our Heavenly Father is far more merciful, infinitely more charitable, than even the best of his servants, and the Everlasting Gospel is mightier in power to save than our narrow finite minds can comprehend.

---

6. Joseph Fielding Smith, "Elijah the Prophet and His Mission," a discourse delivered under the auspices of the Genealogical Society of Utah, Oct. 13, 1920, at the Assembly Hall, Temple Block, Salt Lake City, Utah, *Utah Genealogical and Historical* Magazine, Vol. XII, No. 1, January 1921, 20, accessed February 6, 2021, https://babel.hathitrust.org/cgi/pt?id=njp.32101042555944&view=1up&seq=8.

The Prophet Joseph Smith declared—and he never taught more comforting doctrine—that the eternal sealings of faithful parents and the divine promises made to them for valiant service in the Cause of Truth, would save not only themselves, but likewise their posterity. Though some of the sheep may wander, the eye of the Shepherd is upon them, and sooner or later they will feel the tentacles of Divine Providence reaching out after them and drawing them back to the fold. Either in this life or the life to come, they will return.

They will have to pay their debt to justice; they will suffer for their sins; and may tread a thorny path; but if it leads them at last, like the penitent Prodigal, to a loving and forgiving father's heart and home, the painful experience will not have been in vain. Pray for your careless and disobedient children; hold on to them with your faith. Hope on, trust on, till you see the salvation of God.[7]

The binding and sealing ordinances of the temple truly give us hope in an imperfect world that the Savior, through the power of His infinite Atonement, will make all imperfections related to the family right in the eternities.

Women are fully contributing participants in every aspect of the plan of salvation, as exemplified by the valiancy of Mother Eve. The story and doctrine of the temple would be incomplete without the story of women. Eve was the crowning achievement of all creation, and she is symbolic of all women. A woman is the daughter of a Heavenly Mother, with all the divine potential to become like Her. Eve was an equal partner or a "help meet" for her husband, as are all women for their husbands.

The Hebrew roots translated as "help meet" are (1) *Ezer*, meaning to save, to be strong, or to do something for another that they cannot do for themselves, and (2) *K'negdo*, meaning equal to or even with.[8]

---

7. Orson F. Whitney, Conference Report, April 1929, 110.
8. Beverly Campbell, Eve and the Choice Made in Eden, 24–25.

Thus, she was Adam's equal in strength, beauty, and power. She gives him the strength he did not have on his own, which is the intended role of all women in the family and the world.

Although the rest of the Christian world criticizes Mother Eve for the choice made in Eden, we learn in the restored gospel of Jesus Christ and the temple the necessity of this choice and the great blessings that have come because of it.[9] Eve, with her unique gifts and divine insight, discerned what needed to occur to fulfill the command that she and Adam received to "multiply and replenish the earth."[10] The only way to keep this first command was to transgress the second by eating the forbidden fruit.

As the "mother of all living,"[11] her unique capability was to carefully consider and then courageously choose the higher of the two laws she received, which higher law would bring life into the world. "The woman saw that the tree was good . . . a tree to be desired to make her wise."[12]

Eve saw a higher way—the family way—and helped her family choose it. Of this courageous act, she insightfully said, "Were it not for our transgression we never should have had seed, and never should have known good and evil, and the joy of our redemption, and the eternal life which God giveth unto all the obedient."[13] All mothers have this precious gift of aligning to God's divine will when faced with difficult choices, and they bless the world by it.

This noblest role of "mother" is much more expansive than we might ordinarily consider. Sister Sheri L. Dew, a former counselor in the Relief Society General Presidency and a sister who never married, insightfully taught,

When we understand the magnitude of motherhood, it becomes clear why prophets have been so protective of woman's most sacred role. While *we* tend to equate motherhood solely

---

9. See 2 Nephi 2:22–25; Moses 5:10–11.
10. Genesis 1:28.
11. Genesis 3:20.
12. Moses 4:12.
13. Moses 5:11.

with maternity, in the Lord's language, the word *mother* has layers of meaning.

Of all the words they could have chosen to define her role and her essence, both God the Father and Adam called Eve "the mother of all living"—and they did so *before* she ever bore a child. Like Eve, our motherhood began before we were born. Just as worthy men were foreordained to hold the priesthood in mortality, righteous women were endowed premortally with the privilege of motherhood.

Motherhood is more than bearing children, though it is certainly that. It is the essence of who we are as women. It defines our very identity, our divine stature and nature, and the unique traits our Father gave us.[14]

Eve is symbolic of all women and their vital role in giving life and strength—physical, mental, emotional, and spiritual—to their family, the Church, and the world around them.

Without the gifts, talents, and fully accepted participation by women in the family and the kingdom of God, all our efforts would be restricted, and our progress would be halted. Of the divine role of women, President Gordon B. Hinckley taught,

Woman is God's supreme creation. Only after the earth had been formed, after the day had been separated from the night, after the waters had been divided from the land, after vegetation and animal life had been created, and after man had been placed on the earth, was woman created; and only then was the work pronounced complete and good.

Of all the creations of the Almighty, there is none more beautiful, none more inspiring than a lovely daughter of God who walks in virtue with an understanding of why she should do so, who honors and respects her body as a thing sacred and divine, who cultivates her mind and constantly enlarges the horizon of her understanding, who nurtures her spirit with everlasting truth. God will hold us accountable if we neglect

---

14. Sheri L. Dew, "Are We Not All Mothers?" Conference Report, October 2001.

His daughters. He has given us a great and compelling trust. May we be faithful to that trust.[15]

Sister Elaine S. Dalton, a former Young Women General President, likewise taught of the great role of all women in Heavenly Father's plan:

We are daughters of God. We are not ordinary women. We were born to be leaders. Yet the world would make you think you are insignificant or that there is a certain mold you have to fit. And, according to the world, if you don't fit that mold, you really don't have any influence and you really aren't of any worth.

That is an absolute lie. Every one of us on the earth today has been reserved to be here now during the winding up scenes in preparation for the Savior's Second Coming. We have been prepared and chosen and reserved to be here now, and that is a divine compliment.[16]

Women have been and will always be critical to the Father's plan to save all His children. We must all remember and cherish this sacred truth.

Having a loving husband and father in the family unit and a righteous priesthood holder in the kingdom of God is essential. Adam was created as the first man, and he is emblematic of all righteous husbands, fathers, and priesthood holders. The temple amply models righteous manhood. These portrayals show us how Heavenly Father acts with His family and His kingdom, so we do the same. A man is the son of a Heavenly Father, with all the divine potential to become like Him.

15. Gordon B. Hinckley, "Our Responsibility to Our Young Women," *Ensign*, September 1988.
16. Elaine S. Dalton, *No Ordinary Women* (Salt Lake City: Deseret Book, 2016), 21–22.

In the world, the husband is often harsh and condescending, and the father is often absent or abusive. The gospel of Jesus Christ teaches, and the temple shows, how a loving, active husband and father operates and presides. He demonstrates care and concern for his wife and seeks input and complete collaboration with her. He shows forth obedience and submission to His God, reverence for the sacred, and meek confidence in authorized servants. President Howard W. Hunter counseled the brethren,

> A man who holds the priesthood accepts his wife as a partner in the leadership of the home and family with full knowledge of and full participation in all decisions relating thereto. . . . Presiding in righteousness necessitates a shared responsibility between husband and wife; together you act with knowledge and participation in all family matters. . . . Tenderness and respect—never selfishness—must be the guiding principles in the [marriage] relationship between husband and wife.
>
> Each partner must be considerate and sensitive to the other's needs and desires. Any domineering, indecent, or uncontrolled behavior in the [marriage] relationship between husband and wife is condemned by the Lord. . . . A man should always speak to his wife lovingly and kindly, treating her with the utmost respect. Marriage is like a tender flower, brethren, and must be nourished constantly with expressions of love and affection.[17]

To the men of the Church, President Monson further warned, "Men, take care not to make women weep, for God counts their tears."[18]

Priestcrafts abound in mortality.[19] In contrast, the temple shows how a righteous priesthood holder operates. He shuns evil and seeks

---

17. Howard W. Hunter, "Being a Righteous Husband and Father," Conference Report, October 1994.
18. Thomas S. Monson, "That We May Touch Heaven," Conference Report, October 1990.
19. A priestcraft is a person receiving money for his spiritual work—for preaching the gospel and delivering ordinances of salvation.

that which is holy. He selflessly serves, seeking no monetary reward for his sacred gospel knowledge. He seeks God through revelation. He is tender and loving in his ministry, yet bold and courageous in the face of adversity and temptation.

These are the intended traits and characteristics of righteous men. They are modeled after our Heavenly Father and Jesus Christ, our perfect exemplar of what a righteous man can and should be.

God gave us the eternal commandment to multiply and replenish within the bounds of a family under God's law. With the family at the center of His plan, the Father has emphasized and protected its creation and continuity. He commanded us to "be fruitful, and multiply, and replenish the earth."[20] This mandate to multiply and replenish is an eternal commandment, one only His heirs will continue to obey into the eternities. Procreative desires and capabilities are the part of the human experience that enables families to form. Their divine purpose is to bring children into a family, where spouses are married according to God's law.

These feelings and desires are deeply personal, and they affect us intensely. They intertwine with our *mortal* identity, and they can affect our understanding and perception of our *eternal* identity and destiny as sons or daughters of God. The source or type of our procreative instincts is generally less relevant than what we choose to do with them. Therefore, the Father's covenant children must understand, accept, and live within the divinely appointed bounds for their procreative abilities.

The law of chastity stands as the Father's standard of behavior for His children, and we covenant to obey it in the temple. It states we only use our procreative ability within His law of marriage. This law is a firm boundary on the path to godliness because creating life is our Heavenly Parents' most sacred ability. It exists to guard virtue, a mighty enabler of spiritual power.

Unfortunately, the powerful emotional nature of procreative feelings and their ties to our identity tempt us to misuse them. Our fallen

20. See Genesis 1:22, 28; Moses 2:22, 28; Abraham 4:22, 28.

bodies and minds work against us, which requires us to intentionally discipline and control our procreative appetites. When left unchecked and unbounded, these desires can become carnal "lusts of the flesh"[21] rather than feelings with divine purpose.

The adversary actively entices us to use our procreative ability outside of God's law. [22] He preys upon our carnal desires and any personal weaknesses to morally destroy us and thwart the plan of salvation, which centers on the eternal family. He will capitalize on any opportunity to tempt us to violate virtue, a most serious sin.[23] He does not care about the pain or agony he causes us or our loved ones.

He will use any means possible to his advantage to carry out his plan of distraction, distress, and destruction through assaults on the law of chastity. The adversary will tempt us to break our covenants, devalue commandments, or mistreat those who fall short of the Lord's standards for any reason. He will strive to create contention, discord, and a lack of empathy in all aspects of this sacred law.

The solution to all these difficulties is Jesus Christ and His infinite Atonement. When we have sincerely done all that is possible to align to the will of God, seek peace and healing when issues occur, and show love and empathy toward any heart-wrenching or seemingly impossible situation related to this law, we must trust that the Savior will somehow make any undesirable or unfair issues right at some point. Our submissiveness to God and our love of neighbor in these cases is the key to our salvation and theirs. Elder D. Todd Christofferson of the Quorum of the Twelve lovingly taught,

> In reality, the best way to help those we love—the best way to love them—is to continue to put the Savior first. If we cast ourselves adrift from the Lord out of sympathy for loved ones

---

21. 1 Nephi 22:23.
22. Violations of the law of chastity include "adultery" or "anything like unto it," such as pornography or any other lewd or immoral thoughts, words, or acts. (See Doctrine and Covenants 59:6.) However, victims of sexual abuse, rape, incest, or other sexual offenses and exploitation have not violated the law of chastity. They are victims, not sinners, and they should be treated with kindness, compassion, empathy, and love as we help them heal.
23. See Alma 39:5.

who are suffering or distressed, then we lose the means by which we might have helped them. If, however, we remain firmly rooted in faith in Christ, we are in a position both to receive and to offer divine help.

If (or I should say when) the moment comes that a beloved family member wants desperately to turn to the only true and lasting source of help, he or she will know whom to trust as a guide and a companion. In the meantime, with the gift of the Holy Spirit to guide, we can perform a steady ministry to lessen the pain of poor choices and bind up the wounds insofar as we are permitted. Otherwise, we serve neither those we love nor ourselves.[24]

Each person's path to healing and peace when coping with any issues concerning morality is unique and deeply personal. It takes patience and wisdom throughout the process for all involved. Perhaps, like the father and mother of the prodigal, we will recognize that healing may have already begun even as the person is still away from home in "a far country," distanced from loving associates or the Lord's standards. Or, perhaps like the prodigal's brother, we may need healing for our hearts and attitudes as we seek to accept someone who faces an unexpected path or makes an unwise choice.

Our wisdom and compassion for the healing process—which includes patience and understanding during a period when the person is symbolically or literally "yet a great way off" and feels disconnected—may be the very act that opens the door for the person to reconnect again. Kindness and acceptance can pave the way for an eventual, joyous return at some point, wherein we may find the person spiritually "alive again."[25]

As we patiently and kindly accept others' realities and challenges, it can be hard to discern when changes are occurring within a person currently away from the gospel path. We must simply keep loving and

---

24. D. Todd Christofferson, "Saving Your Life," Church Educational System Fireside, September 14, 2014, accessed February 26, 2021. https://www.churchofjesuschrist.org/broadcasts/article/ces-devotionals/2014/01/saving-your-life?lang=eng.

25. See Luke 15:11–32 for the parable of the prodigal son.

ministering to them and hold tight to the gospel ourselves. By continuing to burn our light as brightly and lovingly as possible, we will enable a person trying to kindle his or her light and return, repent, and heal in the process.

QUESTIONS TO CONSIDER

1. What did you learn about the family during your last visit to the temple? How can that understanding help you in your current family situation?
2. What does the temple teach us about the equal partnership between husband and wife? In what way is that understanding applicable to you?
3. How can your temple covenants help you love and serve your family?

NOTES AND INSIGHTS

_____

_____

_____

_____

_____

_____

_____

_____

_____

Section 3

Divine Helps and Warnings

We are not alone on our journey through mortality. Our Heavenly Parents provided us with divine helps to aid us on our voyage. They include His priesthood power and keys, His Church organization, and His divine truth. Most importantly, they include personal revelation, His direct voice to us. Through His servants and His voice, the Father also gives us divine warnings to keep us out of danger.

When we were married in the Atlanta Georgia Temple in 1992, we could have never imagined the trek that would lie ahead. Full of faith—yet young and naïve—we embarked on what is now a thirty-year journey.

Although we knew we were on our own, we never felt alone. In addition to our families, we always had loving Church members, leaders, and friends to assist us when we needed it. We felt protected by our temple covenants and the divine truths of the gospel, which enabled us to solve our problems in a way that was consistent with the Father's will. We leaned on our patriarchal blessings—which our Father specifically designed for each of us. They acted as a personal compass when we seemed lost amid the confusion of the moment.

Most importantly, we consistently sought our Heavenly Father in prayer, especially when our most heartbreaking moments came upon us. His still, small voice guided and comforted us through it all. Our family saying is, "When times are tough, the Bujnowskis go to their knees." This approach has gotten us through the may ups and downs of our family life.

The doctrine and principles of this section will remind you of your divine helps and warnings. Pay particular attention to them. Learn from the temple about them. They will guide you, empower you, and keep you safe on life's arduous and often spiritually dangerous journey. Successfully navigating it will depend on your willingness and your preparedness. Remember, you are not alone!

Chapter 14

Priesthood Power

"To receive the blessings, power, and promises of the priesthood in this life and the next is one of the great opportunities and responsibilities of mortality."

—Neil L. Anderson[1]

This chapter covers priesthood power, which is taught extensively during temple ordinances. Temple power is priesthood power for both men and women. So, we must learn how to access and use it from the temple. Here, we summarize the Lord's glorious priesthood power, given to men and women through ordinances and ordinations.

Personal Application: Julie

Aaron and I have served in many leadership positions in the Church. In each, we were blessed as we served under the direction of those with priesthood keys. Both of us have felt the priesthood power that comes from these callings.

When Aaron was called as our bishop, I watched those keys in action. They enabled him to lead our ward, giving him strength

---

1. Neil L. Anderson, "Power in the Priesthood," Conference Report, October 2013.

and insight far beyond his natural gifts and talents. When he was released after serving as a bishop twice, we both watched those keys pass to two other worthy men who served with distinction.

When I was called to serve as stake Relief Society president, I was set apart by a loving stake president with priesthood keys. He delegated authority for me to preside over the stake Relief Society. I felt the priesthood power that came with my call. I will share one experience of how it manifested in my service.

Shortly after I was called, the stake president gave me the assignment to organize a stake women's conference, which had not been done in over a year due to the pandemic. I began to ponder and pray about what the Lord wanted us to do for our sisters and what theme we should have for the conference. Then, we met as a presidency to discuss how to organize the conference.

After counseling together, I suggested to my presidency that I felt impressed that the theme should be "Peace Through Christ." I had considered many options, but my mind kept turning back to this specific theme. I asked them to share their thoughts. My first counselor, who was the previous president's secretary, told me that this was the theme that they had considered before the pandemic. This experience was a witness to me of the spiritual power that comes when we are set apart and operate under the keys of the priesthood.

As we learn to use the priesthood authority and power we receive through ordinances, ordinations, or callings, we can find great blessings and do a great deal of good in the kingdom and the world.

The priesthood is the power of God held by mortals, which gives us the power to become like Him. In the temple, we learn about, experience, and receive the fulness of the priesthood.[2] "The priesthood is the power and authority of God. 'It has always existed and will continue to exist without end.'[3] Through the priesthood, Heavenly Father

---

2. See Doctrine and Covenants 124:28.
3. See Alma 13:7–8; Doctrine and Covenants 84:17–18.

accomplishes His work 'to bring to pass the immortality and eternal life of man.'[4] God grants authority and power to His sons *and* daughters on earth to help carry out this work."[5]

The priesthood has been delegated to humankind to enable them to carry out His work of salvation. It allows God's children to act on His behalf in that great effort. It gives them the power to administer the ordinances of salvation and comfort and act in His name as they serve in positions of authority. The priesthood is the power to bring the Atonement's blessings—via sacred ordinances and personal ministering—to all Heavenly Father's children, including ourselves.

Like so many other things, the priesthood is a gift of God and a privilege to hold. It carries solemn obligations and responsibilities. The scriptures describe, and the temple portrays, God the Father, His Son, and their authorized delegates using priesthood authority to bless the lives of God's children.

The Lord gave us two priesthoods: the Aaronic and the Melchizedek.[6] The Aaronic Priesthood is the "lesser priesthood" and "has power in administering outward ordinances."[7] Its power and authority are "to hold the keys of the ministering of angels, and to administer the outward ordinances, the letter of the gospel, the baptism of repentance for the remission of sins."[8] Offices of the Aaronic Priesthood include bishop, priest, teacher, and deacon. Its ordinances are baptism and the sacrament. Although Aaronic Priesthood holders had always performed baptisms outside the temple, in 2017, the First Presidency announced that Aaronic Priesthood holders could also perform baptisms for the dead within temples, once again placing them in a position to carry out temple ordinances and "offer again

---

4. Moses 1:39.

5. General Handbook, Chapter 3: Priesthood Principles, Introduction, accessed February 6, 2021; emphasis added, https://www.churchofjesuschrist.org/study/manual/general-handbook/3–priesthood-principles?lang=eng#p1.

6. See Doctrine and Covenants 107.

7. Doctrine and Covenants 107:14.

8. Doctrine and Covenants 107:20.

an offering unto the Lord in righteousness"[9] as was done during the time of the Old Testament.

The Melchizedek Priesthood holds the "right of presidency, and has power and authority over all the offices in the church."[10] Its power and authority are "to hold the keys of all the spiritual blessings of the church."[11] Its offices include Apostle, Seventy, patriarch, high priest, and elder. Its saving ordinances are confirmation and receipt of the Holy Ghost and the temple ordinances of endowments and sealings. Its enabling and comforting ordinances are the blessing and naming of children, blessings of healing, and the dedication of homes, places of worship, and graves.

During the period of the Great Apostasy, the Lord took the priesthood from the earth. However, the priesthood was restored to Joseph Smith. He and Oliver Cowdery received the Aaronic Priesthood under the hand of John the Baptist, the last legal administrator of this priesthood before Christ, on May 15, 1829.[12] In June of 1829, Joseph and Oliver received the Melchizedek Priesthood and were ordained Apostles by Peter, James, and John, who were the last legal administrators of this priesthood after Christ's death and resurrection.[13]

The restoration of the priesthood opened the ability for all God's children to receive all the ordinances of salvation, including sacred temple ordinances.

We receive priesthood authority and power with an oath and covenant. Individuals who are faithful in "obtaining" priesthood authority and power do so with an "oath and covenant."[14] We should recognize that individuals "obtain" this oath and covenant through both *ordinances* and *ordinations*.

---

9. See Doctrine and Covenants 13 and Doctrine and Covenants 128:24. This modern "offering" is the record of our dead. The administrative change in 2017 fulfilled the prophecy in Doctrine and Covenants 13 that the sons of Aaron would "offer again an offering unto the Lord in righteousness."
10. Doctrine and Covenants 107:8.
11. Doctrine and Covenants 107:18–19.
12. See Doctrine and Covenants 13.
13. See Doctrine and Covenants 18:9.
14. Doctrine and Covenants 84:33–42.

Ordinances enable a person to obtain priesthood power via a covenant. *Ordinations* to priesthood offices enable a person to deliver priesthood power via a priesthood ordinance. This statement does not diminish those who hold priesthood offices. However, it elevates all who receive priesthood ordinances. Therefore, all God's covenant children have access to the precious blessings that stem from the priesthood's oath and covenant through ordinances *and* ordinations.

The Savior makes the *oath*. He gives a sure promise to deliver the blessings associated with the faithful receipt and use of the priesthood and its ordinances. An oath is a one-way assurance that He will not break His promise. In ancient times, an oath was a most serious commitment, one which the person would rather die than break. The Savior demonstrated His level of commitment to His oath by giving His life to fulfill it.

The Savior and the persons receiving priesthood authority both make a *covenant*, where promises are made on both sides of the agreement. The recipients promise to receive the priesthood worthily and to magnify it. The Savior promises to sanctify them, to renew their bodies, and to have them become the sons of Moses and Aaron and the seed of Abraham. The ultimate promise received by those who bear the priesthood is to receive "all [the] Father hath."[15]

We must keep our priesthood covenants to partake of these precious blessings. Of keeping priesthood covenants, President Spencer W. Kimball taught, "One breaks the priesthood covenant by transgressing commandments—but also by leaving undone his [or her] duties. Accordingly, to break this covenant one needs only do nothing."[16]

Priesthood keys direct the work of salvation. Temple ordinances portray how those with presiding keys operate, both personally and through delegated ministers who act on their behalf. We should understand what these keys are and how they operate because they are how all blessings—including the most precious blessings of the temple—are unlocked for us.

---

15. Doctrine and Covenants 84:38.
16. Spencer W. Kimball, *Teachings of Spencer W. Kimball*, 497.

Priesthood keys are distinct from the priesthood itself. From the *General Handbook* of the Church we learn, "Priesthood keys are the authority God has given to priesthood leaders to *direct* the priesthood on behalf of God's children. The use of all priesthood authority in the Church is directed by those who hold priesthood keys. (See Doctrine and Covenants 65:2). Under the direction of the President of the Church, priesthood leaders receive keys so they can preside in their areas of responsibility."[17]

As with physical keys, priesthood keys lock and unlock blessings. We observe the role of those with priesthood keys in the administration and approval of all ordinances and in the administration of the Church. Priesthood keys are central to the work of the temple.

The keyholder oversees and organizes the work of salvation, allowing members to serve under his direction by receiving delegated authority to act on his behalf. Revelation always comes through the appropriate line of priesthood authority and keys, either directly or through delegation.

Priesthood keys were restored to the earth in our dispensation through the prophet Joseph Smith on April 3, 1836, in the Kirtland Temple. In a marvelous revelatory event, four glorified beings appeared to Joseph and Oliver, each holding specific keys required for the work of salvation to progress.

Jesus Christ: The Savior was the first to appear to Joseph Smith and Oliver Cowdery.[18] Jesus Christ holds all keys of the priesthood, of which He delegates specific keys to men. Two keys that He uniquely holds are the keys of resurrection and redemption. He has not entrusted these keys to us, but He stands alone with them as our final Judge and Advocate.

---

17. General Handbook, Chapter 3: Priesthood Principles, 3.4.1 and 3.4.1.1, Priesthood Keys; emphasis added, accessed February 6, 2021, https://www.churchofjesuschrist.org/study/manual/general-handbook/3-priesthood-principles?lang=eng#p1. Section 3.4.1.1 delineates which Church leaders hold keys.
18. See Doctrine and Covenants 110:2–10.

Moses: Moses appeared to Joseph and Oliver, bringing the spirit of Moses or the spirit of missionary work with him.[19] He committed to them the keys of the gathering of Israel or the keys to preach the gospel. These are the keys of missionary work, which are used to open nations of the earth for the preaching of the gospel and to oversee the work of missionaries throughout the world.

Elias: A personage identified as Elias appeared to Joseph and Oliver, bringing the spirit of Elias or the spirit of ministering and caring for others with him.[20] He committed to them the keys to ministering and administering the Abrahamic covenant or the new and everlasting covenant. These keys hold the power to administer the priesthood, its covenants, and its ordinances in every nation.

Elijah: The Old Testament prophet Elijah appeared to Joseph and Oliver, bringing the spirit of Elijah or the spirit of temple and family history work with him.[21] He committed to them the keys of sealing, a long-prophesied event.[22] The sealing keys provide the power to "bind on earth . . . [and] in heaven."[23] Through these keys all ordinances are given eternal validity and that all declarations by the prophet are honored by God.[24] Most importantly, these are the keys whereby families are sealed for time and all eternity.

---

19. See Doctrine and Covenants 110:11.
20. See Doctrine and Covenants 110:12. This Elias may have been Noah. See Joseph Fielding Smith, *Answers to Gospel Questions* (Salt Lake City: Deseret Book, 1960), Vol. 3, 138–141.
21. See Doctrine and Covenants 110:13–15.
22. In the first divine message to Joseph Smith after the First Vision, Moroni quoted from Malachi 3 and 4, stating, "I will reveal unto you the Priesthood, by the hand of Elijah the prophet" (see JS—H 1:36–39). This visit by Elijah in Kirtland fulfilled this long-awaited prophecy.
23. Matthew 16:19.
24. For example, when Elijah (see 1 Kings 17:1) or Nephi (see Helaman 10:6) sealed the heavens, causing a famine.

Many Church members do not fully understand the extensiveness of the sealing power. President Joseph Fielding Smith taught, "Elijah came to restore to the earth, by conferring on mortal prophets duly commissioned of the Lord, the fulness of the power of priesthood. This priesthood holds the keys of binding and sealing on earth and in heaven of *all* the ordinances and principles pertaining to the salvation of man, that they may thus become valid in the celestial kingdom of God."[25]

In the final verse of Doctrine and Covenants 110, Elijah tells Joseph Smith and Oliver Cowdery, "The keys of this dispensation are [now] committed into your hands."[26] These keys are still in force because they were passed from Joseph to the Quorum of the Twelve. Upon Joseph's death, the quorum directed the affairs of the Church until a new prophet was set apart.

This process has continued in an unbroken chain from that time until today, allowing the work of salvation to continue without interruption. This work will go on until "the great and dreadful day of the Lord"[27] when the Savior Himself will return to preside over the work personally.

We experience a priesthood "order" in the Lord's kingdom.
We experience order and organization to the bestowal, usage, and management of the priesthood by Heavenly Father's children. This defined approach is called "the order of the priesthood." Priesthood order follows the order of heaven. We learn and observe this order in the temple.

The process and order in the temple and the Church's administration follow this pattern. Ordinances are approved and delivered in an orderly way. We also observe this order in the following administrative pattern: A person with keys gives direction, others act, and those who act provide a report to those in authority.

---

25. Joseph Fielding Smith, *Doctrines of Salvation* (Salt Lake City: Bookcraft, 1955), 2:117; emphasis added. See also Helaman 10:4–7.
26. Doctrine and Covenants 110:16.
27. Ibid.

The specified method of conducting priesthood affairs includes the following activities: the use of keys to direct the work; the use of counselors in a presidency; the use of councils made of both men and women in directing the work; issuing directions; returning and reporting of results; the common consent required to undertake actions that use priesthood keys, including ordinations and callings; and the use of specific language and actions to perform priesthood ordinances.

The word "order" also refers to a group of people with a social relationship. Men and women have that relationship in their respective quorums and classes. Adult sisters enjoy each other's company in the Relief Society, which sister leaders govern with priesthood authority and using priesthood principles. The same is true of young women in their classes, which are overseen by youth sister leaders who receive priesthood authority when they are set apart in their callings. Men and young men belong to quorums, where they have a fraternal relationship. This association provides unity and deep connections, uplifting and sustaining us in our walk through life.

Both men and women can access priesthood authority and power as part of the "order of the priesthood." Both men and women administer ordinances in the temple, teaching us the reality of access to priesthood authority and power for both, albeit uniquely delivered to and administered by each gender based on their distinct, divine roles in the plan of salvation.

Both men and women receive priesthood power and authority (1) when they receive all the *ordinances* of salvation, but most importantly when they receive the ordinances of the temple, and (2) when they are given authority and set apart to *callings* administered under the keys of the priesthood. However, ordinations to priesthood offices and calls to positions with priesthood keys are only given to men. The relatively limited number of callings with priesthood keys are extended only when individuals are called of God by one who has authority.[28]

---

28. See Hebrews 5:4; Ex. 28:1; Articles of Faith 1:5.

Regarding *ordinances*, Doctrine and Covenants 84:20 states, "In the ordinances, the power of godliness is manifest."[29] This "power" is priesthood power, which all covenant children receive with each successive ordinance, beginning at baptism and culminating in the ordinances of the temple. Because men *and* women receive ordinances, they both access priesthood power through them.

Regarding callings, Elder Dallin H. Oaks, current President of the Quorum of the Twelve, stated, "We are not accustomed to speaking of women having the authority of the priesthood in their Church callings, but what other authority can it be?"[30] Because men *and* women receive callings, they both access priesthood power through them.

Specifically, in the temple, we receive the "fulness of the priesthood."[31] What is this *fulness*? Priesthood fulness is that both men *and* women can obtain *all* the highest priesthood ordinances and covenants that allow them to receive the blessings of the Atonement of Jesus Christ, become like their Heavenly Parents by developing all godly traits, and eventually return to live with them again.

Priesthood "fulness" cannot exist without men and women *both* receiving priesthood authority and power in the temple, which is a culmination of covenants they make as ordinances are received along the covenant path. The covenant path is the priesthood path for both men and women.

Sister Sheri L. Dew, a former counselor in the Relief Society General Presidency, taught us of the glorious blessing both men and women have of accessing priesthood power:

> The blessings of the priesthood are available to every righteous man and woman. We may all receive the Holy Ghost, obtain personal revelation, and be endowed in the temple, from which we emerge "armed" with power. The power of the priesthood heals, protects, and inoculates all of the righteous against the powers of darkness. Most significantly, the fulness

---

29. The definition of "manifest" is "clear or obvious." (See "Manifest," *Oxford Dictionary of English* [Oxford: Oxford University Press, 2010], 1077).
30. Dallin H. Oaks, "The Keys and Authority of the Priesthood," Conference Report, April 2014.
31. See Doctrine and Covenants 124:28.

of the priesthood contained in the highest ordinances of the house of the Lord can only be received by a man and woman together.[32]

President Russell M. Nelson recently expanded and deepened these thoughts when he said,

> Every woman *and* every man who makes covenants with God and keeps those covenants, and who participates worthily in priesthood ordinances, has direct access to the power of God. Those who are endowed in the house of the Lord receive a gift of God's priesthood power by virtue of their covenant, along with a gift of knowledge to know how to draw upon that power. The heavens are just as open to women who are endowed with God's power flowing from their priesthood covenants as they are to men who bear the priesthood.[33]

Because the temple is the conduit of the fulness of priesthood power for all God's children, men and women should prioritize its importance by receiving its ordinances and regularly returning to renew their covenants.

The order of the priesthood in the Church and the hierarchy of organizations in the world are distinct. In the world, the concepts of hierarchy and ascendency prevail, while in the Lord's kingdom, the concepts of order and duty prevail. This difference is no more apparent than in the temple, where we uniformly call all patrons "brother" and "sister," and no one seeks titles or ascendency. The temple is, indeed, a house of order.

In a hierarchical system, a person receives more power the higher he or she ascends. Dominance is its currency. The world arranges itself this way in governments, businesses, and volunteer organizations. Greater responsibility, position, and authority mean greater

---

32. Sheri L. Dew, "It Is Not Good for Man or Woman to Be Alone," Conference Report, October 2001.
33. Russell M. Nelson, "Spiritual Treasures," Conference Report, October 2019; emphasis added.

rewards and recognition for the individual. Therefore, we commonly witness people who attempt to ascend for more significant positions and power in worldly organizations.

In contrast, the Lord emphasizes and recognizes *order*, not *hierarchy*, in His kingdom. Humility, duty, and worthiness are His focus, and charity is His currency. The Savior organized His Church in an orderly way, with leaders over groups of people and with individuals given various callings and assignments, the design of which benefits the kingdom and provides opportunities for personal growth. The Lord expects every person to learn and do his or her duty.[34] And He expects all to be worthy.

Although various callings have broader and narrower spans of responsibility, we do not ascend or descend when moving between callings, meaning the Lord does not recognize or reward callings differentially. To put it another way, although we find a *hierarchy of responsibility* in mortality for people who serve in the structure of the Church, we will not find a *hierarchy of reward* in eternity.

Priesthood power and spiritual blessings are available to all men and women with callings, irrespective of the broadness or narrowness of his or her responsibilities. The Primary teacher and the bishop each receive spiritual blessings, even if the scope of their callings is different. Despite these structural differences, there should always be order and respect among and between callings and assignments. We model this divine approach in the administration and delivery of ordinances in the temple.

This arrangement in the kingdom is vastly different from that of the world. As the Lord taught through Isaiah, "For as the heavens are higher than the earth, so are my ways higher than your ways, and my thoughts higher than your thoughts."[35]

Order in the Lord's kingdom engenders submissiveness to God and humility in our ministry. We recognize that we are all merely branches of the True Vine and that we must all work within our specified sphere of influence and simultaneously respect the authority of others. As Elder Dallin H. Oaks, current President of the Quorum

---

34. See Doctrine and Covenants 107:99.
35. Isaiah 55:9.

of the Twelve, taught, "We do not 'step down' when we are released, and we do not 'step up' when we are called. There is no 'up or down' in the service of the Lord. There is only 'forward or backward,' and that difference depends on how we accept and act upon our releases and our callings."[36]

As we remember this order in the Church, we will be more able to serve and be served with authenticity and love, each person knowing his or her duties and appreciating those of others.[37]

Priesthood order in the kingdom and in the family are different. We use priesthood and priesthood keys in the administration of the Church. We also use priesthood authority and power in the family as modeled in the temple, but the approach in the family is distinct from the procedure in the Church.

The Church has presiding authorities through whom revelations and decisions come. They counsel with and receive input from others, but the final decision always rests upon the presiding officer at each Church level.

In the family, the father and mother are equal partners in all decisions and actions related to their family unit. Although the Lord encourages a father to "preside . . . in love and righteousness,"[38] his authority is *not* independent of his wife, *nor* is it superior to hers. He only has authority *with* her; he does not have authority *above* her. They must make joint decisions and act together as one.

This divine partnership in the family is taught abundantly in the ordinances of the temple. Of the equal role of men and women in the family, Elder Dallin H. Oaks, current President of the Quorum of the Twelve, has also taught,

> The concept of partnership functions differently in the family than in the Church. The family proclamation gives this beautiful explanation of the relationship between a husband

---

36. Dallin H. Oaks, "The Keys and Authority of the Priesthood," Conference Report, April 2014.
37. See Doctrine and Covenants 107:99.
38. "The Family: A Proclamation to the World," *Ensign*, Nov. 1995, 102.

and a wife: While they have separate responsibilities, "in these sacred responsibilities, fathers and mothers are obligated *to help one another as equal partners.*"[39]

President Spencer W. Kimball said this: 'When we speak of marriage as a partnership, let us speak of marriage as a full partnership. We do not want our LDS women to be silent partners or limited partners in that eternal assignment! Please be a contributing and full partner.'[40] . . . When priesthood authority is exercised in that way in the patriarchal family, we achieve the 'full partnership' President Kimball taught.[41]

The family runs best when both parents share in all decision-making, jointly seeking guidance from the Lord to manage its affairs. This three-way partnership—the father, the mother, and the Lord—provides the spiritual power and safety needed to navigate life's dangerous waters.

Righteous choices are needed to receive priesthood authority and power. Priesthood authority and power operate on the principle of agency and worthiness, as modeled in the temple where all blessings are contingent on our faithfulness. The Lord requires a choice to seek priesthood ordinances and ordinations from one who has authority,[42] and then a person must exhibit righteous choices to qualify for and be worthy of his or her ordinances or ordinations.

Similarly, when a person in authority calls someone and offers him a position with priesthood keys, this person must make choices to qualify as being worthy of that authority. Anyone who is extended and accepts a calling or assignment using those keys must similarly be worthy of that call to receive its associated priesthood authority and power. This principle applies to both men and women called to positions of authority.

---

39. Ibid; emphasis added.
40. Spencer W. Kimball, *The Teachings of Spencer W. Kimball*, 315.
41. Dallin H. Oaks, "Priesthood Authority in the Family and in the Church," Conference Report, October 2005; emphasis added.
42. See Abraham 1:1; Hebrews 5:4.

The *authority* of the priesthood and the *power* of the priesthood are different. The *authority* of the priesthood is the right and the privilege to represent our Heavenly Father in the administration of the gospel and its ordinances. The *power* of the priesthood is the spiritual strength to carry out those responsibilities effectively.

By analogy, the *authority* of the priesthood is like an engine with all its powerful moving parts that can make the machine function, and the *power* of the priesthood is like fuel that provides the energy and the vitality to allow the engine to exert its strength.

We *administer* the gospel with the authority of the priesthood, and we *minister* to individuals with the power of the priesthood. Through our *authority* we deliver the ordinances of the gospel and administer in our various callings, but through our spiritual *power* we realize and deliver the benefits of the Atonement.

The Lord testified, "The redemption of Zion must needs come by *power.*"[43] Redemptive power in the Atonement comes through power in the priesthood. Of this priesthood power, Elder Boyd K. Packer, formerly of the Quorum of the Twelve, taught,

> We have done very well at distributing the authority of the priesthood. We have priesthood authority planted nearly everywhere. . . . But distributing the authority of the priesthood has raced, I think, ahead of distributing the power of the priesthood. The priesthood does not have the strength that it should have and will not have until the power of the priesthood is firmly fixed in the families as it should be.[44]

Elder Packer's statement is not an *indictment* but an *invitation* to bring down power in the priesthood to our families and our Church units. When we realize that this power comes in and through the Atonement of Jesus Christ, we will be infinitely more able to call its blessings down on our families and on our friends and neighbors.

Men and women alike share the responsibility to actualize the power of the priesthood. Both need this power to call down the

---

43. Doctrine and Covenants 103:15; emphasis added.
44. Boyd K. Packer, "The Power of the Priesthood," Conference Report, April 2010.

blessings that flow from gospel ordinances, and both require an additional measure of power as they minister in their priesthood responsibilities and callings.

How do we receive this priesthood power?

The Lord taught this "one lesson"—the most important of all lessons regarding priesthood power—to us in the Doctrine and Covenants.[45] *The one lesson is this: The rights of the priesthood[46] are inseparably connected with the powers of heaven[47] and these powers are only handled or controlled using the "principles of righteousness."*[48] Put simply, a person cannot receive the power of the priesthood unless he or she is worthy of it. That worthiness comes as he or she keeps the commandments and develops the character traits of godliness. These characteristics are the key to priesthood power.

Choices that exhibit any amount of unrighteous dominion will cause a priesthood holder, persons who have received a priesthood ordinance, or a person called to a calling to lose priesthood power.[49] When they give in to natural man or natural woman tendencies or temptations, they cease becoming like their Heavenly Parents, and they start becoming "carnal, sensual, and devilish."[50] When this happens—even in the smallest amount—then "the heavens withdraw themselves; the Spirit of the Lord is grieved; and when it is withdrawn, Amen [or farewell] to the priesthood or the authority [and power] of that [person]."[51]

May we all become and remain worthy to receive priesthood power via ordinances, ordinations, and callings!

---

45. See Doctrine and Covenants 121:34–46.
46. The "rights of the priesthood" are the ordinances, calls, or ordinations that men and women receive.
47. The "powers of heaven" are the spiritual gifts, godly traits, and spiritual influence that come from God.
48. The "principles of righteousness" are the authentic acts of humble and meek compliance with the commandments of God, with the voice of the Spirit, and with the direction given by those with priesthood keys.
49. See Doctrine and Covenants 121:34–38.
50. Alma 42:10.
51. Doctrine and Covenants 121:37.

QUESTIONS TO CONSIDER

1. What did you learn about priesthood and priesthood power during your last visit to the temple? How can that understanding help you receive this power in your life?
2. How do your temple covenants provide you with priesthood power? How can you keep from losing it? In what ways can you use priesthood power to bless the lives of others?
3. What can you learn from the temple about priesthood in the family? How can you use your priesthood power to bless your family this week?

NOTES AND INSIGHTS

_____

_____

_____

_____

_____

_____

_____

_____

_____

_____

Chapter 15

Our Discipleship and Social Relationships

"Discipleship brings purpose to our lives so that rather than wandering aimlessly, we walk steadily on that strait and narrow way that leads us back to our Heavenly Father."

—James E. Faust[1]

This chapter covers our discipleship and our social relationships, tenets of the temple and the gospel that sustain and enable us on life's journey. *What* we do as disciples of the living Christ and *who* we do it with are paramount to our eternal progress. Disciples of Christ are His followers. They seek to do as He did and, ultimately, become as He is. As we strive to be His faithful disciples, our social relationships sustain us, even as our personal efforts propel us forward along the covenant path.

Personal Application: Aaron and Julie

We have always enjoyed the friendship and fellowship of the members in our wards and stakes. They have strengthened our Christian discipleship and encouraged us to be faithful to our

---

1. James E. Faust, "Discipleship," Conference Report, October 2006.

covenants. Whether we are together at service projects, chili cook offs, dances, or other activities, we found joy in our Church relationships. Most memorable are the times we could be together at the temple.

On one occasion, we went to the Dallas Texas Temple with our ward's Primary—one of many times we had this experience.[2] The children walked around the building, and then they went inside to hear a message from a member of the temple presidency. They sat on steps inside the foyer while he spoke to them. When he was finished, they sang "I Love to See the Temple."[3]

The hearts of everyone who heard were touched. Patrons arriving for their temple worship stopped to listen to these sweet children sing. Their song was a testimony of the Lord's house. We all loved them even more because of this experience. All were edified during this tender activity. Among others we've participated in, this event fulfills the injunction to "meet together oft,"[4] which encourages our faithful discipleship.

These types of social experiences in our church units enable us to have our "hearts knit together in unity and in love one towards another,"[5] which bless us all.

The temple encourages and enables faithful discipleship. Disciples of Jesus Christ are His followers—those who seek to act like Him and, ultimately, become like Him. He or she is "a follower of Jesus Christ who lives according to Christ's teachings."[6] Temple covenants allow us to voluntarily bind ourselves to Him, a defining characteristic of discipleship. Temple teachings help Jesus's disciples to apply His teachings in our everyday lives, slowly enabling us to develop the character of Christ.

---

2. Story used with permission.
3. "I Love to See the Temple," *Children's Songbook* (Salt Lake City: The Church of Jesus Christ of Latter-day Saints, 1989), 95.
4. Moroni 6:5.
5. Mosiah 18:21.
6. "Disciple," *Guide to the Scriptures*, 2013.

All promised blessings depend on our faithfulness. We receive myriad promised blessings as we make covenants, both in and out of the temple. We also receive them in our patriarchal blessings. All are contingent upon our faith, faithfulness, and willing compliance with their associated covenants and commandments. Our agency is the key to unlock these precious blessings.

The Father has great appreciation and gratitude for our sincere and diligent efforts. When disciples strive to live righteously, the scriptures teach that they are "favored of God."[7] The word "favored" expresses Heavenly Father's gratitude for our sincere efforts. Through simple means, the temple also portrays the Father's appreciation for our obedience, diligence, and quick observance of His commands, either directly or through authorized servants.

Ultimately, He will express His gratitude directly to us when we appear before Him at the Final Judgment. If we are faithful, He will tell us, "Well done, thou good and faithful servant: thou hast been faithful over a few things, I will make thee ruler over many things: enter thou into the joy of thy lord."[8]

Prayer delivers spiritual power to us when sincerely and worthily expressed. Prayers are a form of worship for faithful disciples and any child of God because they draw us close to our Father in Heaven. They are the means for expressing gratitude, petitioning favors and blessings, and seeking guidance. Prayer is a conduit of spiritual power.[9] The prayer that is part of temple ordinances is mighty. It models the power we can generate when we accompany prayer by sincere, heartfelt expression and worthy actions.

In those temple prayers, we unify in our love for one another, our gratitude for blessings received, our expressed desire for blessings needed, and our joint recollection of covenants made and kept, all of which is a gate to open the powers of heaven. Submitting the names

---

7. 1 Nephi 17:35.
8. Matthew 25:21.
9. See Doctrine and Covenants 21:7.

of persons with needs for those prayers is another way to minister to the living through the ordinances for the dead.

Personal Application: Aaron and Julie

A faithful couple in one of our wards taught us the power of prayer.[10] This good couple tried many years to have natural-born children. However, they were unsuccessful. They had attempted every possible medical technique to enable them to have children of their own, but all those efforts were to no avail.

Undeterred by these difficulties, they moved forward in faith and decided to adopt children. They adopted a wonderful, active boy. After a few years, they were fortunate to adopt another wonderful little boy. They were delighted to have two boys that they could love and raise in righteousness. They felt very blessed for that opportunity. They had peace in the direction of their family, despite their difficulties in growing it.

Then, a miracle occurred. Without any medical interventions, the wife became pregnant. This blessing was completely unexpected! They were excited, but they were also wary, as they had a previous pregnancy that had not progressed to completion.

However, this time the pregnancy progressed without complications. After nine months, they gave birth to a healthy baby girl with red hair, just like her father. She was a sweet, precious miracle to this faithful family.

We can vividly recall the first day they came to church with their little daughter. It was a fast Sunday. After the bishopric turned over the meeting for testimonies by members, the mother was the first one to stand up. She walked up to the front of the chapel, gently holding her little girl in her arms, wrapped in a soft white blanket.

We waited with anxious anticipation for her testimony. We knew of her many years of faithfully praying, working, and waiting to have a natural-born child. We also knew of her faithful

---

10. Story used with permission.

discipleship in our ward. The Spirit was powerful even before she began to speak.

She walked up to the podium and said these six simple yet very powerful words: "I know that God answers prayers." She closed in the name of Jesus Christ and then sat down.

There was not a dry eye in that congregation. We had witnessed a modern-day miracle. After many years of anxious anticipation, their day of blessings had come. Because they also had their two adopted sons to bless their lives, theirs was an abundant day indeed.

After they moved away, we found out that this sweet family had a second natural-born child, another girl. Following so many years of waiting for blessings, there now seemed to be, as Isaiah prophesied, "no end" to the increase in peace for this family.[11]

The power of prayer, fueled by faith, led to these precious blessings. Our loving Heavenly Father offers each of us this power when we sincerely pray to Him.

The Father's work is one eternal round. The work of the Father in perfecting His children is eternal; it continues and repeats itself in each successive generation. His work is one eternal round.[12] For example, we are reminded in the temple and in the scriptures that this world is one of many the Father has created, that He will forgive again and again when we seek repentance after we sin, and that an adversary has provided opposition in every phase of existence and in every world the Father has created.

Repetition is another part of the Lord's eternal round. We go to the temple and experience the same ordinances repeatedly. We receive the sacrament each week, we read the scriptures multiple times, and we repent often. Repetition enhances and reinforces the principles we are to learn.

Yet another meaning of "one eternal round" is that we can start keeping one divine principle, and it will always lead to all others.

---

11. See Isaiah 9:7.
12. See Alma 7:20; 37:12.

Therefore, we can start by keeping any principle of godliness, and eventually, we will keep them all as we progress. This principle connects all truths together, so our discipleship becomes complete.

If a person wants to concentrate on faith, for example, his or her study and diligence will lead to all other principles of the gospel. If that person focuses on temple work, he or she will eventually feel the need to share the gospel, to live a more worthy life, and, eventually, do all other things the Lord commands. Therefore, we should not fret over the starting point of our discipleship. With faithfulness to one true doctrine or principle, all of them will eventually come into view.

We experience gospel sociality both now and in the eternities. The interaction, brotherhood and sisterhood, and friendly and kindly relationships between God's children outside of the family unit are important and invigorating. They bring joy and support to us. We experience this sociality in our stakes, wards, and branches, and we see it enhanced in the temple, where individuals who are worthy and who have left behind unkind thoughts and feelings interact and serve together in a holy environment. In these relationships, we "fellowship" one with another. This sociality will exist among us in the eternities.[13]

Fellowship means we commune together, have a social relationship, enjoy one another's company, strive to work together for a common cause, become friends and brothers and sisters in the gospel and in the Church, teach each other, minister to and serve one another, and love one another. These earthly relationships are a model of the sociality we will have in the celestial kingdom,[14] which is a holier and more refined social relationship.

Priesthood quorums and Relief Societies are organizations designed to amplify and systematize our fellowship and to encourage unity. They provide opportunities for interaction and structures for support. Ultimately, they assist us in becoming more like our Heavenly Parents. Sister Julie B. Beck, a former Relief Society General President, taught,

---

13. Helaman 6:3.
14. See Doctrine and Covenants 130:2.

Quorums and Relief Societies are to teach our Heavenly Father's sons and daughters and inspire them to prepare for the blessings of eternal life. Our Father sees the potential of his sons and his daughters to be family leaders. Therefore, everything we do in quorums and Relief Societies is to help the Lord with his mission of preparing his children for the blessings of the eternal life he envisions for us. In these settings we are meant to learn how to become part of our Heavenly Father's eternal family. . . . The quorum and the Relief Society should help us become who our Heavenly Father needs us to become.[15]

The prophet Joseph Smith taught, "By union of feeling we obtain pow'r with God."[16] Our fellowship one with another in our quorums, classes, and activities is how we develop those unifying feelings one towards another. When we do, we receive the power to become like Him.

QUESTIONS TO CONSIDER

1. How do your temple covenants strengthen your discipleship? How does your discipleship enable you to draw spiritual power from your temple covenants?
2. In what ways can worshipping in the temple enable you to build social relationships with members of your branch, ward, or stake?
3. How can you use the power of prayer to address a challenge you are currently facing?

15. Julie B. Beck, "Why We Are Organized into Quorums and Relief Societies," BYU Devotional address, Jan. 17, 2012, Brigham Young University, Provo, UT, accessed Jan. 31, 2021, https://speeches.byu.edu/talks/julie-b-beck/why-we-are-organized-into-quorums-and-relief-societies/.
16. Joseph Smith, "Minutes and Discourse, 9 June 1842," 61, *Joseph Smith Papers*, https://www.josephsmithpapers.org/paper-summary/minutes-and-discourse-9–june-1842/1.

NOTES AND INSIGHTS

_____

_____

_____

_____

_____

_____

_____

_____

_____

Chapter 16

Divine Truth, Authorized Ministers, and Revelation

"The more closely you follow divine guidance, the greater will be your happiness here and for eternity— moreover, the more abundant your progress and capacity to serve."

—Richard G. Scott[1]

In this chapter, we will discuss the relationship between truth, divine ministers, and revelation, which are points of doctrine that facilitate what we take from the temple. The temple teaches pure truth and enables us to recognize it, either via authorized ministers or through the Holy Ghost. Divine guidance via the Holy Spirit is among our most precious blessings. It leads us to truth and helps us receive blessings for ourselves and others.

The temple is a house of revelation. We must understand how revelation works so we can recognize the voice of the Lord and distinguish it from any false voices we may encounter. We can witness great blessings when we follow His voice. Sadly, we can miss opportunities

---

1. Richard G. Scott, "How to Obtain Revelation and Inspiration for Your Personal Life," Conference Report, April 2012.

or even be led astray if we do not. We designed this chapter to help you on your journey to acquire, understand, and apply truth.

Personal Application: Aaron

When I was a young Boy Scout living in Savannah, Georgia, I had an experience that taught me the importance of divine guidance. While camping, we went for a hike to do some exploring, and I became separated from the other boys. I wandered through the forest, trying to find my way back to camp. However, after unsuccessfully navigating through the trees and underbrush, I did not find any trails or roads. I was lost.

Scared, I knelt and prayed for guidance. The impression came to reach into the pouch on my belt. I felt a compass that I had forgotten I had. I was impressed to travel in a specific direction along one of the compass points. I had no idea if this was the right direction. However, I acted on the feeling, and I eventually found a road that led back to my camp. I was grateful to feel the prompting of the Spirit and then to have the faith to trust in His guidance, even when I was unsure of exactly where I should go.

In the years that have followed since that time, I have had many other experiences of hearing and responding to the voice of the Spirit. Each time I trust His promptings, His voice becomes more apparent, and my faith in the path He lays out for me grows.

One such event occurred when I was serving as bishop. One evening while praying before going to bed, I received the strong impression to text a member of our ward who had been going through some difficulties.

I interrupted my prayer to send her a quick text. I wrote, "Your son told me that things are tough right now. You're in my prayers."

She replied, "Thank you. I'll take your prayers; mine don't seem to be working right now."

I replied, "They are working. That's why the Lord told me to reach out to you. He knew that you were having trouble hearing Him, but he knew you could hear me. Be patient through it all." The next day, she sent me this text:

Thank you so much. This is a tender mercy that I will write down and remember. Last night as I was praying, I'm afraid that I had a total meltdown. I told Him that I felt like He wasn't with me anymore even though these last couple of weeks have been as hard as any in the last year.

I was upset at Him and impatient. But I asked for a tender mercy to know He was there—something that I could actually hear and not have to try and interpret. It was very shortly after that when you texted. So, once again, thank you so much for being the answer to my prayers.[2]

I feel so blessed to have been an instrument in the Lord's hand in blessing this good sister. If I had not acted on the voice of the Spirit when I was a Boy Scout and then acted on His voice many times afterward, I would not have been prepared to help this sister in the very moment of her distress.

The temple testifies of pure truth and warns against partial truth. The temple establishes that pure, unvarnished truth exists and that its source is Heavenly Father. The scriptures also teach that pure or absolute truth—things "as they really were, really are, and really will be"—exists.[3]

The Lord invites us to find and embrace it. He warns against mixed truths, where the natural man or woman's ideas blend with eternal truths found in the scriptures and the words of living prophets. Living prophets have also warned against the false concept of relative truths, or the philosophy that what is true is based only on perception and perspective.

The existence of absolute truth requires a Savior's existence because, as imperfect humans, we can never fully live them. We need an Advocate and Sanctifier to plead our cause and offer us freedom

---

2. Story shared with permission.
3. Jacob 4:13.

from spiritual bondage when we fail to live according to those truths. Without Him, we would be forever lost and outside of the presence of the Father.

Perhaps some argue for relative truth because they don't fully understand the infinite and eternal nature of the Atonement of Jesus Christ and the power it gives Him to offer us redemption when we violate absolute truths. Each of us must do our best to seek out, discover, and live according to the absolute truths of God, seeking forgiveness when we fail and ministering to others who, likewise, fail in their efforts.

We must seek out, discover, and heed divine truth. The temple invites us to seek divine truth or spiritual knowledge. Doing so, we will be protected from the sophistries of mortal men and women and from the designs and deceptions of devils. Joseph Smith taught, "Knowledge does away [with] darkness, suspense and doubt, for where knowledge is there is no doubt nor suspense nor darkness. . . . In knowledge there is power."[4]

How do we acquire spiritual knowledge or divine truth? Elder Richard G. Scott, formerly of the Quorum of the Twelve, taught, "To acquire spiritual knowledge and to obey it with wisdom, one must: [1] In humility, seek divine light. [2] Exercise faith in Jesus Christ. [3] Hearken to His counsel. [4] Keep His commandments. As spiritual knowledge unfolds, it must be *understood, valued, obeyed, remembered,* and *expanded*."[5]

We should never forget that although truth is better than error, not all truth will lead us back to our Heavenly Parents. We can discover much truth by scientific and secular means. The Lord encourages us

4. Joseph Smith, *The Words of Joseph Smith*, 183. See also Doctrine and Covenants 130:19.
5. Richard G. Scott, "Acquiring Spiritual Knowledge," Conference Report, October 1993, emphasis original.

to "seek ye out of the best books words of wisdom,"[6] which includes every good and worthy subject.[7]

However essential and factual these secular truths are, they will not enable us to reach our eternal destiny of becoming more like our Heavenly Parents, as will divine truths from God. As sons and daughters of God, we are commanded to seek out and live eternal truth, enabling and enhancing our spiritual progression. Becoming distracted by the flood of myriad secular facts enabled by the information economy will cause us to be "ever learning, and never able to come to the knowledge of [divine] truth."[8]

Therefore, we should always give priority to seeking divine truth or spiritual knowledge from trusted sources. As encouraged and portrayed in temple ordinances, the outcome of our diligent searching will be to find ourselves and to find our God.

Doctrine and principles are never-changing, while applications and practices are ever-evolving. In the temple, we learn eternal doctrine and principles. Because the Father and Son are eternal,[9] the doctrine and principles they teach are eternal and *never* change. These doctrine and principles are divine truths. Hence, He can say, "I am the same, yesterday, today, and forever."[10] He is the same in three ways: (1) His character, characteristics, and attributes never change; (2) He always has the same purpose, "to bring to pass the immortality and eternal life of man;"[11] and (3) He teaches doctrine and principles that never change.[12]

However, what *does* change are the applications, practices, or policies required to use His divine nature, carry out His holy purpose, and

---

6. Doctrine and Covenants 88:118.

7. See Doctrine and Covenants 88:78. Here, the Lord encourages us to study chemistry, biology, astronomy, geology, geography, political science, history, law, and every other secular subject.

8. 2 Timothy 3:7.

9. See Moses 7:35.

10. See 2 Nephi 27:23; 29:9.

11. Moses 1:39.

12. Never changing doctrine and principles include agency, truth, atonement, baptism, repentance, grace, mercy, judgment, and so on.

use His sacred doctrine and principles across time, cultures, and geographies. These adjustments allow for inspired customization of how truth is delivered for specific needs or circumstances. This approach enables Him to simultaneously ground His plan in eternal doctrine and adapt His actions to particular needs. Elder David A. Bednar of the Quorum of the Twelve has taught,

> A *gospel doctrine* is a truth—a truth of salvation revealed by a loving Heavenly Father. Gospel doctrines are eternal, do not change, and pertain to the eternal progression and exaltation of Heavenly Father's sons and daughters. ... Gospel doctrines answer the question of *"why?"* . . .
>
> A *gospel principle* is a doctrinally based guideline for the righteous exercise of moral agency. Principles are subsets or components of broader gospel truths. Principles provide direction. Correct principles always are based upon and arise from doctrines, do not change, and answer the question of *"what?"* . . . A principle is not a behavior or a specific action. Rather, principles provide basic guidelines for behavior and action. . . .
>
> *Applications* are the actual behaviors, action steps, practices, or procedures by which gospel doctrines and principles are enacted in our lives. Whereas doctrines and principles do not change, applications appropriately can vary according to needs and circumstances. Applications answer the question of *"how."*[13]

The temple sets forth divine, unchanging doctrine and principles and provides an allegorical and symbolic model for their application. The scriptures also repeatedly show how men and women of faith apply unchanging doctrine and principles to the unique and changing circumstances of their lives. We, too, must apply these divine doctrine and principles from the scriptures in our own lives.

For example, the presentation, processes, and policies of the temple endowment and sealing ordinances have been modified over time to ensure enhanced application for the contemporary time in which God's

---

13. David A. Bednar, *Increase in Learning* (Salt Lake City: Deseret Book, 2011), 151–156; emphasis added.

children live. However, the basic covenants, doctrine, and principles of those ordinances have not changed. Thus, the Father can weave the never-changing thread of gospel doctrine into the ever-changing fallen mortal world in which his sons and daughters must live.

We grow and become like Him in the experience of discovering and holding onto eternal doctrine and then making inspired and specific applications. When we encounter a unique situation, generally, we do not need new doctrine. We most likely need a new application of established doctrine, which we must prayerfully discover and act upon. The ability to do this consistently and effectively across myriad experiences is the foundation of wisdom. The choice to do this without a complete understanding or with partial knowledge is the foundation of faith.

The temple is our pattern for learning and applying doctrine and principles, wisely and with faith. Much of the inspiration that may come to us in the temple is likely to be guidance on how to *apply* gospel doctrine or principles to a specific issue or situation we currently face. Thus, the insights gained are most often new, personal applications suited to our particular circumstance.

We must only receive truth from God's authorized ministers. The temple reinforces the role of God's authorized ministers, individuals whom He has sent to deliver truth. The Father has always sent His servants to bring the truth to His children so they can have confidence that what they receive and learn is true and pure. We remain safe as we seek truth from them.

Authorized ministers will be sent of God, called by those with the keys of the priesthood in the proper line of authority, and publicly and openly sustained by the body of the Church by "common consent."[14] Anyone claiming authority outside of those requirements is not properly authorized to "preach the gospel and administer in the ordinances thereof."[15]

We could call this principle the "gate principle." The Lord taught us this principle in the Doctrine and Covenants: "For verily I say

---

14. Doctrine and Covenants 26:2.
15. Articles of Faith 1:5.

unto you, that he that is ordained of me shall *come in at the gate* and be ordained as I have told you before, to teach those revelations which you have received and shall receive through him whom I have appointed."[16]

True messages and instructions come through this authorized gate. Revelation from God will always flow through this proper line of priesthood authority. Any impressions for areas outside of a person's stewardship are not from God.

A prophet is a spokesman, someone who speaks on God's behalf. He is the Lord's "gate" for the whole world. The Hebrew word for prophet is *nabi*, which means "one who is called."[17] In Greek, the word for prophet is *prophetas*, which also means "to speak on behalf of." Our modern prophet is the Lord's current spokesman.

We also sustain our current prophet as a "seer" and a "revelator." A seer is "a person authorized of God to see with spiritual eyes things that God has hidden from the world . . . [who] knows the past present and future."[18] A revelator makes known the mind and will of the Lord, showing things as they really are, really were, and really will be.[19]

Many voices in the world seek to lead us down various paths. When we heed the voice of the prophets or others authorized by them, we will remain safe because they know the path ahead.

We should follow the prophet to remain safe on life's path. Elder Marion G. Romney, formerly of the Quorum of the Twelve and the First Presidency, once said, "I have never hesitated to follow the counsel of the Authorities of the Church even though it crossed my social, professional, or political life."[20] As our Primary children sing, "Follow the prophet; he knows the way!"[21]

16. Doctrine and Covenants 43:7; emphasis added.
17. "Nabi," www.biblehub.com, accessed June 6, 2021, https://www.biblehub.com/hebrew/5030.htm.
18. "Seer," *Guide to the Scriptures*, 2013.
19. See Jacob 4:8, 13.
20. Marion G. Romney, Conference Report, April 1941, 123.
21. "Follow the Prophet," *Children's Songbook*, 110.

Authorized ministers find those seeking truth and help them on their journey. The temple models the actions of authorized ministers. Those whom the Lord calls to be ministers of righteousness must be diligent, loyal, and exact in their ministry. They are sent by Him to find all who seek truth. They have the special call to assist those who are wrestling with their faith or struggling with doubt and uncertainty.

As modeled in the temple, our efforts are best led by councils and presidencies to ensure spiritual safety as leaders counsel together. The temple models faithful adherence to instructions given with the need to report performance and outcomes. The salvation and healing of other sons and daughters of God depend on our unified, coordinated efforts.

In every ordinance in the temple, a helper will guide the patron through the process. This ministering duty is symbolic of the heavenly help we receive—by either seen or unseen helpers—throughout our lives. No one in the temple is left alone. All are helped at every step by friends, family members, or temple workers who love, care for, and lead them along. These actions are a pattern of divinity to provide help and guidance along the covenant path, which we will experience repeated on our spiritual journey.

We must diligently seek truth directly from God via revelation. The temple is a place of revelation. Revelation is how God makes known His will to us. It is how He communicates with us. To "reveal" is to uncover something hidden. In the case of messages from God, what is hidden is His will for us. When we need answers in our lives, revelation can make known the mind and will of God for us. Revelation is the only way to know God. As Elder Bruce R. McConkie taught, "God stands revealed or he remains forever unknown."[22]

The Holy Ghost is the means by which God speaks directly to us. He communicates with us via thoughts to our minds or positive

---

22. Bruce R. McConkie, "The Lord's People Receive Revelation," Conference Report, April 1971. See also Bruce R. McConkie, "Upon This Rock," Conference Report, April 1981.

feelings in our hearts.[23] Each of us must recognize how we "hear" His precious voice.

The Father wants us to seek Him. "Seek ye me, and ye shall live."[24] President Russell M. Nelson has emphatically pleaded,

> We live in a world that is complex and increasingly contentious. . . . If we are to have any hope of sifting through the myriad of voices and the philosophies of men that attack truth, we must learn to receive revelation. . . .
>
> In coming days, it will not be possible to survive spiritually without the guiding, directing, comforting, and constant influence of the Holy Ghost.
>
> My beloved brothers and sisters, I plead with you to increase your spiritual capacity to receive revelation. . . . Choose to do the spiritual work required to enjoy the gift of the Holy Ghost and hear the voice of the Spirit more frequently and more clearly.[25]

The temple is an amplifier of revelation, and it will help us do what President Nelson invited—to increase our spiritual capacity to receive revelation. Our spiritual safety depends on it!

Two sources of power influence the world: The Good and the Bad. The temple confirms that opposing sources of spiritual information and revelation exist in the world. One is good, and one is bad.[26] The figure on the following page shows these sources of inspiration. The Holy Ghost and the Light of Christ are good influences, and the natural man or woman and the adversary are bad influences.

---

23. See Doctrine and Covenants 8:2–3.
24. Amos 5:4.
25. Russell M. Nelson, "Revelation for the Church, Revelation for our Lives," Conference Report, April 2018.
26. See 1 Corinthians 14:10.

Good Influences

Prototype: Christ
Central Attributes: Meekness and Humility (Matthew 11:29)
"Nevertheless, not my will, but thine be done" (Luke 22:42).

Holy Ghost
- We are given the gift of the Holy Ghost after baptism.
- His companionship and guidance are contingent on our worthiness.
- He prompts us to act on things we cannot see, hear, or understand with our natural senses.
- His influence is much more expansive: He comforts, teaches, reveals, sanctifies, and empowers.
- He is a source of light.

Light of Christ
- The Light of Christ is our conscience. All sons and daughters of God are given the Light of Christ to guide them.
- This light is the influence of Christ that pulls all mankind to do good. As we do good, the Light of Christ increases. As we disobey, it diminishes.
- It will prompt us to choose the good in what we can see in front of us.
- Our conscience is a recipient of the light from Christ.

If we are not careful, it is possible to spend too much of our lives just living off the Light of Christ and never enjoying the more precious blessings of the Holy Ghost. This will put us in danger of being pulled toward the natural man and woman and the adversary.

Bad Influences

Prototype: Lucifer
Central Attribute: Pride
"Surely, I will do it" (Moses 4:1).

Natural Men and Women
- Our mortal bodies have natural appetites that oppose virtues and desires of the spiritual man or woman.
- Natural men and women are enemies to God (see Mosiah 3:19). They instinctively feel pride, anger, hatred, selfishness, fear, frustration, impatience, and so on. They are biased by their own desires.
- In many cases, inappropriate thoughts, words, or deeds are simply due to the natural man or woman.

Adversary
- The adversary is an actual being who rebelled in the premortal existence and was cast down, along with one-third of the premortal spirits.
- They continue to actively work to oppose the Father.
- He and his followers attempt to deceive and distract us through their influence, which mimics and opposes the Holy Ghost.
- They amplify the tendencies of the natural man and woman.

The natural opposition to good tries to pull us away from Jesus Christ throughout our lives.

Sources of Revelatory Influence

Understanding how to recognize and respond to the Holy Spirit and differentiate it from the Light of Christ, the feelings and biases of the natural man or woman, and the adversary's influence is key to our knowing and doing the will of the Father. Revelation is our pathway to spiritual safety in a world of myriad opposing voices.

Good Influences

Individuals who have been baptized and confirmed receive the gift of the Holy Ghost. This ordinance entitles them to the companionship and guidance of the Holy Spirit, which is a most precious gift. He leads us to Christ and all that is good.

The Holy Spirit always invites and never coerces. His promptings are gentle and mild. His voice is "a still voice of perfect mildness," as a "whisper."[27] It is a "still small voice."[28] It edifies and brings peace.

All humankind has the light of Christ. It is the source of every good and honorable act. The goodness we see in the world as individuals seek to alleviate pain and suffering, raise money for charitable causes, and behave in numerous other good and decent ways are all due to this light.

Meekness and humility are the cardinal attributes required by us to receive and discern revelation. Because of them, we submit our will to His. They generate faith, hope, and charity and enable all the virtuous and positive feelings, including peace, love, kindness, and benevolence.

Heeding the light of Christ is *good*; hearing and recognizing the voice of the Spirit is *better*; responding to the promptings and warnings of the Holy Ghost is *best*. If we spend too much time only under the good and honorable influence of the light of Christ and not the higher influence of the Holy Ghost, we may be in danger of eventually being led off the covenant path by the natural man and woman or the adversary.

---

27. Helaman 5:30.
28. 1 Kings 19:12.

Bad Influences

Mortals are "natural men and women." They are influenced by the fallen mortal world and their fallen mortal bodies. Many of our negative impressions and impulses may simply come from the natural man and woman's internal desires and not from any outside influence of the adversary.

The adversary and the spirits who were cast out with him are the strongest source of evil in our fallen world. They are real beings intent on our destruction. They are a constant source pulling us away from Heavenly Father.

Pride is a core attribute of the natural man and woman. It leads to self-gratification, pleasure-seeking, the desire for recognition, and the craving for power. It is a source of anger, jealousy, and hypocrisy. Pride is the chief barrier to divine revelation and discernment. It is centered on self instead of on God. It leads to sin, which creates a further barrier to revelation and discernment. Pride was the core trait of the adversary, and he uses it to tempt and influence men and women.

The Lord gave us a divine pattern for discerning good from evil in spiritual impressions and visitations. To assist us in discerning good from evil, the Lord has given us specific instructions in the temple and the scriptures to properly discern both *impressions* and *visitations*. *Impressions* are the thoughts and feelings we experience; *visitations* are visits from spirit beings in person or in dreams. The temple and the scriptures teach us how to discern between good and bad sources of these *impressions* or *visitations*.[29]

Impressions

Spiritual impressions can be difficult to discern because they are still and small, and they flow through the channel of emotions. Other things can prompt emotions, such as physical or emotional stimuli

---

29. See Doctrine and Covenants 8:2–3; 9:7–9; 10; 11:12–14; 28; 41; 43; 45; 46; 50; 52:14–18; 85:6; 93 for the keys to discerning impressions. See Doctrine and Covenants 129 for the keys to discerning visitations. See also 1 John 4:1–3; Moroni 7:5–17.

or hormonal triggers. Another difficulty can come in waiting for the proper message or in missing the proper message because it is fleeting, faint, or delayed. So, we must look to the patterns of discernment provided by the Lord to distinguish between these sources.

Recognizing impressions from God: The simple truth taught in the scriptures is that messages from God bring feelings of love, joy, peace, happiness, light, kindness, gentleness, faith, hope, patience, endurance, longsuffering, understanding, and every other positive feeling. They edify, uplift, and encourage and will be in harmony with the accepted revelations of the Church, will be aligned with the decisions of its constituted authorities, and will lead us to Christ and His Church.

Heavenly impressions have a divine stillness, a unique sense of calm. This stillness is His peace. The Lord taught Moroni, "Whatsoever thing persuadeth men [and women] to do good is of me; for good cometh of none save it be of me."[30] He further taught Joseph Smith that His Spirit "leadeth to do good—yea, to do justly, to walk humbly, to judge righteously; and this is my Spirit. . . . [He] shall enlighten your mind, which shall fill your soul with joy. . . . And then shall ye know, or by this shall you know, all things."[31]

Recognizing impressions from other sources: Messages from sources not of God—including our own thoughts, emotions, or biases—bring with them feelings of hatred, despair, contention, anger, sadness, darkness, unkindness, harshness, frustration, irritability, impatience, intolerance, confusion, and every other negative feeling. They drag down, degrade, and discourage and will be out of harmony with accepted revelations of the Church, will be misaligned with the decisions of its constituted authorities, and will lead us away from Christ and His Church.

Impressions from bad sources have an uneasiness about them, a lack of stillness. As Moroni taught, "Whatsoever thing persuadeth men [and women] to do evil, and believe not in Christ, and deny him,

---

30. Ether 4:12.
31. Doctrine and Covenants 11:12–14.

and serve not God, then ye may know with a perfect knowledge it is of the devil . . . for he persuadeth no man [or woman] to do good."[32]

Visitations

We find the process for discerning spiritual visitations in Doctrine and Covenants 129. We learn that eternal beings without physical bodies or eternal beings with glorified bodies could appear in a visitation. When this occurs, we must discern if the messenger is of God or not.

A righteous being will not deceive us. He or she will come and deliver the assigned message and leave. If we extend an arm to shake hands, the being will respond and shake our hand if he or she has a glorified body. If not, the message will be delivered, and the messenger will depart. An unrighteous being will try to deceive us by any means necessary. If the person has no body, he or she will try to shake our hand when we extend our arm, but we will feel nothing.

The Lord gave us a divine pattern for discerning an authorized minister from one not sent from God. In the temple, we learn that the Lord is concerned that His servants distinguish between His voice and other voices. He also wants us to recognize an authorized minister who has the Spirit of the Lord from one who does not. There may be some who are called and properly authorized but who are inwardly actuated by other influences.

The Lord warned, "You cannot always tell the wicked from the righteous."[33] Therefore, to aid us in this process of discerning good from evil, the Lord gave to us "a pattern in all things that [we] may not be deceived."[34] This pattern enables us to discern if a person has the Spirit of the Lord or is being affected by other influences. A person with the Spirit of the Lord does the following:[35]

---

32. Moroni 7:17.
33. Doctrine and Covenants 10:37.
34. Doctrine and Covenants 52:14.
35. See Doctrine and Covenants 52: 14–19 for the pattern for discernment given to us by the Lord.

1. *Prays for guidance.* The person understands the need to look to our Father in Heaven for help, seeking guidance by sincerely praying and not just by saying a prayer.

2. *Has a contrite spirit.* The person is humble and repentant, recognizing his or her imperfections and understanding his or her dependence on the Savior for all things.

3. *Obeys the Lord's ordinances.* The person exactly complies with the laws and ordinances of the gospel, making and keeping sacred covenants to the best of his or her ability.

4. *Speaks with a language that is meek.* The person is kind and gentle. He or she is in control of natural desires, personal influence and power, emotions, and the tongue. He or she endures persecutions and sufferings without complaint or resentment.

5. *Speaks with a language that edifies:* The person uplifts and builds others up. He or she never tears others down or uses language that is biting or harsh.

6. *Trembles under the power of God.* The person is sensitive to the whisperings of the Spirit and feels the power of the positive emotions that come from Him.

We are assured that "by this pattern, [we] can know the spirits in *all cases* under the whole heavens."[36] The phrase "all cases" indicates that this pattern can be used in our church, employment, and community interactions.

The blessings received when we follow this pattern are (1) we are made strong, meaning we can handle difficult situations, trials, burdens, or antagonistic statements, and (2) we bring forth fruits of praise and wisdom, meaning we accomplish the Lord's work because others recognize the validity of the message.[37]

We must distinguish truth from error, light from darkness, and divine guidance from other sources, a sometimes difficult task. As portrayed in the temple, the Father seeks to communicate with us and to guide us from beyond the veil, which requires meekness, humility, and

---

36. Doctrine and Covenants 52:19.
37. See Doctrine and Covenants 52: 17.

faith on our part. Messages that pierce the veil come through spiritual impressions, spiritual visitations, or the teachings of mortal ministers.

The Lord admonishes us, "Believe not every spirit, but try the spirits whether they are of God: because many false prophets are gone out into the world."[38] We must test every theory, doctrine, or philosophy by the Spirit and by the standard of the doctrine of Christ, and we must try every thought, feeling, or prompting to ensure it comes from the Lord. Elder Boyd K. Packer, formerly of the Quorum of the Twelve, warned,

> Be ever on guard lest you be deceived by inspiration from an unworthy source. You can be given false spiritual messages. There are counterfeit spirits just as there are counterfeit angels (see Moro. 7:17). Be careful lest you be deceived, for the devil may come disguised as an angel of light [or a true impression].
>
> The spiritual part of us and the emotional part of us are so closely linked that it is possible to mistake an emotional impulse for something spiritual. We occasionally find people who receive what they assume to be spiritual promptings from God, when those promptings are either centered in the emotions [of the natural man or woman] or are from the adversary.[39]

Distinguishing between *impressions* from the Lord or other sources is difficult due to (1) the stillness and smallness of the Holy Spirit's voice and its primary communication channels of thoughts and emotions, which can be confounded with our own or with other sources of thoughts and emotions, (2) our own mortality and imperfections, which block those sacred channels, and (3) the subtlety and sophistry of the adversary's approach, which mimics true revelation. Spiritual *visitations* have their danger of deception as well for those few who are fortunate enough to have them.

In addition to the adversary's influence, our own mortal biases can affect our ability to hear and respond to the still, small voice of the Spirit. Each of us uses logic, our past experiences, and our natural

---

38. 1 John 4:1.
39. Boyd K. Packer, "The Candle of the Lord," *Ensign*, January 1983, 55–56.

senses to make decisions. In decisions requiring divine guidance, these temporal guides are necessary, but they can also hinder us. Our biased natural perception can dull or block our spiritual senses. So, we must trust our spiritual senses and not our natural senses.

In speaking of the difficulties related created by our own biases, Elder Dallin H. Oaks, current President of the Quorum of the Twelve, has taught,

> Each of us is influenced strongly by our own desires and preferences. We may even mistake these influences as the ratification or prompting of the Holy Ghost. It is therefore significant when we feel prompted to do something contrary to our personal preference. That is good evidence of authenticity.
>
> Conversely, a feeling that seems to confirm a person in some action he or she strongly desires should be received with caution and subjected to more than one test of validity. In that circumstance a person could well ask himself [or herself], 'Am I humbly submitting myself to the will of my Heavenly Father and asking for his guidance, or am I proudly submitting my will to my Heavenly Father and asking for his approval?' Humility is more likely to receive inspiration; pride is more likely to be deceived and fall.[40]

We must recognize these difficulties so they don't become barriers to receiving revelation from God.

Personal Application: Aaron

An aviation example helped me understand the danger of relying in our own biases.[41] A friend who flies airplanes once told

---

40. Dallin H. Oaks, "I Have a Question: How can I distinguish the difference between the promptings of the Holy Ghost and merely my own thoughts, preferences, or hunches?" *Ensign*, June 1983, 27.
41. My father was a manufacturing engineer who worked in aviation his whole career after being discharged from the Air Force. He was passionate about airplanes, even giving Julie a picture of a classic P51 Mustang called "Unruly Julie" for a wedding gift.

me that pilots are taught a fundamental principle—always trust your instrumentation, especially at night or while flying through cloud cover.[42]

They learn that without a visual reference, the natural senses of the body can be easily deceived due to the motion of the plane. The gyroscope that each of us has as part of the inner ear to control balance can send the brain incorrect signals while in flight. Some pilots can become so disoriented that they fly their airplanes upside down without realizing it.

This situation occurred to an Air Force pilot named Major Peter S. Smith on January 15, 2008. Major Smith lost track of the horizon and became so disoriented that his senses could not tell him if he was flying upside down or flying level. Poor usage of his instrumentation compounded his dangerous situation. He was so confused that he increased the steepness of his dive because he thought he was turning upward. Fortunately Major Smith realized that there was a problem, and he was able to eject from the aircraft before it crashed, which saved his life.[43]

As stated in the FAA's Instrument Flying Handbook, "The only effective way to counter these false sensations is to recognize the problem, disregard the false sensations, and while relying totally on the flight instruments, use the eyes to determine the aircraft attitude [its orientation in relation to the horizon]."[44] *This principle could have helped him avoid danger.*

The Holy Ghost is the sure spiritual instrumentation that helps us keep on the correct course and keeps us out of danger. However, we must trust in and respond to the signals that He gives us, or we can quickly go astray. We cannot trust in our natural senses alone.

---

42. Story used with permission.
43. Asif Shamim, "Pilot Disorientation Results of Florida F-16 Crash," March 26, 2008, accessed February 20, 2021, https://www.f-16.net/f-16–news-article2801.html.
44. Instrument Flying Handbook, FAA-H-8083–15B, US Department of Transportation Federal Aviation Administration, 2012, Chapter 3: Human Factors, 3–3, accessed February 20, 2021. https://www.faa.gov/regulations_policies/handbooks_manuals/aviation/media/FAA-H-8083–15B.pdf.

The Savior Jesus Christ is our sure spiritual foundation. Keeping our eyes on Him will always lead us back to the Father and will keep our orientation toward our heavenly destination sure and true.

The gift of discernment enables us to distinguish good from evil. The spiritual gift called "the gift of discernment" enables us to distinguish between good and bad sources of impressions and revelations. It is a gift of the Holy Ghost.[45] The Guide to the Scriptures states, "[Discernment means] to understand or know something through the power of the Spirit. The gift of discernment is one of the gifts of the Spirit. It includes perceiving the true character of people and the source and meaning of spiritual manifestations."[46]

Therefore, discernment is the gift to tell whether the source of spiritual communications is from the Father through the Holy Ghost, from the Light of Christ, from one of His designated or authorized messengers, or from some other source. It is one of our most precious and essential spiritual gifts, one that keeps us safely on the right path and away from spiritual danger. This need for discernment is modeled explicitly in the temple, which encourages us to develop and use this gift when we leave. Of this gift, President George Q. Cannon, formerly of the First Presidency, taught, "The gift of discerning of spirits not only gives men and women who have it the power to discern the spirit with which others may be possessed or influenced, but it gives them the power to discern the spirit which influences *themselves*."[47]

Actively seeking the precious gift of discernment is a key to our spiritual safety. It will enable us to recognize good and avoid evil. When fully developed, the way to judge will be "plain . . . as the daylight is from the dark night."[48]

---

45. See Doctrine and Covenants 46:23.
46. "Discernment, Gift of," *The Guide to the Scriptures*, 2013.
47. George Q. Cannon, *Gospel Truth: Discourses and Writings of President George Q. Cannon*, comp. Jerreld L. Newquist (Salt Lake City: Deseret Book, 1974), Vol. 1, 199; emphasis added.
48. Moroni 7:15.

If we find it challenging to obtain or use the precious gift of discernment for spiritual impressions or visitations, we can take solace in this encouragement by Elder Richard G. Scott, formerly of the Quorum of the Twelve:

> What may appear initially to be a daunting task will be much easier to manage over time as you consistently strive to recognize and follow feelings prompted by the Spirit. Your confidence in the direction you receive from the Holy Ghost will also become stronger.
>
> I witness that as you gain experience and success in being guided by the Spirit, your confidence in the impressions you feel can become more certain than your dependence on what you see or hear."[49]

Fortunately, we can be assured that promptings from God will be persistent and will be recognized by the gift of discernment if we will "apply [ourselves] unto it."[50] When we remember and act upon these points of doctrine and admonitions, the Lord promises we will be kept safe from deception.

Divine truth is given line upon line, requiring us to wait for blessings and instructions from God. A key to discerning truth is understanding God's pattern of pace in delivery. In most instances, God does not give us His truths in their entirety at the beginning of a search. They are generally given "line upon line, precept upon precept; here a little and there a little,"[51] which develops faith. The temple models this method of delivery. This process is no different for prophets and apostles as it is for us. They, too, are taught in a line-upon-line way. When contemporary questions arise, they must also seek divine guidance and direction for what to do.

---

49. Richard G. Scott, "To Acquire Spiritual Guidance," Conference Report, October 2009.
50. Doctrine and Covenants 8:4.
51. Doctrine and Covenants 128:21.

When we seek blessings or truth, we must "wait upon the Lord."[52] His timing may be different than ours, and His methods may be different than we had anticipated. We should recognize and "count our many [small] blessings"[53] even as we wait for the larger blessings or greater understanding we hope to receive. We must continue to faithfully seek answers and blessings from His hand— either directly or through authorized ministers—and not succumb to or settle for instruction or gifts from other sources. Destruction awaits those who rush down "forbidden paths" [54] instead of waiting for divine guidance.

Promptly acting upon spiritual promptings delivers the Lord's intended blessings. The temple encourages us to act on the instruction we receive. Heeding spiritual guidance from our Heavenly Father through the Spirit is the only meaningful way to receive His blessings or avoid dangers that He wants us to circumvent. President Thomas S. Monson taught, "We watch. We wait. We listen for that still, small voice. When it speaks, wise men and women obey. Promptings of the Spirit are not to be postponed."[55]

At times, "it is easy to give heed to the words of Christ."[56] This can happen when we receive a clear impression, when the path ahead seems desirable, or when the obstacles seem readily avoidable. However, acting on spiritual promptings can, at times, be more difficult. The Spirit's direction to us may conflict with our own desires, even if they are good desires, or they may be inconvenient. As with Jonah of the Old Testament, Heavenly Father may want us to go one direction when we want to go in the completely opposite direction.[57]

---

52. Isaiah 40:31.
53. "Count Your Blessings," *Hymns*, No. 241.
54. 1 Nephi 8:28.
55. Thomas S. Monson, *Live the Good Life* (Salt Lake City: Desert Book, 1988), 59.
56. Alma 37:44.
57. In the book of Jonah, Jonah wanted to go to Tarshish instead of Ninevah, where the Lord had commanded him to go.

Another difficulty we may face is that the answer can become confounded by the myriad other choices that we are considering. If this occurs, we should follow our first impression. The Prophet Joseph Smith taught, "If you will listen to the *first promptings* you will get it right nine times out of ten."[58]

Whether the direction is easy or challenging, we must have faith to accept our Father's will for us. When we have faith and follow spiritual guidance, we act on the "evidence of things not seen."[59] Although the first few steps ahead or even the final outcome may not be seen by us, we can be assured that we will receive a witness "after the trial of our faith."[60]

We must persevere through periods of doubt and uncertainty, which builds faith. As modeled in the temple, spiritual learning and discovery is a step-by-step process. It includes periods where divine guidance is not given or where questions are left unresolved. Because the Father's method for teaching His children happens line upon line and progresses slowly over time, we can become impatient or even doubtful in that divine process.

Unfortunately, our reaction to the holy, refining process of seeking for and finding divine truth can sometimes lead to a "wrestle" of faith, wherein a son or daughter of God feels the significant pull of doubt and uncertainty.

Doubts may occur because a person only "know[s] in part"[61] and "see[s] through a glass darkly"[62] on difficult or troubling issues. They can form due to the waiting process as the Lord delivers His answers in His time. Doubts may also arise because individuals misunderstand or are unaware of the divine patterns in the delivery of

---

58. Joseph Smith, as recorded in diary of Charles L. Walker, 902, documented in Truman G. Madsen, *Joseph Smith the Prophet* (Salt Lake City: Deseret Book, 1989), 103; emphasis added.
59. Hebrews 11:1.
60. Ether 12:6.
61. 1 Corinthians 13:9.
62. 1 Corinthians 13:12.

truth,[63] and they "murmur because they [know] not the dealings of that God who had created them."[64] Other times, people can become troubled by the imperfections in the restoration of the gospel due to imperfect people who simply make mistakes in performing the Lord's perfect work.

In these times, our seeking becomes most important. We should persevere in seeking truth, remain loyal to authorized sources of truth, "lay aside"[65] our doubts until they are resolved, either in this life or the next, and continue moving forward in faith in Jesus Christ and with hope for the peace that will come. Indeed, faith has always been and will always be the core principle in our search for truth.

Despite our efforts, many of us may still be wrestling with our faith. Our wrestle may have even come to a critical point—to a "crisis of faith." Faith, by its very definition, means some things are unknown to us. However, the term "faith crisis" refers to that critical point where those unknowns become so powerful that they threaten to overcome faith.

We should not judge others who are wrestling, nor should we harshly judge ourselves if we are wrestling. We should count these struggles as refining experiences that will sanctify us and build a solid foundation of faith. The reasons and rationale for a person's doubts are as complex and individual as each son or daughter of God. So, we should be patient and kind.

However, we must all remember that we will "receive no witness until *after* the trial of [our] faith."[66] Our wrestles and even our crises—however extended they may be—might be among those needed trials. As Sister Sheri L. Dew, a former counselor in the Relief Society General Presidency, taught,

> Spiritual wrestling leverages the strength of true doctrine to overpower our weaknesses, our wavering faith, and our lack of knowledge. Spiritual wrestlers are seekers. They are men

---

63. Those divine methods include delivering truth line upon line, through the still small voice, or through authorized ministers.
64. 1 Nephi 2:12.
65. Alma 32:36.
66. Ether 12:6.

and women of faith who want to understand more than they presently do and who are serious about increasing the light and knowledge in their lives. . . . When we have unresolved questions, our challenge does not lie in what we think we know. It lies in what we don't YET know. . . . The Lord needs men and women who know how to get answers. . . . He needs men and women who are willing to engage in the wrestle.[67]

As we engage in the wrestle and continue to seek for truth, we should "with surety hope for a better world . . . which hope cometh of faith, maketh an anchor to the souls of men [and women], which would make them sure and steadfast, always abounding in good works, being led to glorify God."[68] Let us work and wait for that hope to come.

Ultimately, these exercises of faith—however difficult—will develop in us the character of Christ. Elder Hugh B. Brown, a former member of the First Presidency, taught, "Wherever in life great spiritual values await [our] appropriation, only faith can appropriate them. [People] cannot live without faith, because in life's adventure the central problem is character-building—which is not a product of logic, but of faith in ideals and sacrificial devotion to them."[69]

Let us be patient as our character develops through tests of our faith.

QUESTIONS TO CONSIDER

1. How does the Holy Ghost teach you? How do you hear Him? How might you apply that approach while in the temple to receive personal revelation?

2. What did you hear from Him during your last revelatory experience in the temple? What did you do with that divine direction?

67. Sheri L. Dew, *Worth the Wrestle* (Salt Lake City: Deseret Book, 2017), 22–23, 31–32.
68. Ether 12:4.
69. Hugh B. Brown, Conference Report, October 1969, 105.

3. What keeps you from hearing the voice of the Spirit? How can you avoid those things?
4. What can you do while you wait for an answer from the Lord? How can your temple covenants help you as you wait?

NOTES AND INSIGHTS

Chapter 17

Evil and the Adversary

"You have the power to overcome the adversary. The adversary, however, is aware of who you are. He knows of your divine heritage and seeks to limit your earthly and heavenly potential."

—Peter M. Johnson[1]

Thus chapter covers evil and the adversary. We approach this topic with care and caution, only presenting the insights that will enable us to avoid spiritual danger. The temple is the house of Jesus Christ, but it warns us of the reality of the adversary and instructs us on how to avoid and reject his advances. We hope you heed the warnings and warn others of spiritual danger. We wrote this somber chapter with that purpose in mind.

Personal Application: Aaron and Julie

The adversary is a predator who seeks to destroy us. The experience of two good friends taught us how to avoid danger when a predator is nearby.[2] Our friends live on the Gulf Coast. One

---

1. Peter M. Johnson, "Power to Overcome the Adversary," Conference Report, October 2019.
2. Story used with permission.

summer day, their family went to the beach to enjoy themselves. The two younger children played in the sand, building sandcastles, while their oldest child decided to take a boogie board into the surf.

As our friends sat on the shore watching their children play, the wife noticed something moving in the water behind their daughter. She looked more closely, and to her horror, she realized it was a shark circling behind her daughter! The predator was outside of her daughter's line of sight as she floated on the boogie board, so she was unaware of the danger.

Saying a quick prayer, the mother immediately ran to the water. However, she felt impressed to stop short of rushing out into the surf after her daughter, which could have agitated the shark. Instead, she began to yell frantically for her daughter to come to the shore. She did not want to tell her daughter why she was screaming because she did not want her to become too frightened to act.

At first, the girl ignored her mother, not realizing the danger lurking near her. However, our friend kept yelling and motioning for her daughter to return to the shore. Eventually, the girl made her way back to the safety of the sand.

Understandably shaken, our friend grabbed her daughter in a tight embrace and, only then, told her about the danger that was so awfully close. As the family packed up to leave, a fisherman came by and asked if he needed to call the coast guard. He said that he had been in the area all morning and had seen the shark in the water earlier. He also saw our friend's daughter in the water and, hearing the screams and knowing that the shark was near, supposed that she had been bitten.

Our friends were stunned by his admission. If the fisherman had known that there was danger nearby, why had he not warned them earlier? Why did he not come to help when he knew that there was a child in the water? Why had he not acted? They left the beach that day, thanking their Father in Heaven for safety and deliverance that morning on the shores of the Gulf Coast.

Spiritual dangers lurk around us in much the same way as this shark circled our young friend. Like her, we often do not

306

recognize the dangers that are so close to us—dangers that, without intervention by a loving, vigilant parent or friend, could result in devastating spiritual injuries.

We must be vigilant to keep ourselves "from the [spiritual] snares"[3] that might snag and harm us. We must be more like our young friend's parents, who acted to protect the safety of their children, and less like the inattentive fisherman, who did not act when he knew danger was near. Only then will we escape the adversary's predatory actions.

We will experience the effects of good and evil in mortality. The temple and the scriptures confirm the reality of God and His Son and the existence of an adversary who opposes them. The Book of Mormon is "Another Testament of Jesus Christ."[4] However, this sacred book also confirms the reality of evil and of an adversary who pervades it.[5] It warns us to be aware of our spiritual enemy—an active adversary who seeks our destruction. Prophets in the Book of Mormon and other ancient and modern prophets had their encounters with evil, which further warn us and prepare us.

The prophet Moses experienced a firsthand encounter with evil when he went to a high mountain to seek the Lord.[6] After Moses experienced a face-to-face encounter with the Lord, the adversary appeared. Moses called upon God to receive strength and then dismissed Satan.[7]

Joseph Smith had a similar encounter.[8] He went to the woods to seek an answer from the Lord. As he prayed, he experienced opposition from the adversary. As he was about to sink into despair and destruction, a light delivered him.[9]

---

3. Psalm 141:9.
4. Scholars estimate that Jesus is referenced every 1.7 verses in The Book of Mormon. He is referred to by one hundred different names. (See Susan Ward Easton, "Names of Christ in the Book of Mormon," *Ensign*, July 1978.)
5. See Helaman 6:26–31; Ether 8:25; Mor. 5:18; 3 Nephi 2:3, 6:15.
6. See Moses 1 for the full account.
7. See Moses 1:20, 22.
8. See Joseph Smith—History 1:13–17.
9. Joseph Smith—History 1:15–16.

Joseph had "learned for himself"[10] about the reality of good and evil, just like Moses. Of Joseph's personal experience with both, Elder John A. Widtsoe, formerly of the Quorum of the Twelve, taught,

> This contest with evil was necessary. Knowledge comes by comparisons and contrasts. By light we know darkness, by good we know evil; by successive, comparative steps man [and woman] moves into a larger knowledge. . . . There was fine pedagogic purpose in Joseph's battle with evil, as it gave him a contrast with the glory he was about to experience. Every seeker for truth must expect to battle with untruth.[11]

We, too, should expect to have such opposing experiences to learn for ourselves these same realities and become wiser children of God.

We will experience the enticement of money and its power and influence while in mortality. The temple warns us about the negative influence of money. Pride rules in the mortal world, and the love of money is a core issue of pride. "The love of money is the root of all evil."[12]

We learn in the Church's self-reliance efforts and observe in the temple that disciples must strive to have sufficient for their needs and must use their excess to help and to enable others, not to use it for self-aggrandizement. Riches and wealth themselves are not evil; however, the *use* of wealth and the *desire* for it can be evil.

Unfortunately, the allurement of riches and wealth is the source of much evil in our world. So much contention, so much betrayal, and so much immorality can be traced back to the desire for riches and wealth. People are willing to trade anything—including their good name and their morals—for riches and their corollary evil, recognition, or popularity.

We must guard against any misuse of or an overt yearning for riches and wealth by seeking first the things of righteousness. As Jacob

---

10. Joseph Smith—History 1:20.
11. John A. Widtsoe, *Joseph Smith: Seeker After Truth, Prophet of God* (Salt Lake City: Bookcraft, 1951), 12.
12. 1 Timothy 6:10.

taught his sons, "*Before* ye seek for riches, seek ye for the kingdom of God. And *after* ye have obtained a hope in Christ ye shall obtain riches, *if ye seek them*; and ye will seek them for *the intent to do good*— to clothe the naked, and to feed the hungry, and to liberate the captive, and administer relief to the sick and the afflicted."[13]

Individual apostasy will inevitably occur if we do not live up to our covenants, if we break the commandments, and if we reject the Lord, His Spirit, or His servants. The Lord warns us of what will happen if we depart from the true covenant path. The scriptures are full of warnings and exhortations to stay on the covenant path and not depart from it. The temple has similar warnings.

Disobedience and rebellion prevent us from developing the characteristics of godliness. We, instead, develop traits like those of the adversary. These traits grow out of the foundation of pride. They include hatred, anger, bias, jealousy, prejudice, self-absorption, self-pleasure, maliciousness, manipulation, coercion, dishonesty, deception, cowardice, and every other negative character trait we witness among natural men and women in mortality. Eventually, if we continue down this rebellious, unrepentant path, the adversary "will seal [us] his,"[14] for we will have become like him.

If left unrepented, willful disobedience eventually leads to apostasy, which is a full departure from faith in the Lord Jesus Christ coupled with a desire to fight against truth and to gather or organize others in our fight. When we make choices that either rebel actively against light and truth or that cause us to dwindle passively, personal apostasy can and will occur.

Apostasy is different than a simple difference of opinion between a member and a Church leader. President George Q. Cannon, formerly of the First Presidency, taught,

---

13. Jacob 2:18–19; emphasis added.
14. Alma 34:35.

A friend . . . wished to know whether . . . we considered an honest difference of opinion between a member of the Church and the authorities of the Church apostasy. . . .

We replied that we had not stated that an honest difference of opinion between a member of the Church and the authorities constituted apostasy; for we could conceive of a man [or a woman] honestly differing in opinion from the authorities of the Church and yet not be an apostate; but we could not conceive of a man [or a woman] publishing those differences of opinion, and seeking by arguments, sophistry and special pleading to enforce them upon the people to produce division and strife, and to place the acts and counsels of the authorities of the Church, if possible, in a wrong light, and not be an apostate, for such conduct was apostasy as we understood the term.

We further said that while a man [or a woman] might honestly differ in opinion from the authorities through a want of understanding, he [or she] had to be exceedingly careful how he [or she] acted in relation to such differences, or the adversary would take advantage of him [or her] and he [or she] would soon become imbued with the spirit of apostasy, and be found fighting against God and the authority which He had placed here to govern His Church.[15]

We should ever be on guard against apostasy, which begins with disobedience and rebellion. These actions create a dark and slippery path that leads to spiritual destruction.

We should understand the traits and characteristics of the adversary, who seeks our utter destruction and provides opposition to our progress, to recognize and avoid his influence. We learn in the temple and the scriptures the genuine existence of the enemy of all righteousness. We learn the constancy of his influence and presence

---

15. George Q. Cannon, *Gospel Truth: Discourses and Writings of President George Q. Cannon*, comp. Jerreld L. Newquist (Salt Lake City: Deseret Book, 1974), Vol. 2, 267–277.

in mortality. We also learn how to gain power over the author of the works of darkness and evil, which is only in and through the name of Jesus Christ. We learn his many names, roles, and characteristics to recognize him and his influence, so he will not ensnare us.

In the premortal world, the adversary was named Lucifer, which is Latin for "light-bringing" or "light-bearer." He was an angelic "son of the morning" who fell.[16] He rebelled against Heavenly Father's plan in the premortal world, taking a third of the spirits with him, which caused great sadness among the sons and daughters of God, "for the heavens wept over him."[17]

Following his fall, he was called Perdition, which means "destruction or loss." In Hebrew, he is called Satan, meaning "adversary" or "accuser." In Greek, he is called the devil, meaning "accuser" or "slanderer," for he "accused them before our God day and night."[18]

He is a contender and is the "father of contention,"[19] using and promulgating anger and strife among the Saints and in the world. He is a usurper, seeking to steal power for himself.[20]

He is a liar and a deceiver,[21] and he has been so "from the beginning."[22] He is the "father of all lies."[23]

He is the "destroyer"[24] who goes "to and fro in the earth" looking to "destroy . . . without cause." [25] He sought to destroy agency in the premortal realm,[26] and he continues his relentless pursuit today.

He is a predator, seeking his prey night and day without ceasing. In 1 Peter we read, "Your adversary the devil, as a roaring lion,

16. Isaiah 14:12; 2 Nephi 2:17.
17. Doctrine and Covenants 76:26–27.
18. Revelation 12:10.
19. 3 Nephi 11:29–30.
20. See Doctrine and Covenants 29:36.
21. See Doctrine and Covenants 52:14.
22. Doctrine and Covenants 93:25.
23. See 2 Nephi 2:18; 9:9; Ether 8:25; Moses 4:4. In contrast the Savior is called the "fountain of all righteousness" (Ether 8:26).
24. See Doctrine and Covenants 61:19; Helaman 8:28.
25. Job 2:2–3.
26. See Moses 4:3.

walketh about, seeking whom he may devour."[27] He has also been a "murderer from the beginning."[28]

He seeks to make all men and women "miserable like unto himself."[29] He is "the author of all sin" who works and plots "from generation to generation according as he can get hold upon the hearts of the children of men."[30]

The adversary's self-absorption, narcissism, and overconfidence are poignantly taught and displayed in the temple and throughout the scriptures. He could be called "the prince of pride." He embodies all that is loathsome, all that is abhorrent, all that is deceptive, all that is pompous and aggrandizing, all that is destructive, and all that is evil.

The scriptures and the temple expose his deceptions and his methods of operating. These methods include the following tactics: [31]

- Using partial truths mixed with full lies.
- Using a friendly or accommodating approach before a wrong choice is made and then using guilt and shame after a wrong choice is made.
- Using isolation to divide us from our source of power and strength and to cause us to feel alone and depressed.
- Using anger, contention, and strife to "stir up" people and to drive away love and peace.
- Using comparison to drive enmity and division.
- Using great swelling words to dominate the conversation.
- Finding alternative ways to deceive if his first attempts are not successful.
- Customizing the approach and the temptation to the personality of the person.

---

27. 1 Peter 5:8.
28. John 8:44.
29. 2 Nephi 2:27.
30. Helaman 6:30.
31. See Genesis 3:1–7; 2 Corinthians 11:14; 1 Peter 5:8; 2 Nephi 2:17–18, 9:9,28, 24:12–17, 26:22–23, 28:20–22, 32:8; Mosiah 4:14; Helaman 6:21–31, 16:22; 3 Nephi 6:15, 10:63, 11:29, 18:18; Moroni 7:17; Ether 8:18–26; Doctrine and Covenants 10:20–28, 29:36, 50:2–3,18,23,31–33, 76:25–30, 93:25, 39; Moses 1, 4, 5:13,21–31, 6:49.

- Using the allurement of money, power, and popularity to achieve his ends.

The adversary's actions and attacks against the Saints and the world are a continuation of the war that began in the premortal world. President Wilford Woodruff taught,

> There are two powers on the earth and in the midst of the inhabitants of the earth—the power of God and the power of the devil. . . . When God has had a people on the earth, it matters not in what age, Lucifer, the son of the morning, and the millions of fallen spirits that were cast out of heaven have warred against God, against Christ, against the work of God, and against the people of God.[32]

An awareness of this continued war and its participants will give us a greater chance to win our personal battles with our spiritual enemies.

The adversary's attacks on the Saints and the entire world are intense and constant. The temple demonstrates the constancy of the adversary's influence in our lives. The Lord warned the Saints that "Satan thinketh to overpower your testimony."[33] His attacks on testimony are a continuation of his premortal war, where we overcame him by the "word of [our] testimony."[34]

He seeks to overpower our small, simple testimonies with a tidal wave of half-truths, lies, innuendo, deceptions, emotions, and direct threats, all of which try to overwhelm the "small means" and "simple things" the Lord uses in His work.[35]

The scriptures describe the effects of the adversary's "overwhelming" attacks on our testimony as "mighty winds," "shafts in the

---

32. Wilford Woodruff, October 5, 1896 general conference, cited in *Collected Discourses of Wilford Woodruff, Vol. 5* (Salt Lake City: Deseret Book, 2017), Deseret Bookshelf eBook.
33. Doctrine and Covenants 10:33.
34. Revelation 12:11.
35. See 1 Nephi 16:29; Alma 37:6–7, 41.

whirlwind," and "his hail and his mighty storm."[36] These are appro-priate descriptors. Below, we liken his attacks to these weather-related events.

Mighty winds have a constant force. They do not back down or bend, and they can sweep us away. Some spiritual attacks on testi-mony are just as relentless.

The whirlwind or tornado appears suddenly with great force. These spiritual attacks appear suddenly and have a tremendous influence on a specific and small number of people.

Shafts in the whirlwind are those sharp objects that pierce or blunt objects that bludgeon amidst the whirling storms of life. These are the specific, personal, heart-piercing, soul-wrenching attacks that affect us personally and privately, ones only we feel or understand. These are deeply personal events, designed to refine us and to deepen our testimony and our resolve. However, if we are not built upon the rock of Jesus Christ, they will cut us to the core and cause us to doubt and eventually fall.

Hail are those sudden showers of hard attacks that pelt us intensely with the intent to damage. They appear suddenly and do much damage.

The "mighty storm" is an attack from the adversary comparable to a hurricane. It is large and damaging, but it is predictable. We can limit casualties from this type of attack by appropriate preparation and by taking the early, known means of escape. Unfortunately, it will affect many people simultaneously and create widespread damage because of its scope and scale.

The adversary attacks God's children in multiple ways. The adversary has myriad ways and methods of conducting his attacks and of creating spiritual damage. They align with his roles as a fallen angel, an accuser, a contender, a usurper, a liar and deceiver, a destroyer and predator, and a murderer.

---

36. Helaman 5:12.

Fallen angel

Because the adversary was a former "son of the morning," the temple portrays his familiarity with true, authorized ministers of righteousness, which is a warning to all such ministers.[37] His disdain of authority generally and of the Father specifically are demonstrated. He hates all who have been born into the world with physical bodies, but he most hates those who valiantly defended the Savior and who thwarted his plan in the premortal world.

Unlike us, he has not lost his memory of the premortal world, and he uses this asymmetry of knowledge and information about us to his advantage in customizing his attacks on each of us personally. President George Q. Cannon, formerly of the First Presidency, taught,

> Some have called him *the* son of the morning, but here it is *a* son of the morning—one among many, doubtless. This angel was a mighty personage, without doubt. The record that is given to us concerning him clearly shows that he occupied a very high position; that he was thought a great deal of, and that he was mighty in his sphere, so much so that when the matter was debated concerning the earth and the plan of salvation, he was of sufficient importance to have a plan, which he proposed as the plan by which this earth should be peopled and the inhabitants thereof redeemed.
>
> His plan, however, was not accepted; but it was so plausible and so attractive that out of the whole hosts of heaven one-third accepted his plan and were willing to cast their lot with him. [Moses 4:1–4; D&C 29:36–37.] *Now, the difference between Jesus and Lucifer was this: Jesus was willing to submit to the Father.*[38]

---

37. See Acts 19:15.
38. George Q. Cannon, *Gospel Truth: Discourses and Writings of President George Q. Cannon*, comp. Jerreld L. Newquist (Salt Lake City: Deseret Book, 1974), Vol. 1, 4–5; emphasis added.

He detests us because he remembers our valiancy in fighting him. He is a narcissist who hates to lose and hates those who caused him to lose. So, his attacks will be personal, making him very dangerous.

Accuser

Because he is an accuser, the adversary accuses disciples of Christ of myriad things. His accusations are varied and intense. They include accusing us of being forever lost due to sin, not being good enough, being strange and peculiar, not being accepted, being too good, being foolish and naïve, and so on. He also tempts us to accuse others of these same things.

Satan accuses "sacred" things of being "secret." His accusations of secrecy are nothing more than doubt cloaked in the mask of openness and transparency. He also accuses sacred things of being silly, charging those who believe them as being foolish.

The scriptures warn that he "make[s] a man [or a woman] an offender for a word, and lay[s] a snare for him that reproveth in the gate, and turn[s] aside the just for a thing of nought."[39] He takes Church leaders' statements or historical events out of context and uses those events against them and the work. He also pulls historical events forward in time and measures them against today's cultural and legal standards as evidence of their impropriety.

The great accuser uses believers' errors and humanity as evidence that the divine work they are performing is not true or not inspired. Or worse, he actively lays traps for believers to prey upon their humanity and imperfections. Then, he uses those mistakes as evidence that the entire work is untrue and the person is unworthy. Tragically, he obscures the positive intent of believers, accusing them of negative intent.

The devil, who is a supreme narcissist, rails against correction and calls to repentance, accusing those who make them of being harsh, unkind, and hateful. To feign justness, he misapplies social justice to justify sin and to accuse believers of lacking love and empathy. Alternatively, he tempts people to discriminate, ignore social justice,

39. Isaiah 29:21.

and disregard love and empathy by having them judge inappropriately and by having them accuse others of disobedience under the guise of their own self-righteousness or superiority.

The adversary cleverly pulls attention away from the vast, overwhelming good happening in the Lord's kingdom and in the world by emotionally hyper-focusing on a few issues or inconsistencies, which become an obsessively over-emphasized distraction. Simultaneously, he obscures the historical and the current contradictions and even open evil in other organizations or people, overemphasizing their good to draw people away from the Lord's kingdom.

Under the deceptive guise of outrage for real and perceived problems, he accuses the work as being off course, and then he entices men and women to "steady the ark,"[40] meaning to make inappropriate and unsanctioned corrections of Church leaders, doctrine, and policy when they do not have priesthood keys or authority. He encourages people to band together to accusatorially push for policy and doctrinal changes in a time line that suits them instead of expressing their concerns and questions individually and waiting for change to come through revealed channels. When needed change does eventually come, he accuses Church leaders of bending to social pressure, whereas the truth is they are merely responding to contemporary needs.

To ridicule the Saints, he dismisses previous personal spiritual experiences as "mind washing" or "group think," accusing people who have felt them of being foolish puppets. The Prophet Joseph Smith taught, "The devil has great power to deceive; he will so transform things as to make one gape at those who are doing the will of God."[41]

Contender

The adversary's chief tactic in all his accusations is the use of contention and anger. The phrase "stir up" is used repeatedly in the scriptures to describe the agitation that the chief contender causes. He strives to "rage in the hearts of the children of men"[42]—to cause them to have a flood of emotions inspired by some cause or issue (just or

---

40. See 2 Samuel 6:6–7; Doctrine and Covenants 85:8.
41. Joseph Smith, *Teachings of the Prophet Joseph Smith*, 227.
42. 2 Nephi 28:20.

not) that overwhelms their sense of logic and decorum and destroys their loyalty to God, His kingdom, or His servants.

The core of his anger is his enmity or hostility toward all Heavenly Father's sons and daughters. This enmity is founded in his extreme pride. He seeks to stir Father's children up against all that is good, righteous, and wholesome. He aims to pit them one against another. These actions cut them off from the Holy Spirit and obscure the Light of Christ, overwhelming them with the negative emotion of anger, which blocks divine guidance and even common decency.

Any time anger is present, the Holy Spirit leaves. Anger is a clear indication the adversary is at work. Anger is one of the adversary's most used and most effective tools because it draws on negative emotions driven by chemicals in the body, which are hard to control, and take much time to dissipate physiologically. He uses our mortal bodies against us and begins to imprint these physiological emotions onto our spirits, such that he drags them down and binds us with them.

The Savior warned, "He that hath the spirit of contention is not of me, but is of the devil, who is the father of contention, and he stirreth up the hearts of men [and women] to contend with anger, one with another. Behold, this is not my doctrine, to stir up the hearts of men with anger, one against another; but this is my doctrine, that such things should be done away."[43]

Usurper

Because he is a usurper, we learn of his attempts to steal or usurp power, authority, and recognition from those to whom they rightfully belong and those who have legitimately and diligently qualified for them. His ultimate purpose—to gain power for himself at our expense—is openly presented in the scriptures and the temple as a warning.[44]

His followers are similarly infatuated with power, so we are warned and forewarned "against the rulers of darkness of this world,

---

43. 3 Nephi 11:29.
44. See Isaiah 14:13–14; Doctrine and Covenants 29:36; Moses 4:1.

against spiritual wickedness in high places"[45] and against the "evils and designs which do and will exist in the hearts of conspiring men [and women] in the last days."[46]

Be warned that the adversary will use any means necessary to achieve his goal—to usurp all power for himself by destroying agency. Agency is an insult to him because its existence means he cannot control an individual. In his extreme narcissism, he pathologically seeks to point all power and control to himself. He knows the best way to do this is subtlety because open, forced coercion is generally met with resistance, whereas indirect, small deceptions will likely be missed or even embraced. In this way, he is the ultimate manipulator.

Liar and Deceiver

Because he is a liar, he promulgates falsehoods in every way possible. He uses partial truths, which are falsehood cloaked in truth, and he uses complete lies. He is devoid of integrity, and he strives to destroy all men and women's integrity by influencing them to lie.

Because he is a deceiver, the adversary attempts to have us believe things that are not true—the lies he has told. He revels in deceit. He strives to obscure, hide, twist, change, and only partially disclose facts and truth to gain an advantage and put himself at the center of people's lives. He deceives in every way possible, and he encourages men and women to be duplicitous and deceitful just as he is.

The adversary is the most subtle of all the creatures God created.[47] Subtle means "making use of clever and indirect methods to achieve something."[48] He is called the "cunning one."[49] Cunning means "having or showing skill in achieving one's ends through deceit or evasion."[50]

---

45. Ephesians 6:12.
46. Doctrine and Covenants 89:4.
47. See Moses 4:5; Alma 12:4.
48. "Subtle," *Oxford Dictionary of English* (Oxford: Oxford University Press, 2010), 1776.
49. 2 Nephi 9:39.
50. "Cunning," *Oxford Dictionary of English* (Oxford: Oxford University Press, 2010), 426.

At times, the adversary confronts people with open sin and rebellion, "stir[ring] them up to anger against that which is good."[51] But most often, he uses clever and indirect means for achieving his efforts to deceive. As distinguished Christian author C. S. Lewis observed, "The safest road to Hell is the gradual one—the gentle slope, soft underfoot, without sudden turnings, without milestones, without signposts."[52]

He uses "cunning," "snares," and "wiles"[53] in his subtle deceptions. *Snares* are traps—both seen and hidden—intended to lure or tempt someone into harm or error. *Wiles* are evil strategies employed in manipulating or persuading someone to do what he wants.

His subtle approach includes multiple tactics. He deceivingly distributes temptation over time and across people with the single intent of destroying an individual or a group of individuals. He pacifies to "lull them away unto carnal security," making them think nothing is wrong and that "all is well."[54] Other times, he flatters them, telling them, "I am no devil, for there is none."[55]

The adversary often uses flattery as a form of deception. He flatters people by playing to their egos, telling them that they are very righteous when they are not. He convinces them that they are keenly wise when they depend on their own or others' wisdom instead of God's wisdom.

This smooth enemy convinces people that they are socially just when they deny commandments or, alternatively, that they are faithful when they are dogmatic. He cunningly convinces them they are united when they only unite with those who are like them, or when they reject anything that disagrees with their personal views.

Alarmingly, this adulating antagonist convinces the self-righteous that they tell the "truth" when they are just hurtful, not empathizing with another's feelings, trials, or problems. Especially damaging are their comments cast at those who have been hurt or victimized by

51. 2 Nephi 28:20.
52. C. S. Lewis, *The Screwtape Letters* (London: William Collins, 2015), 61.
53. Helaman 3:29.
54. 2 Nephi 28:21.
55. 2 Nephi 28:22.

another person. The adversary delights in their pain and in flattering the proud into being the unsympathetic source of sorrow.

The adversary lures us with things that appear to be enticing but are harmful. He uses popularity and charm to entice and attract men and women into sin. President James E. Faust, formerly of the First Presidency, warned us that the chain that the adversary holds is enticing to lure us into his clutches:

> Much of what comes from the devil is alluring and enticing. It glitters and is appealing to the sensual parts of our nature. His message sounds so reasonable and easy to justify. His voice is usually smooth and intriguing. If it were harsh or discordant, nobody would listen, nobody would be enticed. Some of Satan's most appealing messages are: Everyone does it; if it doesn't hurt anybody else, it's all right; if you feel there is no harm in it, it's okay; it's the "cool" thing to do.
>
> Satan is the greatest imitator, the master deceiver, the arch counterfeiter, and the greatest forger ever in the history of the world. He comes into our lives as a thief in the night. His disguise is so perfect that it is hard to recognize him or his methods. He is a wolf in sheep's clothing.[56]

The great deceiver also transforms himself into an "angel of light" to deceive us,[57] which means he does anything he can to influence men and women by appearing to be a legitimate source of truth. He makes evil appear to be good, and what is damaging appear to be helpful or enjoyable. He corrupts all that is good, pure, and plain. "He rewardeth you no good thing."[58]

As a subtle but sharp artifice, Lucifer provides counter-promptings to the Saints and to the world, seeking to influence them subtly as if he were the Spirit of the Lord. He will mimic every good and righteous thing he can to deceive men and women. However, he cannot mimic peace, which is the primary way the Spirit communicates. The

---

56. James E. Faust, "The Devil's Throat," Conference Report, April 2003.
57. See 1 Corinthians 11:14; 2 Nephi 9:9.
58. Alma 34:39.

Savior is the Prince of Peace, and the adversary cannot copy this special, divine stillness that can only come by the Spirit of the Lord.

The adversary's closest counterfeit to divine peace is simple familiarity with our personal biases or comfort with the status quo when trying to make a decision. He will attempt to make us feel comfortable about making no change even as the Lord leads us down a road that may make us personally uncomfortable. We must remember that divine peace can come even amid personal discomfort. We must discern the difference between the comfort of personal preference and the peace of divine guidance.

We must be wary of any false promptings! They do not produce His unique peace. They do not align with gospel principles. They do not align with counsel given through leaders with keys. They do not align with known doctrine. President Joseph F. Smith warned us of the adversary's ability to mimic truth:

> Let it not be forgotten that the evil one has great power in the earth, and that by every possible means he seeks to darken the minds of men [and women] and then offers them falsehood and deception in the guise of truth. Satan is a skillful imitator, and as genuine gospel truth is given the world in ever increasing abundance, so he spreads the counterfeit coin of false doctrine. Beware of his spurious currency, it will purchase for you nothing but disappointment, misery and spiritual death. The 'father of lies' he has been called, and such an adept has he become through the ages of practice in his nefarious work, that were it possible he would deceive the very elect.[59]

The adversary uses myriad other deceptions to trick men and women. He tries to convince us that sin is the path to happiness. He strives to make us feel unloved, unwanted, and unappreciated. He wants us to believe we are unimportant and assume any good we have ever done is spoiled or overshadowed by our imperfections, by our failures, or by the lack of appreciation of others. He works tirelessly to obscure every truth, to hide every source of joy, to spoil every pleasant

---

59. Joseph F. Smith, Ed. John A. Widtsoe, *Gospel Doctrine* (Salt Lake City: Deseret Book, 1986), 376.

and good thing, to fracture every relationship, to minimize every success, and to cast doubt on every divine truth.

In all his subtlety and deception, the adversary slowly binds people as he "leadeth them by the neck with a flaxen cord, until he bindeth them with strong cords forever,"[60] which achieves his goal of destroying agency. Moses saw all these diabolical actions of the adversary and warned that the evil one "had a great chain in his hand, and it veiled the whole face of the earth with darkness; and he looked up and laughed, and his angels rejoiced."[61] This smirking gaze into heaven is his prideful way of gloating to the Father of his successes and his deceptions.

Destroyer and Predator

Because he is a destroyer and a predator, the adversary seeks to ruin, sabotage, devastate, and eradicate anyone striving to do good. He seeks "the misery of all mankind"[62] by extinguishing hope and replacing it with discouragement and despair. He preys upon any weakness, any lapses, and any inattentiveness in his efforts.

One of his chief targets in his efforts to destroy us is our bodies. He has no physical body, so he entices us to misuse our bodies so we will "be miserable like unto himself."[63] Elder David A. Bednar of the Quorum of the Twelve has taught, "One of the ultimate ironies of eternity is that the adversary, who is miserable precisely because he has no physical body, invites and entices us to share in his misery through the improper use of our bodies. The very tool he does not have and cannot use is thus the primary target of his attempts to lure us to physical and spiritual destruction."[64]

Because he has no family, Satan also seeks to destroy the family, the temple, and temple work, which binds families together for eternity. The family always has and always will be a prime target in

---

60. 2 Nephi 26:22.
61. Moses 7:26.
62. 2 Nephi 2:18.
63. 2 Nephi 2:27.
64. David A. Bednar, "Watchful Unto Prayer Continually," Conference Report, October 2019.

his destructive efforts. Capitalizing on family members' inherent weaknesses and imperfections, he tries to amplify them to tear the family apart.

The adversary preys upon strengths by turning them into sources of pride and comparison. Comparison is one of his most subtly destructive tools, both within the family and without. It generates enmity—hostility toward another. Enmity destroys relationships.

He wants men and women to compare differences instead of aligning on strengths, dividing genders. He wants teenagers and adults or middle-aged adults and seniors to have intergenerational misunderstandings. He wants people to have feelings of racial, ethnic, cultural, or religious superiority, which cause them to discriminate or look down on others due to the color of their skin, the traditions of their culture, or nature of their beliefs. He urges discrimination of along any dimension that creates differences between God's children.

The adversary's destructive attacks get more intense the spiritually stronger we become. The Prophet Joseph Smith taught, "The nearer a person approaches the Lord, a greater power will be manifested by the adversary to prevent the accomplishment of His purposes."[65] This statement should serve as a warning to all faithful disciples who are growing in their testimony.

Murderer

Because he is a murderer, he seeks to destroy the physical, spiritual, emotional, mental, and reputational lives of all the children of God.[66] He does this with malice and with forethought of how to accomplish any of these most despicable deeds. As a sociopath, he takes great pleasure in these murderous acts. The Lord laments that "the devil

65. Joseph Smith cited in Orson F. Whitney, *Life of Heber C. Kimball* (Salt Lake City: Bookcraft, 1967), 132.

66. The Talmud equates embarrassing another person with murder (see Rabi Ari Enkin, "Embarrassing Others," www.outorah.org, https://outorah. org/p/49535/#_ftn1, accessed May 24, 2021).

laugheth, and his angels rejoice because of the slain sons and daughters of my people."[67]

The adversary has no compassion and no empathy. He does not care who gets hurt, damaged, or heartbroken—either directly or collaterally—in his nefarious schemes. He pays no regard to those with disabilities or disparities; all are considered targets or pawns in his evil designs. He will drain the physical, mental, emotional, and spiritual life out of anyone to suit his purposes. And he will do it as slowly and as painfully as he can, for he delights in our misery.

One of his murderous tools is secret combinations, whereby people organize and bind themselves by oaths to achieve their selfish purposes. The most sinister secret combination intends to "murder and get gain."[68] He influences individuals to create and join these organized efforts. They are particularly dangerous because they are secretive and methodical.

We can conquer the adversary and his hosts if we call on the unquestionable power of God. We learn in the scriptures that the adversary is an "old serpent,"[69] which means he is ancient and his techniques are well established. He has been tempting the sons and daughters of God for many millennia. Therefore, we should be warned. We are neither more intelligent nor more experienced than him.

We learn that he and his minions are all about and ever-present. As written in the book of Helaman, "We are surrounded by demons, yea we are encircled about by angels of him who hath sought to destroy our souls."[70] The Lord warned us, "Watch, for the adversary spreadeth his dominions, and darkness reigneth."[71]

Because of the adversary's cunning and strength, we cannot conquer him and his hosts on our own. However, if we are faithful and "watchful unto prayer continually,"[72] we can have the power of God

---

67. 3 Nephi 9:2.
68. See 2 Nephi 9:9; Helaman 6:21–31; Ether 8:9, 15–26; Moses 5:29–31, 51–52.
69. Mosiah 16:3.
70. Helaman 13:37.
71. Doctrine and Covenants 82:5.
72. Alma 34:39.

on our side and can have guidance from the Spirit, who is older and more experienced, and who knows the mind of God.

With Him, we will "not be led away by the temptations of the devil."[73] We will be protected and sustained because "they that be with us are more than they that be with them."[74] God and his hosts will not fail us nor forsake us, but we must choose to come to Him for His protection to be in force.

The Lord promises us, "My wisdom is greater than the cunning of the devil."[75] How do we capitalize on that comforting promise?

First, we must choose to heed His "watchmen on the tower,"[76] which includes parents, Church leaders, and other ministering disciples. If we do not listen to them, we put ourselves in danger. However, if the watchmen fail in their duties, dire consequences can ensue.

Personal Application: Aaron and Julie

In 2009, our family went to Hawaii and stayed on the island of Oahu, where we visited the Pearl Harbor memorial site. Following the tour, we wondered why the Japanese attack was so successful.

According to records, although radar operators reported observing a target echo larger than anything they had ever seen, an untrained officer to whom they issued the report presumed that the scheduled arrival of six B-17 bombers was the source of the massive radar signal. Therefore, there was a failure to notify the fleet of the incoming danger adequately.[77] This failure of the watchmen on the tower resulted in the loss of thousands of lives.

Likewise, our spiritual watchmen and watchwomen must be ever vigilant in their sacred duties, or we could experience devastating consequences. President Harold B. Lee admonished them,

73. Alma 34:39.
74. 2 Kings 6:16.
75. Doctrine and Covenants 10:43.
76. See Ezekiel 33:7; Doctrine and Covenants 101:44–58.
77. See Gordon W. Prange, *At Dawn We Slept: The Untold Story of Pearl Harbor* (New York: Penguin Books, 1981), 500–501.

> *In [Isaiah 21:11] the Lord asked: "But watchman, what*
> *of the night? Watchman, what of the night?" suggesting*
> *that more to be feared than the enemies that come in*
> *the daytime that you can see are the enemies that come*
> *in the night. . . .*
>
> *There are insidious forces among us that are constantly*
> *trying to knock at our doors and trying to lay traps for*
> *our young men and women, particularly those who are*
> *unwary and unsophisticated in the ways of the world. . . .*
> *Watchmen, be alert to the "dangers of the night"![78]*

Let all who are watchmen and watchwomen be alert and raise the alarm of warning!

Second, we must choose to "lay hold upon the word of God, which is quick and powerful, which shall divide asunder all the cunning and the snares and the wiles of the devil."[79] The word of God—the scriptures, the words of living prophets, and the promptings of the Spirit—will teach us of the tactics, strategies, and disguises of the adversary. It will help us increase our spirituality and will lead us away from temptation. President James E. Faust, formerly of the First Presidency, taught,

> In the future the opposition will be both more subtle and more open. It will be masked in greater sophistication and cunning, but it will also be more blatant. We will need greater spirituality to perceive all of the forms of evil and greater strength to resist it.[80]

Our spirituality will grow as we learn and live the prophets' words and remain faithful to our covenants.

Third, we must take the "way to escape" temptation provided by the Lord that we "may be able to bear it."[81] We must be alert, vigilant,

---

78. Harold B. Lee, "Enemies That Come in the Night," Conference Report, April 1970, 54.
79. See Helaman 3:29; 1 Nephi 15:24.
80. James E. Faust, "The Great Imitator," Conference Report, October 1987.
81. 1 Corinthians 10:13.

and "watch and pray continually, that [we] may not be tempted above that which [we] can bear."[82] We should remember to "resist the devil, and he will flee from [us.]"[83]

Fourth, we must hold tight to all our covenants—most especially our temple covenants. Faithfulness and loyalty to covenants will protect us from the adversary's advances. They give us spiritual strength and priesthood power. They give us knowledge and help us discern good from evil. They are our strongest spiritual armor in the battle with the adversary. With them, we will be "armed with righteousness and with the power of God in great glory."[84]

Ultimately, we must "remember that it is upon the rock of our Redeemer, who is Christ, the Son of God, that [we] must build [our] foundation" so the adversary "shall have no power over [us] . . . because of the rock upon which [we] are built, which is a sure foundation, a foundation whereon if men [and women] build *they cannot fall*."[85] We learn in the temple and the scriptures the adversary will have some victories, but he will eventually be conquered by Jesus Christ.[86]

The Father and the Son have absolute power over evil and will have the ultimate victory over all enemies of righteousness. Our Heavenly Father and His Son's ultimate power is portrayed and reinforced in the temple and in the scriptures, so we, as their agents, understand how to access, use, and manage His sacred power to bless others and protect ourselves. Indeed, "because of the righteousness of his people, Satan has no power."[87]

Disciples of Christ overcome the adversary "by the blood of the Lamb [the Atonement of Jesus Christ], and by the word of their testimony; and [because] they loved not their lives unto death [meaning, they were willing to sacrifice for the kingdom of God and for their

---

82. See Alma 13:28; 3 Nephi 13:15, 18.
83. James 4:7.
84. 1 Nephi 14:14.
85. Helaman 5:12; emphasis added.
86. See Isaiah 14:14–17; Doctrine and Covenants 19:3.
87. 1 Nephi 22: 26.

covenants, which sacrifice demonstrates meekness and humility and draws down spiritual power]."[88]

President Gordon B. Hinckley gave us this encouragement to face our daily battles with the enemy of all righteousness:

> We are engaged in a great eternal struggle that concerns the very souls of the sons and daughters of God. We are not losing. We are winning. We will continue to win if we will be faithful and true. We *can* do it. We *must* do it. We *will* do it. There is nothing the Lord has asked of us that in faith we cannot accomplish. . . .
>
> The war goes on. It is waged across the world over the issues of agency and compulsion. It is waged by an army of missionaries over the issues of truth and error. It is waged in our own lives, day in and day out, in our homes, in our work, in our school associations; it is waged over questions of love and respect, of loyalty and fidelity, of obedience and integrity. We are all involved in it. . . . We are winning, and the future never looked brighter.[89]

The Savior has already won. He conquered sin and death. The battle that now rages is for our souls—whether we will qualify for the blessings of His Atonement so that He can claim us as His own. With Him on our side, we cannot fall, and we cannot fail.

QUESTIONS TO CONSIDER

1. What did you learn about avoiding evil during your last visit to the temple? How can those principles help you at this time in your life?
2. How can your temple covenants protect you from the influence of evil in your life? How can they give you the spiritual power to avoid temptation?

---

88. Revelation 12:11.
89. Gordon B. Hinckley, "The War We Are Winning," Conference Report, October 1986.

3. What does the temple teach you about God's power to overcome the adversary? How can your faith in Him give you the strength to fight your spiritual battles?
4. In what ways are you winning your spiritual battles using your temple covenants?

NOTES AND INSIGHTS

_____

_____

_____

_____

_____

_____

_____

_____

_____

_____

Epilogue

Come and See

"And the blind and the lame came to him in the temple; and he healed them."

—Matthew 21:14

A LIFETIME OF LEARNING

Our great opportunity and responsibility are to seek out, discover, embrace, and apply all the divine and sublime truths taught in the holy temple. This work will require a lifetime of participation, pondering, study, seeking, revelation, teaching, and application on our part.

Learning from the temple takes a lifetime because divine light comes "line upon line, precept upon precept, here a little and there a little."[1] Foundational truths build on each other in succession. Additionally, each phase of our lives provides a new context for learning and applying additional truths. As we discover them, our awareness opens further questions for us to pursue. This process is an eternal round of divine learning that never ends.

---

1. Doctrine and Covenants 128:21.

The Savior described His Church as "true *and* living"[2] Likewise, the temple is true *and* living. It is *authorized* by the Savior as His house, and it is *alive* with priesthood power and continuous revelation, which are available to all who enter.

Consequently, our chief desire should be to come to the temple and seek the Savior there. There, our spiritual education will continue. There, healing will occur. There, we will receive the fullness of priesthood power via covenants, which help us to become like Christ. President Gordon B. Hinckley pled with the Saints,

> I hope that everyone gets to the temple on a regular basis. . . . I know your lives are busy. I know that you have much to do. But I make you a promise that if you will go to the House of the Lord, you will be blessed; life will be better for you. Now, please, please, my beloved brethren and sisters, avail yourselves of the great opportunity to go to the Lord's house and thereby partake of all the marvelous blessings that are yours to be received there.[3]

Our sacrifices and efforts in attending the temple will surely be met with divine blessings.

PREPARE YOURSELF

Elder Boyd K. Packer, formerly of the Quorum of the Twelve, taught, "What we gain *from* the temple will depend to a large degree on what we take *to* the temple in the way of humility and reverence and a desire to learn. If we are teachable, we will be taught by the Spirit in the temple."[4] Our attitude toward our preparatory efforts enables this desire to learn.

We prepare for the temple each time we study the scriptures. Increasing our knowledge and familiarity with the language of and

2. Doctrine and Covenants 1:30; emphasis added.
3. Gordon B. Hinckley, *Teachings of Gordon B. Hinckley* (Salt Lake City: Deseret Book, 1997), 624.
4. Boyd K. Packer, *The Holy Temple* (Salt Lake City: Deseret Book, 1980), 2nd Printing, 1981, 42.

symbols in the scriptures will enhance our ability to discern truth and derive meaning in the temple. Our regular daily scripture study outside of the temple makes our time in the temple much more effective. Therefore, what may appear to be a mundane task is a foundational effort to open extraordinary revelation.

We prepare for the temple each time we pray. Increasing our understanding of the language of the Spirit—how He communicates through feelings and emotions—will prepare us to receive those most precious impressions while in the temple. Regular prayer outside the temple leads to enhanced messages while in it.

We prepare for the temple each time that we seek to apply gospel knowledge in our lives. Irrespective of how we learn, gospel truth consistently applied is the key to our salvation. Why? Because doing so requires us to voluntarily use our agency to act on faith, which slowly builds our Christlike character. If we can act on truth learned *outside* the temple, we will be prepared to act on truth learned *inside* the temple.

SEEK TO BECOME

If pondered and appropriately considered, regularly preparing for and attending the temple—the House of the Lord—will enable us to put Jesus Christ at the center of our lives more consistently. By diligently and thoughtfully seeking Him via temple ordinances and covenants, we will genuinely and eventually become like Him, for we shall see Him as He is.

So, let us go and see what the temple holds. Go often. Go prepared. Go seeking Him in whatever question besets us. Then, leave and apply what the Holy Spirit teaches us. As we do, we will know our Savior, Jesus Christ, in a deeply personal way that we could not otherwise achieve.

The temple insights we presented in this book were only the beginning for us, and we hope they have helped you on your own personal journey. As we wrote, we kept discovering additional temple insights to share, which made finding the "end" of the book difficult. We finally realized that our lifelong journey of spiritual learning from the temple will never end! The information in this book only represents one small piece of our journey, and your time reading, pondering, and applying it only represents a small piece of yours. We recommend that you write down your own insights and impressions as you commence and continue your journey of learning *from* the temple. Those personal records will become a precious resource for you as this book has become for us.

We invite you to continue discovering your own personal temple insights. Precious blessings await!

Works Cited

Anderson, Neil L. "Power in the Priesthood." Conference Report. Salt Lake City: The Church of Jesus Christ of Latter-day Saints, October 2013, https://www.churchofjesuschrist.org/study/general-conference/2013/10/power-in-the-priesthood?lang=eng.

Andrei, Mihai. "Article suggests dragonflies are the most effective predators in the animal world—95% success rate," *ZME Science*, October 9, 2020, accessed June 4, 2021, https://www.zmescience.com/ecology/animals-ecology/article-suggests-dragonflies-are-the-most-effective-predators-in-the-animal-world-95-success-rate/.

Ashton, Marvin J. "On Being Worthy," Conference Report. Salt Lake City: The Church of Jesus Christ of Latter-day Saints, April 198, https://www.churchofjesuschrist.org/study/general-conference/1989/04/on-being-worthy?lang=eng.

At the Pulpit: 185 Years of Discourses by Latter-day Saint Women. Salt Lake City: The Church Historian's Press, 2017, https://www.churchofjesuschrist.org/study/church-historians-press/at-the-pulpit?lang=eng.

Ballard, M. Russell "Suicide: Some Things We Know, and Some We Do Not," *Ensign*, October 1987, https://www.churchofjesuschrist.org/study/ensign/1987/10/suicide-some-things-we-know-and-some-we-do-not?lang=eng.

Beck, Julie B. "Teaching the Doctrine of the Family," Seminaries and Institutes of Religion Broadcast, August 4, 2009, accessed February 6, 2021, https://www.theredheadedhostess.com/assets/uploads/2010/08/2009-beck-teaching-the-doctrine-of-the-family__eng.pdf.

Beck, Julie B. "Why We Are Organized into Quorums and Relief Societies," BYU devotional address, Jan. 17, 2012. Provo, UT: Brigham Young University, accessed January 31, 2021, https://speeches.byu.edu/talks/julie-b-beck/why-we-are-organized-into-quorums-and-relief-societies/.

Bednar, David A. "Accepting the Lord's Will and Timing." *Ensign*, August 2016, https://www.churchofjesuschrist.org/study/ensign/2016/08/accepting-the-lords-will-and-timing?lang=eng.

Bednar, David A. "In the Strength of the Lord," *BYU Speeches*. Provo. Brigham Young University, October 23, 2001, accessed February 6, 2021, https://speeches.byu.edu/talks/david-a-bednar/strength-lord/.

Bednar, David A. *Increase in Learning*. Salt Lake City: Deseret Book, 2011.

Bednar, David A. "Let This House Be Built to My Name." Conference Report. Salt Lake City: The Church of Jesus Christ of Latter-day Saints, April 2020, https://www.churchofjesuschrist.org/study/general-conference/2020/04/44bednar?lang=eng.

Bednar, David A. "Meek and Lowly of Heart." Conference Report. Salt Lake City: The Church of Jesus Christ of Latter-day Saints, April 2018, https://www.churchofjesuschrist.org/study/general-conference/2018/04/meek-and-lowly-of-heart?lang=eng.

Bednar, David A. "Prepared to Obtain Every Needful Thing." Conference Report. Salt Lake City: The Church of Jesus Christ of Latter-day Saints, April 2019, https://www.churchofjesuschrist.org/study/general-conference/2019/04/54bednar?lang=eng.

Bednar, David A. "The Character of Christ." *BYUi Religion Symposium*, January 25, 2003, accessed February 6, 2021, https://www2.byui.edu/presentations/transcripts/religionsymposium/2003_01_25_bednar.htm.

Bednar, David A. "Watchful Unto Prayer Continually." Conference Report. Salt Lake City: The Church of Jesus Christ of Latter-day Saints, October 2019, https://www.churchofjesuschrist.org/study/general-conference/2019/10/22bednar?lang=eng.

Benson, Ezra Taft. "Born of God." Conference Report. Salt Lake City: The Church of Jesus Christ of Latter-day Saints, October 1985, https://www.churchofjesus-christ.org/study/general-conference/1985/10/born-of-god?lang=eng.

Benson, Ezra Taft. Conference Report. Salt Lake City: The Church of Jesus Christ of Latter-day Saints, April 1965, https://archive.org/details/conferencereport1965a.

Brown, Hugh B. Conference Report. Salt Lake City: The Church of Jesus Christ of Latter-day Saints, October 1969, https://archive.org/details/conferencereport1969sa.

Brown, Matthew B. *The Gate of Heaven*. Salt Lake City: Covenant Communications, Inc., 1999.

Brown, Matthew B., and Smith, Paul Thomas. *Symbols in Stone*. Salt Lake City: Covenant Communications, Inc., 2003.

Bujnowski, Aaron M. "Seek This Jesus." Address delivered at the funeral of Kenneth J. Bujnowski, April 9, 2021, https://www.dropbox.com/s/lw1kod-5j6n7e675/Seek%20This%20Jesus.pdf?dl=0.

Bujnowski, John K. "Kenneth John Bujnowski Eulogy," April 9, 2021, https://www.dropbox.com/s/ujbav4d8c7egugm/04.07.21%20Ken%20Bujnowski%20Eulogy.pdf?dl=0.

Campbell, Beverly. *Eve and the Choice Made in Eden.* Salt Lake City: Deseret Book, 2003.

Campbell, Beverly. *Eve and the Mortal Journey.* Salt Lake City: Deseret Book, 2005.

Cannon, George Q. *Gospel Truth: Discourses and Writings of President George Q. Cannon.* Comp. Jerreld L. Newquist. Salt Lake City: Deseret Book, 1974.

Cannon, George Q. "Seeking Spiritual Gifts." *Ensign,* April 2016. https://www.churchofjesuschrist.org/study/ensign/2016/04/seeking-spiritual-gifts?lang=eng.

Children's Songbook. Salt Lake City: The Church of Jesus Christ of Latter-day Saints, 1989.

Christofferson, D. Todd. "As Many as I Love, I Rebuke and Chasten." Conference Report. Salt Lake City: The Church of Jesus Christ of Latter-day Saints, April 2011, https://www.churchofjesuschrist.org/study/general-conference/2011/04/as-many-as-i-love-i-rebuke-and-chasten?lang=eng.

Christofferson, D. Todd. "How Beautiful Thy Temples, Lord." *BYU Family History Fireside—Joseph Smith Building,* March 8, 2002, accessed February 6, 2021, https://brightspotcdn.byu.edu/1f/5b/58a130484e3283ac2932983df9c6/2002-03-08.pdf.

Christofferson, D. Todd. "Saving Your Life." Church Educational System Fireside, September 14, 2014, accessed February 26, 2021, https://www.churchofjesus-christ.org/broadcasts/article/ces-devotionals/2014/01/saving-your-life?lang=eng.

Christofferson, D. Todd. "The Power of Covenants." Conference Report. Salt Lake City: The Church of Jesus Christ of Latter-day Saints, April 2009, https://www.churchofjesuschrist.org/study/general-conference/2009/04/the-power-of-covenants?lang=eng.

Christofferson, D. Todd. "Why Marriage, Why Family." Conference Report. Salt Lake City: The Church of Jesus Christ of Latter-day Saints, April 2015, https://www.churchofjesuschrist.org/study/general-conference/2015/04/why-marriage-why-family?lang=eng.

Christofferson, Thomas H. *That We May Be One: A Gay Mormon's Perspective on Faith and Family.* Salt Lake City: Deseret Book, 2017.

Clark Jr., J. Reuben. *Behold the Lamb of God.* Salt Lake City: Deseret Book, 1962.

Clark Jr., J. Reuben. Conference Report. Salt Lake City: The Church of Jesus Christ of Latter-day Saints, October 1953. https://archive.org/details/conferencereport1953sa/page/n85/mode/2up

Collected Discourses of Wilford Woodruff Vol. 5. Salt Lake City: Deseret Book, 2017. Deseret Bookshelf eBook.

Cook, Quentin L. "Hearts Knit in Righteousness and Unity." Conference Report. Salt Lake City: The Church of Jesus Christ of Latter-day Saints, October 2020, https://www.churchofjesuschrist.org/study/general-conference/2020/10/15cook?lang=eng.

Coppins, McKay. "The Most American Religion," *The Atlantic*, January/February 2021 Issue, Published online December 16, 2020, accessed February 6, 2021, https://www.theatlantic.com/magazine/archive/2021/01/the-most-american-religion/617263/.

Craig, Michelle D. "Eyes to See," Conference Report. Salt Lake City: The Church of Jesus Christ of Latter-day Saints, October 2020, https://www.churchofjesuschrist.org/study/general-conference/2020/10/14craig?lang=eng.

Crowther, Duane S. *Life Everlasting.* Salt Lake City: Horizon Publishers, 2017.

Dalton, Elaine S. *No Ordinary Women.* Salt Lake City: Deseret Book, 2016.

Davidson, Karen Lynn. *Our Latter-day Hymns: The Stories and the Messages.* Salt Lake City: Deseret Book, 2009.

Dew, Sheri L. "Are We Not All Mothers." Conference Report. Salt Lake City: The Church of Jesus Christ of Latter-day Saints, October 2001, https://www.churchofjesuschrist.org/study/general-conference/2001/10/are-we-not-all-mothers?lang=eng.

Dew, Sheri L. "It Is Not Good for Man or Woman to Be Alone." Conference Report. Salt Lake City: The Church of Jesus Christ of Latter-day Saints, October 2001, https://www.churchofjesuschrist.org/study/general-conference/2001/10/it-is-not-good-for-man-or-woman-to-be-alone?lang=eng.

Dew, Sheri L. "Knowing Who You Are—And Who You Have Always Been." Brigham Young University Women's Conference. Marriott Center, Brigham Young University, Provo, Utah, May 4, 2001, accessed January 31, 2021, https://womensconference.ce.byu.edu/sites/womensconference.ce.byu.edu/files/dew_sheri_2.pdf.

Dew, Sheri L. *No Doubt About It.* Salt Lake City: Deseret Book, 2001.

Dew, Sheri L. *Worth the Wrestle.* Salt Lake City: Deseret Book, 2017.

Discover Magazine, accessed January 4, 2021, https://www.discovermagazine.com/the-sciences/bafact-math-the-sun-is-400-000-times-brighter-than-the-full-moon.

Dyer, Alvin R. *Who Am I?* Salt Lake City: Deseret Book, 1973.

Easton, Susan Ward. "Names of Christ in the Book of Mormon," *Ensign*, July 1978, https://www.

churchofjesuschrist.org/study/ensign/1978/07/discovery/names-of-christ-in-the-book-of-mormon?lang=eng.

Ehat Andrew F., and Cook, Lyndon W. *The Words of Joseph Smith*. Salt Lake City: Grandin Book Co., 1991.

"Elder Alvin R. Dyer Dies," *Ensign*, May 1977, https://www.churchofjesus-christ.org/study/ensign/1977/05/news-of-the-church/elder-alvin-r-dyer-dies?lang=eng&adobe_mc_ref=https%3A%2F%2Fwww.churchofjesuschrist.org%2Fstudy%2Fensign%2F1977%2F05%2Fnews-of-the-church%2Felder-alvin-r-dyer-dies%3Flang%3Deng&adobe_mc_sdid=SDID%3D7529C535ADC0919B-4A51FDA014A4A45A%7CMCORGID%3D66C5485451E56AAE0A490D45%2540AdobeOrg%7CTS%3D1641139170

Enkin, Rabi Ari. "Embarrassing Others," www.outorah.org, accessed May 24, 2021. https://outorah.org/p/49535/#_ftn1.

Eubank, Sharon. "By Union of Feeling We Obtain Power with God." Conference Report. Salt Lake City: The Church of Jesus Christ of Latter-day Saints, October 2020, https://www.churchofjesuschrist.org/study/general-conference/2020/10/31eubank?lang=eng.

Faust, James E. "Discipleship," Conference Report. Salt Lake City: The Church of Jesus Christ of Latter-day Saints, October 2006, https://www.churchofjesus-christ.org/study/general-conference/2006/10/discipleship?lang=eng.

Faust, James E. "The Devil's Throat." Conference Report. Salt Lake City: The Church of Jesus Christ of Latter-day Saints, April 2003, https://www.churchofje-suschrist.org/study/general-conference/2003/04/the-devils-throat?lang=eng.

Faust, James E. "The Great Imitator." Conference Report. Salt Lake City: The Church of Jesus Christo of Latter-day Saints, October 1987, https://www.churchofjesus-christ.org/study/general-conference/1987/10/the-great-imitator?lang=eng.

Firmage, Edwin Brown. "Violence and the Gospel: The Teachings of the Old Testament, the New Testament, and the Book of Mormon," *BYU Studies Quarterly Vol. 25 No. 1*. Provo: Brigham Young University, 1985, 6; see also footnote 14. Accessed February 14, 2021, https://byustudies.byu.edu/wp-content/uploads/2020/02/25.1FirmageViolence-ab148ed3-6a69-49aa-9d3c-858130e81b3a.pdf.

Gaskill, Alonzo L. *Sacred Symbols*. Salt Lake City: Cedar Fort, 2019.

General Handbook: Serving in The Church of Jesus Christ of Latter-day Saints. Salt Lake City: The Church of Jesus Christ of Latter-day Saints, 2021, accessed February 6, 2021, https://www.churchofjesuschrist.org/study/manual/general-handbook?lang=eng.

Groberg, John H. "The Power of God's Love." Conference Report. Salt Lake City: The Church of Jesus Christ of Latter-day Saints, October 2004, https://www.churchofjesuschrist.org/study/general-conference/2004/10/the-power-of-gods-love?lang=eng.

Hanks, Marion D. "Forgiveness: The Ultimate Form of Love." Conference Report. Salt Lake City: The Church of Jesus Christ of Latter-day Saints, October 1973, https://www.churchofjesuschrist.org/study/general-conference/1973/10/forgiveness-the-ultimate-form-of-love?lang=eng.

Hardison, Amy. *Understanding the Symbols, Covenants, and Ordinances of the Temple.* Salt Lake City: Covenant Communications, Inc., 2016.

Hinckley, Gordon B. "Excerpts from Recent Addresses of President Gordon B. Hinckley," *Ensign*, January 1998, https://www.churchofjesuschrist.org/study/ensign/1998/01/excerpts-from-recent-addresses-of-president-gordon-b-hinckley?lang=eng.

Hinckley, Gordon B. "My Testimony." Conference Report. Salt Lake City: The Church of Jesus Christ of Latter-day Saints, April 2000, https://www.churchofjesuschrist.org/study/general-conference/2000/04/my-testimony?lang=eng.

Hinckley, Gordon B. "Our Responsibility to Our Young Women," *Ensign*, September 1988. https://www.churchofjesuschrist.org/study/ensign/1988/09/our-responsibility-to-our-young-women?lang=eng.

Hinckley, Gordon B. *Teachings of Gordon B. Hinckley.* Salt Lake City: Deseret Book, 1997.

Hinckley, Gordon B. "The War We Are Winning." Conference Report. Salt Lake City: The Church of Jesus Christ of Latter-day Saints, October 1986, https://www.churchofjesuschrist.org/study/general-conference/1986/10/the-war-we-are-winning?lang=eng.

Hinckley, Gordon B. "To the Women of the Church." Conference Report. Salt Lake City: The Church of Jesus Christ of Latter-day Saints, October 2003, https://www.churchofjesuschrist.org/study/general-conference/2003/10/to-the-women-of-the-church?lang=eng.

Holland, Jeffrey R. "Be Ye Therefore Perfect—Eventually." Conference Report. Salt Lake City: The Church of Jesus Christ of Latter-day Saints, October 2017, https://www.churchofjesuschrist.org/study/general-conference/2017/10/be-ye-therefore-perfect-eventually?lang=eng.

Holland, Jeffrey R. "Lessons from Liberty Jail," CES Fireside. Provo: Brigham Young University, September 7, 2008, accessed February 6, 2021, https://speeches.byu.edu/talks/jeffrey-r-holland/lessons-liberty-jail/.

Holland, Jeffrey R. "Like a Broken Vessel." Conference Report. Salt Lake City: The Church of Jesus Christ of Latter-day Saints, October 2013, https://www.churchofjesuschrist.org/study/general-conference/2013/10/like-a-broken-vessel?lang=eng.

Holland, Jeffrey R. "Waiting on the Lord." Conference Report. Salt Lake City: The Church of Jesus Christ of Latter-day Saints, October 2020, https://www.churchofjesuschrist.org/study/general-conference/2020/10/57holland?lang=eng.

Howell, Elizabeth. "Brightest Stars: Luminosity and Magnitude," accessed January 4, 2021, https://www.space.com/21640-star-luminosity-and-magnitude.html.

Hunter, Howard W. "Being a Righteous Husband and Father." Conference Report. Salt Lake City: The Church of Jesus Christ of Latter-day Saints, October 1994, https://www.churchofjesuschrist.org/study/general-conference/1994/10/being-a-righteous-husband-and-father?lang=eng.

Hunter, Howard W. "The Golden Thread of Choice." Conference Report. Salt Lake City: The Church of Jesus Christ of Latter-day Saints, October 1989, https://www.churchofjesuschrist.org/study/general-conference/1989/10/the-golden-thread-of-choice?lang=eng.

Hymns. Salt Lake City: The Church of Jesus Christ of Latter-day Saints, 1985.

Johnson, Peter M. "Power to Overcome the Adversary." Conference Report. Salt Lake City: The Church of Jesus Christ of Latter-day Saints, October 2019, https://www.churchofjesuschrist.org/study/general-conference/2019/10/54johnson?lang=eng.

Jones, Joy D. "An Especially Noble Calling." Conference Report. Salt Lake City: The Church of Jesus Christ of Latter-day Saints, April 2020, https://www.churchofjesuschrist.org/study/general-conference/2020/04/14jones?lang=eng.

Instrument Flying Handbook. FAA-H-8083-15B. US Department of Transportation Federal Aviation Administration, 2012, accessed February 20, 2021, https://www.faa.gov/regulations_policies/handbooks_manuals/aviation/media/FAA-H-8083-15B.pdf.

Journal of Discourses, 26 vols. London: Latter-day Saints' Book Depot, 1854–1886.

Kimball, Spencer W. *Faith Precedes the Miracle.* Salt Lake City: Deseret Book, 1972.

Kimball, Spencer W. *Teachings of Spencer W. Kimball.* Ed. Edward L. Kimball. Salt Lake City: Deseret Book, 1982.

Kimball, Spencer W. "The Role of Righteous Women." Conference Report. Salt Lake City: The Church of Jesus Christ of Latter-day Saints, October 1979, https://www.churchofjesuschrist.org/study/general-conference/1979/10/the-role-of-righteous-women?lang=eng.

Larsen, Sharon G. "Agency—A Blessing and a Burden." Conference Report. Salt Lake City: The Church of Jesus Christ of Latter-day Saints, October 1999, https://www.churchofjesuschrist.org/study/general-conference/1999/10/agency-a-blessing-and-a-burden?lang=eng.

Lee, Harold B. "Enemies That Come In the Night." Conference Report. Salt Lake City: The Church of Jesus Christ of Latter-day Saints, April 1970, https://archive.org/details/conferencereport1970a.

Lewis, C. S. *The Screwtape Letters*. London: William Collins, 2015.

Ludlow, Daniel H. *Companion to Your Study of the Doctrine and Covenants, Vol. 1*. Salt Lake City: Deseret Book, 1978.

Lyon, Jack M. *Understanding Temple Symbols Through Scripture, History, and Art*. Salt Lake City: Deseret Book, 2016.

Madsen, Truman G. *Joseph Smith the Prophet*. Salt Lake City: Deseret Book, 1989.

Madsen, Truman G. *The Temple: Where Heaven Meets Earth*. Salt Lake City: Deseret Book, 2008.

Maxwell, Neal A. "But a Few Days," Address to CES Religious Educators, September 10, 1982, Salt Lake Palace Assembly Room, accessed February 27, 2021, https://silo.tips/download/but-a-few-days-elder-neal-a-maxwell-of-the-quorum-of-the-twelve-apostles.

Maxwell, Neal A. "If Thou Endure It Well," *BYU Speeches*. Provo, UT: Brigham Young University, December 2, 1984, accessed February 6, 2021, https://speeches.byu.edu/talks/neal-a-maxwell/if-thou-endure-well/.

Maxwell, Neal A. "In Him All Things Hold Together," *BYU Speeches*. Provo, UT Brigham Young University, March 31, 1991, accessed March 31, 2021, https://speeches.byu.edu/talks/neal-a-maxwell/in-him-all-things-hold-together/.

Maxwell, Neal A. "Meek and Lowly," *BYU Speeches*. Provo: Brigham Young University, October 21, 1986, accessed February 6, 2021, https://speeches.byu.edu/talks/neal-a-maxwell/meek-lowly/.

Maxwell, Neal A. "Meekly Drenched in Destiny," *BYU Speeches*. Provo: Brigham Young University, September 5, 1982, accessed February 6, 2021, https://speeches.byu.edu/talks/neal-a-maxwell/meekly-drenched-destiny/.

Maxwell, Neal A. *Not My Will, But Thine*. Salt Lake City: Deseret Book, 2008.

Maxwell, Neal A. *Notwithstanding My Weakness*. Salt Lake City: Deseret Book, 1981.

Maxwell, Neal A. "Swallowed Up in the Will of the Father." Conference Report. Salt Lake City: The Church of Jesus Christ of Latter-day Saints, October 1995, https://www.churchofjesuschrist.org/study/general-conference/1995/10/swallowed-up-in-the-will-of-the-father?lang=eng.

McConkie, Bruce R. *Mormon Doctrine*. Salt Lake City: Deseret Book, 1966.

McConkie, Bruce R. "Obedience, Consecration, and Sacrifice." Conference Report. Salt Lake City: The Church of Jesus Christ of Latter-day Saints, April

1975, https://www.churchofjesuschrist.org/study/general-conference/1975/04/obedience-consecration-and-sacrifice?lang=eng.

McConkie, Bruce R. "The Lord's People Receive Revelation." Conference Report. Salt Lake City: The Church of Jesus Christ of Latter-day Saints, April 1971, https://www.churchofjesuschrist.org/study/general-conference/1971/04/the-lords-people-receive-revelation?lang=eng.

McConkie, Bruce R. *The Probationary Test of Mortality.* Address given at the University of Utah Institute of Religion, January 10, 1982, accessed January 4, 2021, http://www.ldsscriptureteachings.org/2018/07/26/5867-2/.

McConkie, Bruce R. "Upon This Rock." Conference Report. Salt Lake City: The Church of Jesus Christ of Latter-day Saints, April 1981, accessed February 28, 2021. https://www.churchofjesuschrist.org/study/general-conference/1981/04/upon-this-rock?lang=eng.

McKay, David O. cited in Hales, Robert D. "Understandings of the Heart," *BYU Speeches.* Provo, UT: Brigham Young University, March 15, 1988, https://speeches.byu.edu/talks/robert-d-hales/understandings-heart/.

McKay, David O. Conference Report. Salt Lake: The Church of Jesus Christ of Latter-day Saints, April 1969, https://archive.org/details/conferencereport1969a.

Merriam-Webster Dictionary, www.merriam-webster.com, accessed January 7, 2021.

Molyneaux, David. "'Blessed Are the Meek, for They Shall Inherit the Earth'— An Aspiration Applicable to Business?" *Journal of Business Ethics.* Vol. 48. Netherlands: Kluwer Academic Publishers, 2003.

Monson, Thomas S. "Decisions Determine Destiny," *BYU Speeches.* Provo: Brigham Young University, November 6, 2005, accessed January 4, 2021, https://speeches.byu.edu/talks/thomas-s-monson/decisions-determine-destiny/.

Monson, Thomas S. *Live the Good Life.* Salt Lake City: Desert Book, 1988.

Monson, Thomas S. "That We May Touch Heaven" Conference Report. Salt Lake City: The Church of Jesus Christ of Latter-day Saints, October 1990, https://www.churchofjesuschrist.org/study/general-conference/1990/10/that-we-may-touch-heaven?lang=eng.

Monson, Thomas S. "The Call of Duty." Conference Report. Salt Lake City: The Church of Jesus Christ of Latter-day Saints, April 1986, https://www.churchofjesuschrist.org/study/general-conference/1986/04/the-call-of-duty?lang=eng.

Mortensen, Krista Rogers. "You Love, He Saves," *Ensign.* July 2020.

Nelson, Russell M. "Drawing the Power of Jesus Christ into Our Lives," Conference Report. Salt Lake City: The Church of Jesus Christ of Latter-day Saints, April

2017, https://www.churchofjesuschrist.org/study/general-conference/2017/04/drawing-the-power-of-jesus-christ-into-our-lives?lang=eng.

Nelson, Russell M. "Joy and Spiritual Survival." Conference Report. Salt Lake City: The Church of Jesus Christ of Latter-day Saints, October 2016, https://www.churchofjesuschrist.org/study/general-conference/2016/10/joy-and-spiritual-survival?lang=eng.

Nelson, Russell M. "Let God Prevail." Conference Report. Salt Lake City: The Church of Jesus Christ of Latter-day Saints, October 2020, https://www.churchofjesuschrist.org/study/general-conference/2020/10/46nelson?lang=eng.

Nelson, Russell M. "Prepare for the Blessings of the Temple," *Liahona*, October 2010, https://www.churchofjesuschrist.org/study/liahona/2010/10/prepare-for-the-blessings-of-the-temple?lang=eng

Nelson, Russell M. "Revelation for the Church, Revelation for our Lives." Conference Report. Salt Lake City: The Church of Jesus Christ of Latter-day Saints, April 2018, https://www.churchofjesuschrist.org/study/general-conference/2018/04/revelation-for-the-church-revelation-for-our-lives?lang=eng.

Nelson, Russell M. "Spiritual Treasures." Conference Report. Salt Lake City: The Church of Jesus Christ of Latter-day Saints, October 2019, https://www.churchofjesuschrist.org/study/general-conference/2019/10/36nelson?lang=eng.

Nelson, Russell M. "The Atonement." *Conference* Report. Salt Lake City: The Church of Jesus Christ of Latter-day Saints, October 1996, https://www.churchofjesus-christ.org/study/general-conference/1996/10/the-atonement?lang=eng.

Nelson, Russell M. "The Creation." Conference Report. Salt Lake City: The Church of Jesus Christ of Latter-day Saints, April 2000, https://www.churchofjesus-christ.org/study/general-conference/2000/04/the-creation?lang=eng.

Nelson, Russell M. "The Sabbath Is a Delight." Conference Report. Salt Lake City: The Church of Jesus Christ of Latter-day Saints, April 2015, https://www.churchofjesuschrist.org/study/general-conference/2015/04/the-sabbath-is-a-delight?lang=eng.

Nelson, Russell M. "The Temple and Your Spiritual Foundation." Conference Report. Salt Lake City: The Church of Jesus Christ of Latter-day Saints, October 2021, https://www.churchofjesuschrist.org/study/general-conference/2021/10/47nelson?lang=eng

Nelson, Russel M. and Nelson Wendy, W. "Hope of Israel." Worldwide Youth Devotional. Salt Lake City: The Church of Jesus Christ of Latter-day Saints. June 3, 2018. https://www.churchofjesuschrist.org/study/broadcasts/worldwide-devotional-for-young-adults/2018/06/hope-of-israel.58?lang=eng#58

New Testament Seminary Teacher Manual. Salt Lake: The Church of Jesus Christ of Latter-day Saints), "Lesson 134: Philemon," accessed February 6, 2021.

https://www.churchofjesuschrist.org/study/manual/new-testament-seminary-teacher-manual/introduction-to-the-epistle-of-paul-to-philemon/lesson-134-philemon?lang=eng.

Nibley, Hugh W. *Mormonism and Early Christianity*. Salt Lake City: Deseret Book, 1987.

Nibley, Hugh W. *Temple and Cosmos*. Salt Lake City: Deseret Book, 1992.

Nibley, Hugh W. "The Atonement of Jesus Christ, Part 1," *Ensign*, July 1990, https://www.churchofjesuschrist.org/study/ensign/1990/07/the-atonement-of-jesus-christ-part-1?lang=eng.

Oaks, Dallin H. "I Have a Question: How can I distinguish the difference between the promptings of the Holy Ghost and merely my own thoughts, preferences, or hunches?" *Ensign*, June 1983, https://www.churchofjesuschrist.org/study/ensign/1983/06/i-have-a-question/how-can-i-distinguish-the-difference-between-the-promptings-of-the-holy-ghost-and-merely-my-own-thoughts-preferences-or-hunches?lang=eng.

Oaks, Dallin H. "Love and Law." Conference Report. Salt Lake City: The Church of Jesus Christ of Latter-day Saints, October 2009, https://www.churchofjesuschrist.org/study/general-conference/2009/10/love-and-law?lang=eng

Oaks, Dallin H. "Priesthood Authority in the Family and in the Church." Conference Report. Salt Lake City: The Church of Jesus Christ of Latter-day Saints, October 2005, https://www.churchofjesuschrist.org/study/general-conference/2005/10/priesthood-authority-in-the-family-and-the-church?lang=eng.

Oaks, Dallin H. "Taking Upon Us the Name of Jesus Christ." Conference Report. Salt Lake City: The Church of Jesus Christ of Latter-day Saints, April 1985, https://www.churchofjesuschrist.org/study/general-conference/1985/04/taking-upon-us-the-name-of-jesus-christ?lang=eng.

Oaks, Dallin H. "The Challenge to Become." Conference Report. Salt Lake City: The Church of Jesus Christ of Latter-day Saints, October 2000, https://www.churchofjesuschrist.org/study/general-conference/2000/10/the-challenge-to-become?lang=eng.

Oaks, Dallin H. "The Desires of Our Hearts." *BYU Speeches*. Provo: Brigham Young University, October 8, 1985, accessed February 6, 2021, https://speeches.byu.edu/talks/dallin-h-oaks/desires-hearts/. See also *Ensign*, June 1986. https://www.churchofjesuschrist.org/study/ensign/1986/06/the-desires-of-our-hearts?lang=eng.

Oaks, Dallin H. "The Keys and Authority of the Priesthood." Conference Report. Salt Lake City: The Church of Jesus Christ of Latter-day Saints, April 2014, https://www.churchofjesuschrist.org/study/general-conference/2014/04/the-keys-and-authority-of-the-priesthood?lang=eng.

Old Testament Student Manual: Genesis—2 Samuel. Salt Lake City: The Church of Jesus Christ of Latter-day Saints, 1981.

Oxford Dictionary of English. Oxford: Oxford University Press, 2010.

Packer, Boyd K. "Little Children." Conference Report. Salt Lake City: The Church of Jesus Christ of Latter-day Saints, October 1986, https://www.churchofjesus-christ.org/study/general-conference/1986/10/little-children?lang=eng.

Packer, Boyd K. "The Candle of the Lord." *Ensign*, January 1983. https://www.churchofjesuschrist.org/study/ensign/1983/01/the-candle-of-the-lord?lang=eng.

Packer, Boyd K. *The Holy Temple.* Salt Lake City: Deseret Book, 1980.

Packer, Boyd K. "The Instrument of Your Mind and the Foundation of Your Character." *BYU Speeches.* Provo: Brigham Young University, February 2, 2003, accessed February 7, 2021, https://speeches.byu.edu/talks/boyd-k-packer/instrument-mind-foundation-character/.

Packer, Boyd K. "The Mediator." Conference Report. Salt Lake City: The Church of Jesus Christ of Latter-day Saints, April 1977, https://www.churchofjesus-christ.org/study/general-conference/1977/04/the-mediator?lang=eng.

Packer, Boyd K. "The Power of the Priesthood." Conference Report. Salt Lake City: The Church of Jesus Christ of Latter-day Saints, April 2010, https://www.churchofjesuschrist.org/study/general-conference/2010/04/the-power-of-the-priesthood?lang=eng.

Packer, Boyd K. "The Spirit Beareth Record." Conference Report. Salt Lake City: The Church of Jesus Christ of Latter-day Saints, April 1971, https://www.churchofjesuschrist.org/study/general-conference/1971/04/the-spirit-beareth-record?lang=eng.

Packer, Boyd K. "The Temple, the Priesthood." Conference Report. Salt Lake City: The Church of Jesus Christ of Latter-day Saints. April 1993, https://www.churchofjesuschrist.org/study/general-conference/1993/04/the-temple-the-priesthood?lang=eng.

Parkin, Bonnie D. "With Holiness of Heart," Conference Report. Salt Lake City: The Church of Jesus Christ of Latter-day Saints, October 2002, https://www.churchofjesuschrist.org/study/general-conference/2002/10/with-holiness-of-heart?lang=eng.

Parry, Donald W. (Ed.). *Temples of the Ancient World.* Salt Lake City: Deseret Book, 1994.

Perry, Donald W. *175 Temple Symbols.* Salt Lake City: Deseret Book, 2020.

Perry, L. Tom. "The Plan of Salvation." Conference Report. Salt Lake City: The Church of Jesus Christ of Latter-day Saints, October 2006, https://www.churchofjesuschrist.org/study/general-conference/2006/10/the-plan-of-salvation?lang=eng.

Peters, John Durham. "Bowels of Mercy." *BYU Studies Quarterly*, Volume 38, Issue 4, Article 2, October 1, 1999, accessed February 21, 2021, https://scholarsarchive.byu.edu/cgi/viewcontent.cgi?article=3342&context=byusq.

Prange, Gordon W. *At Dawn We Slept: The Untold Story of Pearl Harbor*. New York: Penguin Books, 1981.

Pratt, Parley P. *Key to the Science of Theology*. Salt Lake City: Deseret Book, 1979.

Preach My Gospel. Salt Lake City: The Church of Jesus Christ of Latter-day Saints, 2019. https://www.churchofjesuschrist.org/study/manual/preach-my-gospel-a-guide-to-missionary-service?lang=eng

Prince, Gregory, and Wright, Wm. Robert. *David O. McKay and the Rise of Modern Mormonism*. Salt Lake City: University of Utah Press, 2005.

Rasband, James R. "Ensuring a Righteous Judgment." Conference Report. Salt Lake City: The Church of Jesus Christ of Latter-day Saints, April 2020, https://www.churchofjesuschrist.org/study/general-conference/2020/04/13rasband?lang=eng.

Reeves, Linda S. "Worthy of Our Promised Blessings." Conference Report. Salt Lake City: The Church of Jesus Christ of Latter-day Saints, October 2015, https://www.churchofjesuschrist.org/study/general-conference/2015/10/worthy-of-our-promised-blessings?lang=eng.

Renlund, Dale G. "Infuriating Unfairness." Conference Report. Salt Lake City: The Church of Jesus Christ of Latter-day Saints, April 2021, https://www.churchofjesuschrist.org/study/general-conference/2021/04/25renlund?lang=eng.

Renlund, Dale G. "Our Good Shepherd." Conference Report. Salt Lake City: The Church of Jesus Christ of Latter-day Saints, April 2017, https://www.churchofjesuschrist.org/study/general-conference/2017/04/our-good-shepherd?lang=eng.

Romney, Marion G. Conference Report. Salt Lake City: The Church of Jesus Christ of Latter-day Saints, April 1941, 123, https://archive.org/details/conferencereport1941a/mode/2up.

Scott, Richard G. "Acquiring Spiritual Knowledge." Conference Report. Salt Lake City: The Church of Jesus Christ of Latter-day Saints, October 1993, https://www.churchofjesuschrist.org/study/general-conference/1993/10/acquiring-spiritual-knowledge?lang=eng.

Scott, Richard G. "How to Obtain Revelation and Inspiration for Your Personal Life." Conference Report. Salt Lake City: The Church of Jesus Christ of Latter-day Saints, April 2012, https://www.churchofjesuschrist.org/study/general-conference/2012/04/how-to-obtain-revelation-and-inspiration-for-your-personal-life?lang=eng.

Scott, Richard G. "Jesus Christ, Our Redeemer." Conference Report. Salt Lake City: The Church of Jesus Christ of Latter-day Saints, April 1997, https://www.churchofjesuschrist.org/study/general-conference/1997/04/jesus-christ-our-redeemer?lang=eng.

Scott, Richard G. "To Acquire Spiritual Guidance." Conference Report. Salt Lake City: The Church of Jesus Christ of Latter-day Saints, October 2009, https://www.churchofjesuschrist.org/study/general-conference/2009/10/to-acquire-spiritual-guidance?lang=eng.

Scott, Richard G. "Trust in the Lord." Conference Report. Salt Lake City: The Church of Jesus Christ of Latter-day Saints, October 1995, https://www.churchofjesus-christ.org/study/general-conference/1995/10/trust-in-the-lord?lang=eng.

Shamim, Asif. "Pilot Disorientation Results of Florida F-16 Crash." March 26, 2008, accessed February 20, 2021, https://www.f-16.net/f-16-news-article2801.html.

Smith, Joseph. *History of the Church*. Salt Lake City: Deseret Book, 1980.

Smith, Joseph. *Lectures on Faith*. Comp. N.B. Lundwall. Salt Lake City: Deseret Book, 1835.

Smith, Joseph. "Minutes and Discourse, 9 June 1842," *Joseph Smith Papers*. https://www.josephsmithpapers.org/paper-summary/minutes-and-discourse-9-june-1842/1.

Smith, Joseph. *Teachings of Presidents of the Church: Joseph Smith*. Salt Lake City: Deseret Book, 2007.

Smith, Joseph. *Teachings of the Prophet Joseph Smith*. Comp. Joseph Fielding Smith. Salt Lake City: Deseret Book, 1976.

Smith, Joseph. *The Personal Writings of Joseph Smith*. Comp. D. Jessee. Salt Lake City: Deseret Book, 1984.

Smith, Joseph F. Conference Report. Salt Lake City: The Church of Jesus Christ of Latter-day Saints, October 1916, https://archive.org/details/conferencereport1916sa.

Smith, Joseph F and Widtsoe, John A. (Ed.). *Gospel Doctrine*. Salt Lake City: Deseret Book, 1986.

Smith, Joseph Fielding. *Answers to Gospel Questions*. Salt Lake City: Deseret Book, 1957. Vol. 3.

Smith, Joseph Fielding. Conference Report. Salt Lake City: The Church of Jesus Christ of Latter-day Saints, October 1958, https://archive.org/details/conferencereport1958sa.

Smith, Joseph Fielding. *Doctrines of Salvation*. Salt Lake City: Deseret Book, 1954.

Smith, Joseph Fielding. "Elijah the Prophet and His Mission." *Utah Genealogical and Historical* Magazine, Vol. XII, No. 1, January 1921, accessed February 6, 2021, https://babel.hathitrust.org/cgi/pt?id=njp.32101042555944&view=1up&seq=8.

Snow, Lorenzo. *The Teachings of Lorenzo Snow.* Comp. Clyde J. Williams. Salt Lake City: Bookcraft, 1984.

Taylor, John. *Teachings of Presidents of the Church: John Taylor.* Salt Lake City: Deseret Book, 2001.

The Bible Dictionary. Salt Lake City: The Church of Jesus Christ of Latter-day Saints, 2013, accessed February 6, 2021, https://www.churchofjesuschrist.org/study/scriptures/bd?lang=eng.

The Book of Mormon. Salt Lake City: The Church of Jesus Christ of Latter-day Saints, 2013, accessed February 6, 2021, https://www.churchofjesuschrist.org/study/scriptures/bofm?lang=eng.

The Doctrine and Covenants. Salt Lake City: The Church of Jesus Christ of Latter-day Saints, 2013, accessed February 6, 2021, https://www.churchofjesuschrist.org/study/scriptures/dc-testament?lang=eng.

"The Family: A Proclamation to the World." *Ensign*, November 1995, accessed February 28, 2021. https://www.churchofjesuschrist.org/study/ensign/1995/11/the-family-a-proclamation-to-the-world?lang=eng.

The Guide to the Scriptures. Salt Lake City: The Church of Jesus Christ of Latter-day Saints, 2013, accessed February 6, 2021, https://www.churchofjesuschrist.org/study/scriptures/gs?lang=eng.

"The Living Christ: The Testimony of the Apostles." Salt Lake City: The Church of Jesus Christ of Latter-day Saints, January 1, 2000, accessed February 28, 2021, https://www.churchofjesuschrist.org/study/scriptures/the-living-christ-the-testimony-of-the-apostles/the-living-christ-the-testimony-of-the-apostles?lang=eng.

The New Testament. Salt Lake City: The Church of Jesus Christ of Latter-day Saints, 2013, accessed February 6, 2021, https://www.churchofjesuschrist.org/study/scriptures/ot?lang=eng.

The Old Testament. Salt Lake City: The Church of Jesus Christ of Latter-day Saints, 2013, accessed February 6, 2021, https://www.churchofjesuschrist.org/study/scriptures/nt?lang=eng.

The Pearl of Great Price. Salt Lake City: The Church of Jesus Christ of Latter-day Saints, 2013.

Turner, Aubrey. "Women Gather at Spiritual Retreat, Serve Others," *The Prosper Press*, May 22, 2021, accessed June 6, 2021, https://www.prosper-pressnews.com/story/news/2021/05/22/women-gather-spiritual-retreat-serve-others/5230704001/?fbclid=IwAR16owlFEDbnCkKjdn9xZlJYhLicZ_3j_SYvFSOWfsue-QUJ4kUlUbsmh8c

Whitney, Orson F. *Life of Heber C. Kimball.* Salt Lake City: Bookcraft, 1967.

Widtsoe, John A. *Joseph Smith: Seeker After Truth, Prophet of God*. Salt Lake City: Bookcraft, 1951.

Widtsoe, John A. "Temple Worship," *The Utah Genealogical and Historical Magazine*, Vol. XII, April 1921, 49–64, accessed February 6, 2021, https://babel.hathitrust.org/cgi/pt?id=njp.32101042555944&view=1up&seq=68.

Widtsoe, John A. *The Message of the Doctrine and Covenants*. Salt Lake City: Deseret Book, 1969.

Whitney, Orson F. Conference Report. Salt Lake: The Church of Jesus Christ of Latter-day Saints, April 1929, https://archive.org/details/conferencereport1929a.

Winkel, Richard H. "The Temple Is About Families." Conference Report. Salt Lake City: The Church of Jesus Christ of Latter-day Saints, October 2006, https://www.churchofjesuschrist.org/study/general-conference/2006/10/the-temple-is-about-families?lang=eng.

www.biblehub.com, "Nabi," accessed June 6, 2021. https://www.biblehub.com/hebrew/5030.htm.

www.gotquestions.org, "What is the meaning of the Hebrew Word *hesed*?" Accessed February 14, 2021, https://www.gotquestions.org/meaning-of-hesed.html.

www.physicsbuzzphysicscentral. *The American Physical Society*. "The Physics of Sailing: How Does a Sailboat Move Upwind?" May 12, 2015, accessed February 20, 2021, http://physicsbuzz.physicscentral.com/2015/05/the-physics-of-sailing-how-does.html.